OUTSIDE OF A DOG

OUTSIDE OF A DOG

A Bibliomemoir

Rick Gekoski

CONSTABLE · LONDON

Constable & Robinson Ltd
3 The Lanchesters
162 Fulham Palace Road
London W6 9ER
www.constablerobinson.com

This edition published by Constable,
an imprint of Constable & Robinson, 2009

ISBN 978-1-84529-883-8

Printed and bound in the EU

1 3 5 7 9 10 8 6 4 2

PEFC/16-33-111
CATG-PEFC-052
www.pefc.org

Outside of a dog, a book is man's best friend.
Inside of a dog, it's too dark to read

Groucho Marx

For Vera, Chuck and Dave

CONTENTS

ACKNOWLEDGEMENTS

First thanks are due to my literary agent Peter Straus, for finding the right home for this book, and to Andreas Campomar of Constable & Robinson for supplying it. Both of these friends have been constant sources of encouragement and critical attention.

Sandy Neubauer's enthusiasm meant more than he would know in those early difficult days; Warwick Gould helped me to avoid errors of fact and judgement with regard to W.B. Yeats; Ron Schuchard kindly supplied an obscure Eliot reference; Martin Warner was so generous that he made me want to take back every criticism I have made about academic life, all of the virtues of which come together in him; Tom Rosenthal cast his shrewd but friendly eye on successive drafts, and is absolved from ever having to read this again; Natalie Galustian read with acute sympathy, and kept me going when things got tough; I couldn't find either the time or the energy to write without the staunch support of Peter Grogan, who keeps our business going when my eye is turned in a different direction. I am also indebted to Michael Silverman, Ann Rosenthal, Tim Gilbertson, James Stourton, Mez Packer, Geordie Williamson, Maggie Body, Mary Montgomery, Gina Rozner, Ali Blackburn, Bob Demaria and Mark Everett for helpful advice.

Particular thanks are due to Sam Varnedoe who improves everything that he touches, and whose lovingly assiduous enthusiasm has sustained me throughout.

For Anna, Steve, Bertie and the eagle-eyed Ruthie, so full of love and support. And for Belinda, as ever, and always.

Vera, Chuck and Dave are, of course, the imagined prospective grandchildren in the Beatles' 'When I'm 64'.

RG

INTRODUCTION

THE BATTLE OF THE BOOKS

> How many a man has dated a new era in his life from
> the reading of a book.
>
> Henry David Thoreau, *Walden*

'Lot 147 then. Lovely item!'

The auctioneer's eyes flicked towards the left-hand wall.

A ferrety porter in a green apron pointed out the object.

'Showing here, sir!'

'Who'll start me at £100 then?'

I stood along the left side of the room, my catalogue clutched damply in my hand, trying to look nonchalant. An audience of about fifty people wandered in and out, settled on their chairs, drank coffee from plastic cups. A middle-aged woman in a hat with a red feather bid excitedly on many of the items, waving her catalogue in the air. In the back row a silver-haired man was reading quietly to a toddler.

Our local auction house had weekly sales of sub-antique household furniture, which were great fun for picking up the odd coal scuttle, rocking chair, or threadbare Oriental rug. Occasionally I might spend a tenner on a job lot of books with one or two first editions in it. The pickings were not bad: prosperous towns with large houses often disgorge interesting bric-a-brac. While Leamington Spa's treasures weren't as rich as those of, say, Bath or Cheltenham, there were bargains to be had.

But this was not one of the weekly sales, but the monthly Fine Art Sale, which was not for the likes of me. In 1974 I only made £1,800 a year, and I had never spent more than £16 on an item for the house. I was very nervous, scanning the room for possible competition. A local dealer? Perhaps one of my university colleagues?

'One hundred pounds? £100? Who'll start me at £50 then?' His eyes moved towards the back of the room, where a clutch of dealers were smoking and chatting noisily, apparently paying no attention.

'I have £50.'

He moved upwards slowly in increments of £5. I bided my time, prowling like a nervous lion, ready to pounce. The bidding reached £85 and the pace slowed. I raised my programme in the air, but wasn't noticed. I raised my whole arm. *Me, sir, pick me!*

'New place. £90. Thank you, sir.'

The dealer at the back nodded once more, and I increased my bid to £100. There was a pause as the auctioneer peered round the room. The dealer shrugged and went back to his conversation. The laws of nature were suspended. Time stood still. The gavel poised in the air.

'All done then? Last chance. Do I hear £110? . . . I'll take £105 if you like.'

A final leisurely look, and the gavel hit the podium with a satis-fying crack. I lowered my arm, which had stayed suspended in the air as if I were acknowledging applause after scoring a goal.

I was exultant. The very same item had been offered in a previous Fine Art Sale, at an estimate of £300–£500, and I had watched as it failed to sell. No way could I afford that much for a book-case, however grand. I had a theory though – I had *lots* of theories in those days – which was that large bookcases were white elephants: if a person had a lot of books he was unlikely to have a big house, whereas people with large houses weren't likely accumulators of books. So big bookcases need to find just the right buyer.

That would be me, and this one was a beauty. Made of Victorian mahogany, it divided into six sections, the three top ones fitting on to the slightly protruding bottom sections, making a unit twelve feet long by ten feet high, with fifteen adjustable shelves that would hold, I reckoned, about a thousand books. My then-wife Barbara and I had recently refurbished a gracious Regency terraced house in the middle of Leamington Spa. It had four double bedrooms, a large sitting room with a balcony overlooking the garden and original wide-planked reddish Canadian pine floor-boards, and an undistinguished marble fireplace, which we thought rather posh.

In the process of furnishing the house, the recurrent problem was where to find room for all my books. I was not a book collector, but I acquired them avidly, and for any variety of reasons. I bought books to read immediately, books to read some time in the future, books that were useful for research, books that looked good to me or might look good to others. Many I bought for no reason at all, on one whim or another. And after a time there was nowhere to put them. The alcoves were all shelved, occasional bookcases bedecked the walls of the hallways, bedrooms, kitchen and study. Piles of books grew like spores, and prospered. The house was infested with them.

And now, with the mere raising and eventual lowering of a hand, the problem was solved. I paid £20 to have our new book-case delivered, assembled it on the left-hand wall of the sitting room, opposite the fireplace, and spent a sweaty weekend organ-izing and shelving, constructing an exhibition of my life as a reader. There were books from my high school and undergraduate years, like the tatty but heavily annotated *A Portrait of the Artist as a Young Man*. From my time at Oxford, working copies of all of Matthew Arnold, my annotated Lewis Carroll, long runs of

Lawrence, Joyce and Eliot. And, most significantly, there were my Conrads: all of his books, many in first editions, as well as most of the available critical books on him, which I had used doing my DPhil. Then there were all of the books, with their heavy apparatus of notes, annotations, marginalia and insertions, that I had used while teaching at the University of Warwick: hundreds of volumes of philosophy, psychology and literature, the tools of my trade, each volume weighted with the memory of courses, syllabuses and seminars taught. There were books that charted my various enthusiasms: tomes on Chinese porcelain, a series of books on Oriental painting, shelves full of art books and exhibition catalogues, plus a mass of books about various sports: John Feinstein on golf and basketball, Mike Brearley on cricket captaincy, Hunter Davies on football, George Will on baseball, Nick Faldo on himself.

When, some twenty-five years later, Barbara and I divorced, we came to the neat agreement that she would keep the house and its contents, and I would have our smaller London flat and its contents. The only exception to this admirably simple plan was that I would be allowed to retrieve my books whenever I was able to house them. But a divorce is seldom a simple or amicable thing: people don't do it because they trust each other and know how to negotiate their differences. A year later, when I moved to a larger flat with my new girlfriend Belinda, I rang Barbara to ask when I could pick up the books. Never, she said. She was entitled to the contents of the house, as we had agreed, and if she had once, she acknowledged, allowed me to think of them as mine, she had changed her mind and was keeping them. Given that I had refused to return a Roger Hilton painting that I had given her as a gift, but which was still in London, why should she return my books?

I was stunned. She was quite right about the painting, and I had behaved badly, but I had never expected anything as forensically undermining as the kidnapping of my books. I'd been outsmarted, mugged and denuded of a great treasure. I howled,

I hooted, I imprecated. I cursed Barbara and I cursed God. These weren't books, things of paste and ink and paper. They were as close as I came to a *soul*, they contained my history, my inner voices and connections to the transcendent, and she had excised it, as in Philip Pullman's *Northern Lights*, where children's daemons are surgically removed, and they waste away and die. Ex-wives know where your soft spots are, and this foray was wonderfully exact, as if beamed by micro-surgery into the secret places of my heart.

The books were not of any interest to her. They were mine, they were archaeologically mine. If you dug through and into them, layers of my life were progressively uncovered. What hurt the worst was the loss of my Graham Greenes, which had been Bertie's bottle books. Though Barbara had breast-fed our first child, Anna, by the time baby Bertie was born, some six years later, she had decided that anyone who goes through childbirth deserves a rest. I rather agreed, and was happy to give him his middle-of-the-night feed with a bottle. He would beam up at me, his silver-gold hair radiant as spun moonlight, and slurp away happily. I developed rather a neat posture in which I could tuck him into the crook of my left arm, place the bottle delicately in his mouth, and keep open a paperback Graham Greene in my right hand. I read fifteen of them before Bertie started to sleep through the night.

I later bought, from Greene himself, a set of his *Collected Works*, each of the twenty volumes signed by him, which he'd formerly kept in his flat in Paris. I associated them, naturally enough, with Bertie. They were gone as well.

My books were gone. The effect was tremendous, unexpected, physically distressing. I felt dizzy and nauseous, I kept having to sit down to regain my equilibrium. My books were gone. It prompted the questions, at once psychological and metaphysical: Was I still me? *Who am I, with no books?*

You may think this was an overreaction. It was. Nobody died, yet what I experienced was a form of grief. After the initial pain and disbelief there was an aching sense of loss. If there was something clownishly self-indulgent about this response, the intensity of my reaction was fuelled from other sources, from the accumulated frustration, anger and hurt that the loss of love entails.

But as time passed – we're only talking six months here – what I increasingly and surprisingly felt was no longer a sense of loss, but one of release. All those books, all that dust, all those metres of shelf space crammed higgledy-piggledy with paperbacks with their spines coming off, assorted hardbacks with torn or missing dust wrappers, maps and guidebooks stuffed into corners, bits of stuff and guff and fluff. For a rare book dealer I treat my personal books with shocking disregard. I cram them into shelves, dog-ear pages as I read, remove dust wrappers and then lose them. I suppose I still regard most books, as academics do, as mere objects of utility.

Though there may be comfort in large numbers of books, there's very little beauty. The art dealer Anthony d'Offay, who began his career as a rare book dealer, once told me that of all the serious art collectors he knew 'only two' have large numbers of books anywhere in the house. His point was not that big-hitting art collectors are semi-literate, but that almost all of them regard large assemblages of books as *ugly*. Viewed in this way (you have to skew your head to the side and look carefully) what you see when you look at a lot of books is paper in various stages of decay. Over time it progressively becomes yellowed with age, musty, acidic, bowed or brittle, ready for decomposition. It takes longer for paper than for humans, but the process is the same, and the results similar.

I like to think that when Philip Larkin memorably said 'books are a load of crap', he was not trying simply to shock. Perhaps he was also observing something about books as physical objects, and about the properties – the genesis and eventual decline – of paper? Paper begins when trees are reduced to vatfuls of yucky mulch; the books that are one of the results of this process can fertilize and nourish, to be sure, but there is something ineluctably physical, something that suggests decay and death, something disgusting about them.

And the curious feeling that was gradually unfolding in me, I recognized, was relief. Books, if not exactly crap, were certainly a burden. It felt free to live in a space that wasn't shelved on all sides, surrounded and defined by books. Large numbers of books seem to consume the very air. There's something insistently aggressive about them, something clamorous: '*Look at me! Read me! Remember me! Refer to me! Cite me! Dust me! Rearrange me!*' Perhaps this is why working in libraries has always made me feel anxious. Academic friends reminisce with delight about hours spent in Duke Humfrey's Reading Room at Bodley, the Beinecke at Yale, the Ransom Center at Texas, the old Reading Room at the British Library. I've spent my time in each of them, anxiously plotting an escape.

Too much unread, too much unknown, too poignant the sense of the futility of writing books. The British Library has millions of the damn things. Looking at the stacks I am often struck, not by the range and determination of man's quest for knowledge, but by the utter fatuousness of it all, the vanity.

Samuel Johnson – himself heavily represented in libraries – makes the point with characteristic zest:

> Of many writers who fill their age with wonder, and whose names we find celebrated in the books of their contemporaries, the works are now no longer to be seen, or are seen only among the lumber of libraries which are seldom visited, where they lie only to shew the deceitfulness of hope, and the uncertainty of honour.

My books were gone? What a relief: they'd done their work, and I'd done mine. All of a sudden there was a new sense of lightness. This didn't merely consist of more space in which to hang pictures, it meant that I felt less surrounded by my own history. I was a bookish person. I still am, only without many books. It was a giddy sensation. I felt deracinated, disassociated. And free.

I suppose you need to be a certain age (I was fifty-five) to feel thus unencumbered; I would have taken it worse twenty years before, when I needed the books not merely as working tools, but as objects of self-definition. But now? Now they had become *memento mori*, and I was glad to take my eyes from them. I came to feel that if Barbara hadn't initiated the process, I would (or at least should) have done it myself. I began, even, to feel grateful to her, for releasing me from these fusty appurtenances. She'd always had an acute sense of the fatuousness of academic life. Well, now all those books were *her* problem.

After all, *reading* is what matters, and has always mattered to me. I can't not do it, any more than I can stop eating or breathing. Left on my own for the briefest of moments – on a bus, in the toilet, waiting for the dentist – I am acutely uncomfortable without something, anything, to read. In extremis I take my wallet out and read my credit cards. (One of them has five sevens in the number!) I can't stop reading without feeling anxious, and extinguished: I read, therefore I am.

We are accustomed to talking of things and events 'influencing' our 'development': of the formative power of parental support or abuse, gifted or sadistic schoolteachers, changes of faces and venues, disappointment and delight in the pursuit of love, successes and failures in search of some goal or other. When we think of such experiences we too often neglect the way in which reading, too, has made us. Who would I be abstracted from what I have read, how would I have been formed? If I try to extract some sense of myself now, at the age of sixty-four, which is in some way independent of the myriad effects of my reading, there is only puzzlement. The same sort of bemusement that occurs when I wonder what it would have been like to have been an astronaut or a lion, grown up in Bangladesh or Peru, met an angel or been abducted by aliens.

I am inconceivable without my books. You can't take them away, they are inside me, they are what I am. Yet when the relations between reading and living are considered, it is often in passing, and frequently results in a formulation similar to that once made by Angela Carter: 'You bring to a novel, anything you have read, all your experience of the world.' That's an unremarkable thing to say. What else would you 'bring' to a novel? A prawn cocktail? But if you reverse Carter's formulation, and also claim that you bring to *life* everything that you have read in *novels* – some version of the Emma Bovary thesis – you get a much more interesting, and less studied, topic.

How do books make us? I don't know. Putting the question at this level of abstraction suggests a topic for a psychologist or sociologist, and I have no taste for such generalities. What I want to know is how my books have made me. To recall, to reread and to re-encounter the books that filled my mahogany bookcase, and continue to fill my present self.

What fun to pursue such a train of thought. To go into my (sparsely) book-lined study, turn that reading lamp inwards, and to reflect. To look at those (few) books in the dawning recognition that what they furnish is not a room, but a self.

1

HORTON AND MAYZIE

Then they cheered and they *cheered* and they CHEERED
  more and more.
They'd never seen anything like it before!
'My goodness! My *gracious*!' they shouted. 'MY WORD!
It's something brand new!
IT'S AN ELEPHANT BIRD!!'
Dr Seuss, Horton Hatches the Egg

I like things big. I adore Palladian villas, monumental Mark Rothkos, vases of gladioli, eagles, sixteen-ounce T-bone steaks. I can grasp the attractiveness of cottages, Indian miniatures, lilies of the valley, guinea pigs and roast quail. But it seems to me that, with a little more effort, any of these might make more of itself.

It is of course typically American to equate mere largeness with abundance and generosity. The country has vast spaces and majestic vistas, but that doesn't explain it. So does Tibet, and Tibetans rarely drive Hummers. When I grew up in the 1950s, size was an index of post-war prosperity: developments of four-bedroomed tract houses flourished like (large) mushrooms, cars sprouted fins and expanded in all directions, people gorged on the abundant food, and expanded to inhabit the capaciousness of their domiciles and transport.

I suffer from some of this. But I rather suspect that in my case this predisposition to the outsized is also caused by that admirable pachyderm, Dr Seuss's Horton the Elephant, to whom I was exposed at the impressionable age of four. (Elephants figure in the American imagination in a way that they don't in the European: consider that American attempt to render the small and cute – Dumbo the baby flying elephant.) Horton is himself a symptom of this culture of largeness, but in me he is its cause.

I adored *Horton Hatches the Egg*, one of the lesser known Seuss books, but my favourite by far. The reason for this doesn't entirely reside in the text, which is unforgettably delightful, though hardly more so than many other of the Seuss books. I wonder, all these years later, whether I didn't have, at that time, some obscure recognition that this particular story applied to me?

The poem concerns a charming and winsome, but flighty, bird called Mayzie who, bored by the longeurs of egg-sitting, wishes instead to go on an extended holiday to Palm Beach. She flirtatiously prevails upon the kindly elephant Horton to take her place up in the tiny tree, in spite of his considerable misgivings:

Why of all silly things!
I haven't feathers and *I* haven't wings.
ME on your egg? Why, that doesn't make sense. . .
Your egg is so small, ma'am, and I'm so immense!

He gives in, of course, flattered by her eyelash batting, and reassured by the promise that she will hurry right back. Which of course she doesn't, she's having too much fun.

Stuck up his tree for months, covered by snow and buffeted by wind – you quite understand why Mayzie didn't fancy it – Horton is mocked by his fellow creatures, and eventually towed away, still sitting on his nest, to become the star turn of a travelling circus: *Look at this unnatural, laughable fellow! He thinks he's a bird! He's so fat he must be pregnant!*

The egg, when it eventually hatches under the immeasurable

placidity of Horton, reveals a hybrid creature, representative of both earth and air: a baby elephant with wings. Although Mayzie, visiting the circus when it arrives near Palm Beach, wishes to claim her chick, the baby (complete with tiny trunk – like Mayzie with a penis) flies directly into the arms of the estimable Horton, whom it recognizes as its androgynous progenitor:

> And it should be, it *should* be, it SHOULD be like that!
> Because Horton was faithful! He sat and he sat!
> He meant what he said
> And he said what he meant . . .
> . . . And they sent him home
> Happy,
> One hundred per cent!

I'd beg: *Again! Read it again!* And if it was too late, or I'd asked too often, I'd snuggle up under the covers repeating to myself that final, immensely comforting verse: 'Because Horton was faithful he sat and he sat . . .' I loved this line so passionately, I suspect, because that was how my father, Bernie, was. He loved being at home, was happiest with a book, and an opera in the air. My mother, Edie, was in spirit a Mayzie: she hated sitting around, liked a drink, a fag and a party, loved travelling and seeing the world, had a rage for company and good talk. She didn't so much dislike children as ignore them – they weren't much fun – though she got on better with hers as they became more reasonable and responsive. But motherhood was never, she was happy to acknowledge, entirely her thing.

'Babies? Ugh!' she'd say.

'How do you think that makes me feel, mom?' I would ask.

'You're not a baby now, I can talk to you. I like children when you can talk to them.'

She'd suffered badly from post-natal depression, and my father liked to claim, ruefully but proudly, that he had done much of my mothering: feeding, changing, bathing and putting me to bed and reading at night. My father was that sort of elephant, and my mother that sort of bird. It was a compelling contrast, and if at first glance the dice seem loaded in favour of Hortons, there's a lot to be said for Mayzies. Mine was full of laughter, a great talker and a good listener, engaged, vibrant, attractive. On a good day. But like many Mayzies she was also self-absorbed, suffered violent mood swings, and could be as cruel and critical as she was kind and supportive. And the problem was: you never knew which side of her you were going to meet. She might light on the branch with you and chirp away or, for no obvious reason, peck you in the eye and fly off in a huff. And so childhood, with such a mother, consisted of a constant oscillation between connection and disconnection, elation and despair.

In addition to her regular mood swings, she suffered severe pre-menstrual tension, and could fill the house – indeed, fill the entire neighbourhood – with a bleak and dangerous friability. (To this day I am convinced that I caused it and, indeed, that I am still the cause of *all* pre-menstrual tension.) The lesson was learned painfully early, and continued to inform my sense of women thereafter: when they are more than usually difficult, it is prudent to hide in an upstairs closet. There was nothing more delightful than connection to such a woman, and nothing more dangerous.

One day she disappeared. She'd become rather large, and there was apparently a baby in her tummy, though that seemed preposterous to me. Just like a woman, just like a Mayzie, to fly off and leave you on some obscure mission, and then come back with an adored stranger in her arms. When the week-old Ruthie arrived home, a gigantic vase of orange gladioli appeared on the table in the hall, which is one of my earliest visual memories. I was apparently supposed to be excited by this gratuitous addition to the family, but spent my time in my room twisting coat hangers (I couldn't find any way to attach screws or nails to them) making a 'baby swatter'. My father came up to examine it: 'Quite a good baby swatter. Shall we put it away? I'll read to you, if you want.'

Connection to a man that you could count on one hundred per cent. If Hortons are – let us admit it squarely – perhaps a little unexciting in their placidity and steadfastness, they aren't just out for a good time, they can be counted on. Not in some paltry way, as you might rely on your accountant: Hortons are mature, reasonable and great suppliers of love and reading.

But, sadly, you couldn't just be read to for the rest of your life. *Would you like to learn how to read yourself?* I wasn't so sure. Being read to was better, surely? Faster, more comfortable. I could drift off to sleep lapped by language, hardly aware of the last sentences, though my lips still moved with them. And then, right away, it would be morning. Could anything be better than that?

There was certainly something worse. When you learned to read two unpleasant and frustrating things came together. First of all you didn't get any more *stories*: no Babar and Queen Celeste, no little nuns, no Hansel or Gretel, no Dr Dolittle and his gang of animals. Having inhabited this enchanted realm, I was conscious of some going backwards, a regression, a fall. No stories, no sentences, not even any words. Only the acute sensation of beginning again, puzzling out, the frustration of, say, a native speaker confronted with a foreign tongue.

I began singing and sounding my ABCs, well before they might be assigned the utilitarian task of being made up from sound to word. The first pleasure was simply in mastering the connections, the sounds, the sequences. As if I were learning to count, because B follows A as surely and satisfyingly as two follows one. I would follow my mother around the apartment for hours, counting to a hundred, doing it again, then singing my ABCs, incessantly. It drove her crazy.

But when I got my first reading books, a process was initiated which was rather frightening, consisting of repeated experiences of puzzlement, frustration, and resolution.

C – A – T

Three sounds, in a slow order, then a faster one, as they are elided. What do they mean? Reading begins in anxiety. It is up to me to decipher and decide. *Can I do this?*

A dawning recognition, a smile, a great sense of incipient achievement and relief. *I get it! CAT!*

And on to the next word, and to the yet more creative and complex process of assembling those words into sentences. I am in my pyjamas, sitting on the edge of the bed. It's night-time, the lamp is on, and the milk and Oreo cookies are on my bedside table. I sit on a lap, cuddle and squirm into some mutual organic rhythm, reach out and tentatively touch each letter, secure in the warmth and visceral encouragement of being held. My father smells better than my mother: a cigarette, closets and stuffed teddy smell; mom smells sharper, sometimes she almost stings my nose, with a smell mixed up of metal, marigolds and the wolf enclosure at the zoo.

We'd sound out the words together. The reiterated moments of triumph as one overcomes those spurts of anxiety and learns to read is forever associated, I suspect, with warmth, proximity and physical comfort. People like me, who are compulsive lifetime readers, are unconsciously prompted as we turn the page by memories of this Edenic collaboration, in which the book ultimately replaces the breast or bottle. (Goethe says, 'in all things we learn only from those we love.')

It was particularly hard when, at the same time, often in the same session, my own halting reading of some banal book or other might be interrupted and replaced, before going to sleep, with a chapter from, say, *Dr Dolittle*. Dr Dolittle! That was terrific, even with its paucity of elephants. And *Jack and Jill*? Junk. The lesson of this was obvious, and – learned early – has been a tenet for most of my adult life: never do for yourself what others can do better for you.

It was the same with writing, for learning to read is also learning to write: why bother? Other people were much better at it than me. Let them write and me listen or, if I had to, read. For my earliest efforts at writing were even less interesting than the *Jack and Jill* books on which I painstakingly learned to read. I wrote my first book at the age of six. It consisted of a few sheets of scrappy paper, cut clumsily with scissors into pieces, chunks really, about two inches square, and stapled together. It bore its title in crayon on the front page: *A Friend for Mickey*. The text followed on the next four pages, also inscribed in crayon. It read: 'Once upon a time a boy went wakking down the street to see his friend his friend was a good friend.'

It was probably the product of a task set on a difficult day, buying my mother a few moments' respite from my relentless counting and general fidgetiness. There is something rushed and uncommitted about my fulfilment of the assignment, characteristics that are an abiding part of my nature. But my mother, nonetheless, was sufficiently proud of my little book that it became the foundation document of her Old Age Box. It rather surprised me, rediscovering *Mickey* after she died in 1974, to find myself embarrassed by this palpable reminder of my early lack of anything approaching high intelligence or, at the very least, some small creative spark.

Neither of the above. There was nothing *promising* in *A Friend for Mickey*. If it vaguely echoes – as I later imagined – the opening paragraph about Baby Tuckoo and his friend the moocow of Joyce's *A Portrait of the Artist as a Young Man*, it can only be at the most fundamental archetypal level: an isolated child, the voyage down the road, the search for a boon companion. No, if books were to be a part of my life it was likely that somebody else was going to have to write them.

But once I had read, indeed memorized, the available Dr Seuss books, it wasn't entirely clear what to read next. *Nothing* was as good as them. My parents cast about for tempting material, but their frustration reflected something about the culture in which they found themselves: the choices were limited. There were the Babar books, but he (King of the Elephants!), his Queen Celeste and their children Pom, Flora and Alexander were rather inferior elephants compared to Horton. They didn't hatch a single egg between them. A series of deliciously illustrated books about Madeline and some nuns interested me for a time, but the texts were dull compared to Dr Seuss, and Madeline was too small and inexplicably fond of lining up in rows. No, children were better catered for by the comics (the years 1949/1950 alone saw the first strips of *Peanuts, Beetle Bailey, Pogo* and *Dennis the Menace*), and shortly by that captivating new medium, television, than by the written word.

By the middle of the 1950s the effect of television on reading was becoming evident. We loved *The Howdy Doody Show*, a captivatingly inane programme hosted by a toothy, freckled, red-haired puppet who had absolutely nothing to say for himself. He didn't need to. He was *there*. At the age of four Ruthie, a beautiful and silent child who loitered on the edge of things, partaking rather than participating, was asked, as dessert was being served by our neighbours in the upstairs apartment, if she liked jelly roll?

'I love him!' she replied. 'What channel is he on?'

Within a year we got a TV too, and we spent our time either in front of it, or begging to be in front of it, though there was almost nothing worth watching. But it sure was better than reading.

In 1955, Rudolf Flesch's bestselling book *Why Johnny Can't Read: And What You Can Do About It* caused such national consternation that even *Life* magazine, hardly a bastion of high literary culture, took up the cause. Its answer? We needed more Seuss books! In 1957, the obliging doctor responded with *The Cat in the Hat* and, sure enough, it sold huge quantities. Kids know quality when they see it: to this day 25 per cent of American children read a Dr Seuss title as their first book. But Rudolf Flesch missed the real point, because he thought that American child illiteracy resulted from bad teaching, whereas it is clear in retrospect that the very activity of reading was being superseded. Within a couple of generations, not merely many children, but their parents too, would admit without shame that they have never read a book.

Even one by Dr Seuss. What a deprivation! His characters are so loveably free and wild, perfect embodiments of the lawlessness and egotism of childhood. His world is always in danger of falling apart: he is children's laureate of entropy. Think of the crazy energy of *The Cat in the Hat*, or the infantile omnipotence of *Yertle the Turtle*. It is no surprise to hear that Dr Seuss (like my mom) didn't actually like kids, because both knew you couldn't trust them. Mrs Seuss once admitted that her husband was frightened of children, because he was so worried what they might do or ask next.

That doesn't bother me at all. Many of the greatest writers for or about children didn't like kids much, partly because they understood and respected them so thoroughly, and anxiously knew what they were capable of: not only Dr Seuss, but Beatrix Potter, Charles M. Schulz, and Lewis Carroll (unless they were half-naked little girls). But from such child-phobic writers we get many of the abiding images and ideas that shape our sense of ourselves.

I never thought of myself as one of Dr Seuss's child figures. Though I flew to Horton like that new-born chick, it was the estimable elephant with whom I most identified. His heroism made me swoon with admiration: *'he sat and he sat!'* From which, I rather believe, I derive both a lifetime preference for sitting rather than doing, and a tendency to present myself as bigger and more important than I actually am. Yet I am grateful for my inner Horton, who has otherwise guided me truly and well. Though if I regret anything from our lifetime association it lies in my apparent need, in unconscious acknowledgement of his internal presence, to emulate his waistline. I try to lose weight – in my time I have lost a Horton-amount of weight – but I just don't feel comfortable at an everyday size. It's better to be big.

2

SPRITZING OVER THE BOOKS

my sexual appetite is directed towards myself . . .
A patient of Magnus Hirschfeld,
quoted in his *Sexual Anomalies and Perversions*

At the time of writing *A Friend for Mickey* I was, according to Freud, supposed to be entering that phase of psychosexual development that he called the latency period. I had already failed my Oedipal tests by attaching myself to my father rather than my mother, not to mention identifying with an androgynous elephant-bird, and I didn't do much better at this later stage. Latency is supposed to involve the sublimation of the heightened (oral, anal and phallic) sexual awareness of the infant into other interests and activities, until that reawakening that occurs at puberty.

But it was just the opposite for me. All the polymorphous sexual pleasure and curiosity of the infant continued, thoroughly unsublimated, throughout my later childhood years, in which I could most frequently be found pants down behind a bush with any available child companion, peering and giggling. At least my parents never had to worry where I was. They'd lure me out, covered with leaves rather than embarrassment, and suggest I came in to have something to eat, and maybe read a book.

My mother, Ruthie and I spent the summer holidays in Huntington, Long Island, in her parents' bungalow in Harbor Heights Park, a community of modest dwellings that served as summer retreats for New Yorkers. The bungalow was a ten-minute walk – you could pick blackberries on the way – from Brown's Beach, with its unreliable seaweed-stuffed tides, the oily surface of the water reflecting the sun in brilliant colours. The sand was mucky and unappealing, but there was a small snack bar where you could buy cream soda or root beer, and hotdogs with yummy green relish gone crusty in the heat. I wasn't allowed in the water for an hour after my lunch, or I would get cramps and drown. But lots of other kids were allowed in the water right away, I observed to Granny Pearl, and they didn't drown. She sniffed – her usual form of disapprobation or rebuttal – looked at her watch, and said, '*One hour!*'

The bungalow was entirely without soundproofing, and it was easy to overhear conversations, the everyday intimacies of belching and arguing. There were only two bedrooms. Mom slept on the porch on a sofa-bed, in which dad would join her when he finally arrived to spend a couple of weeks, while Ruthie and I shared a room and bed next to the kitchen. Its great advantage was that the wall that separated it from the kitchen terminated – for no obvious reason – some eighteen inches short of the ceiling. If I stood on the bedstead I could just peer over, and see what was going on. Ruthie was too short, so I sent back reports.

'Granny's in there,' I would whisper.

'What's she doing?'

'Nothing.'

Ricky! Ruthie! Will you go to sleep right now!

There was a tiny third room, hardly more than a cupboard, where *die schwarz* would sleep. Each summer a young coloured woman, supplied by an agency in New York City, would spend the summer in the bungalow, tidying, cleaning and washing up. Granny was frequently exasperated with the help, unsure whether they made life easier or harder. What the poor girls made of it is almost impossible to imagine, and none of us even tried to. The demands of running a kosher kitchen were incomprehensibly arcane to most of them. '*No, no! You don't serve the butter when there is meat on the table. And you don't use these dishes with the meat. How many times do I have to tell you?*'

An imposing woman grown plump in later life, granny had a noble bosom and a bottom that stuck out, a rolled mop of grey hair and an anxiously inquisitive expression on her round powdered face that suggested that the worst was yet to come. My major encounters with her were about food: did I finish my lunch? Had I eaten too much fruit, or too many cookies? Taken all of those candies? Was I a little feverish? Had I done a BM? The spectre of the enema bag loomed. I was *fine*. In tacit acknowledgement of her obsession with anal functioning, my girl cousins, sister and I would periodically inspect each other's bottoms as we ducked behind a bush or tree. 'Hey!' Uncle Freddie would yell over to us, 'if you want to show cookies go somewhere else!' We did. Showing cookies was better, even, than eating them.

I avoided Granny Pearl as best I could. Unlike Poppa Norman she knew nothing of baseball, or making things in the garage workshop, or polishing the Caddy. I adored being with him, watching and helping, or playing 'catched'um-missed'um' with a softball in the garden. He'd played semi-pro baseball, and had a catcher's stocky body, with a thick and hairy torso, short legs, low centre of gravity. He loved Friday nights, shedding his elegant suit and colourful tie when he got to Huntington, spending the weekend puttering round the bungalow. He was great value in short spurts, but tired of the company of children quickly. You could make money out of that. 'First one to fall asleep gets a nickel!' he'd offer. Even in the afternoon I was happy to feign sleep, though I quickly raised the ante to a quarter.

I was the only one of the children who was able to climb the posts of the low white picket fence that surrounded the bungalow, along which poppa placed pots of trailing geraniums, to lever myself up on to the roof. I could overhear the grown-ups talking on the back porch, only they rarely said anything interesting, and when it was, it was likely to be in Yiddish. But I knew that granny's vocabulary – *narishkeit, ganif, mishigas, meshuginah, shlepper, chutzpah, kvetch, tsouris* – demarcated the myriad ways in which life could try and disappoint.

Hidden behind the sloping roof line, I was as invisible as God with a handful of sugared almonds. One time I vanished sufficiently from the collective memory and was allowed to lie up on the roof as the light faded, and the moon came up. In the slow darkness the fireflies' bottoms glowed like embers descended from the canopy of stars. The honeysuckle odour sharpened as the air cooled, and I looked upwards at the meaningless immensity. I felt alarmingly diminished, and reasoned that surely it must end, somewhere. In a wall perhaps? How high would such a wall have to be? How thick? What above? Beneath?

I never repeated the experience. It was too unsettling. I decided to domesticate the roof instead. Often I'd take a cushion from the porch, and a book to read to ward off the silence of those infinite spaces. What did I read? It is hard to remember. Early things always are, you may be thinking. But childhood reading, for an American child of my period, is difficult to recall. To remember an American reading childhood you have to engage in manifold acts of recovery of what is almost irretrievably lost.

This was not true for English children of the same time, at least for the middle and upper-class ones. In the late nineteenth and early twentieth century England had produced a body of children's literature – from Edward Lear and Lewis Carroll through the great period of high Edwardian whimsy: Barrie, Milne, Beatrix Potter, Kenneth Grahame – that became the lingua franca of an English childhood. It was impossible to grow up as an English child in the first half of the twentieth century without reading – indeed without owning – copies of the Alice and Pooh books, *The Jungle Book*, *Peter Pan*, the Beatrix Potters, *The Wind in the Willows*, as well as various *Famous Five*s or *Just William*s.

The message of these was remarkably similar: life may be a little dangerous, but not very; energy is hardly required to combat such dangers; it pays to be shoulder-shruggingly loveable and hapless. Think of Pooh or, indeed, of Bertie Wooster. If the Battle of Waterloo was won on the playing fields of Eton, which supplied the manpower for the next generations of Empire, that Empire was lost between the covers of *Winnie the Pooh*.

I have vague memories of Alfred Olivant's *Bob, Son of Battle* (dogs), *Treasure Island* (parrots and hooks), *King Solomon's Mines* (diamonds) and *Peter Pan* (fairies and crocodiles), but more particular ones of Franklin W. Dixon's Hardy Boys series. The Hardy Boys books were great. There were loads of them, and you could talk about them to your friends, even read them together. Everybody read the Hardy Boys. (Except girls. If you were a girl you read the Nancy Drew books instead. Boys never did that. Nancy Drew was stupid.)

The joy of the Hardy Boys series was not that the individual books were particularly exciting, but that there were so many of them. They were remarkably similar. The two brothers, Joe and Frank, aged seventeen and eighteen and in all respects except hair colour indistinguishable, were boon companions and super sleuths, packers of one-punch knockouts, and energetic associates of their father, an investigative police officer. They could solve any plot devised by a sneaky foreigner, and though frequently thwarted or even kidnapped, they never came to the slightest harm. Neither did the foreigners: all they got was captured by our heroes, and sent off to the pokey, muttering, 'Sacré bleu! Zese 'Ardy boys 'ave done eet again!'

It didn't matter what books I read. The key was to be seen to be reading. If I wasn't up on the roof, I would retreat to my room ('*I'm reading and I need some peace and quiet!*') but I made sure to leave the door open. ('*He's reading and he needs some peace and quiet!*') What I was reading was a *book*. It didn't matter what the book was, and I hadn't the faintest idea that one might be better than another. But to garner credit, to be approved of, left alone, quietly commended, it had to be a book. Comics wouldn't do. Reading books gave the signal that intelligent life was going on: I didn't merely read them, I displayed them like trophies.

I was an anxious boy. Before Ruthie was born we lived in a garden apartment in Alexandria, a suburb of Washington DC where my dad worked as a lawyer for the federal government, and wrote short stories in his (little) spare time. When we went shopping, over the weekend, and needed to split up to pursue different tasks and purchases, I would insist on accompanying which ever parent had the keys to the car.

It may have been in response to this anxiety that my parents sent me to a recently opened progressive school in rural Alexandria. Burgundy Farm Country Day School had been founded by a co-operative of parents in 1946, and was based on Homer Lane's child-centred principles of learning by doing. There was a motivated and engaged staff of young teachers who were called by their first names, an outdoor swimming pool, goats and other farm animals wandering about. We pupils fed the livestock and helped in the general running of the farm, which was presumably intended to establish some organic connection to the natural world. It left me with a life-long aversion to doing the chores, and any relations with animals unless accompanied by gravy and potatoes.

I called my parents Bernie and Edie. They were products of the 1930s: socially committed, progressive, anxious for the world to become a better place, partly by creating in their new family a microcosm of a world in which everyone was treated with respect. Even children. My mother's social work training at the University of Pennsylvania had included large doses of A.S. Neill and Homer Lane, while my father would much rather have been a writer, university teacher, or psychoanalyst than a lawyer. He worked for the federal government's Rural Electrification Administration, and though he argued a case before the Supreme Court he never made much money. My mother was largely at home for the first few years with Ruthie, who'd been born in 1948. It must have been a hard time financially, but neither of them ever complained of it, though mom occasionally joked about being footsore from selling World Book encyclopaedias door-to-door.

While she shlepped her books about I was having fun. There were very few set lessons at school, and children were encouraged to read whatever they liked, and to pursue what interested them most. There were no exams, lots of play, handicrafts and painting, swimming and sports. It was the purpose of such an education to produce children who had their own voices, were not cowed by authority, learned enthusiastically, related to each other generously, and played uncompetitively.

When, in 1954, we moved to Huntington, Long Island, I was barely aware of the reason: as the McCarthy era progressed and the House Un-American Activities Committee began to name and pursue more and more 'communists', my father's position in the government became increasingly untenable. Both of my parents had been 'card-carrying' in the 1930s, like many intelligent young people with a conscience. It was only a matter of time before he was hunted down, humiliated, and fired.

Huntington was the obvious place to go. Poppa Norman and Granny Pearl were there in the summers, and their son Freddie, with his wife Eleanor moved there when he was demobbed from the Navy. There were enough family contacts for my dad, once he passed the bar examination, to find a few clients in his new private practice. Mom could probably get a job at a local social work agency. It would be tough for a while, but there wasn't much choice.

Burgundy Farm aimed to instil self-reliance and confidence, but it certainly didn't prepare me for the Huntington School System. I entered the fourth grade in Woodbury Avenue Elementary School in the way many travellers enter obscure foreign parts, partly intimidated, but fascinated as well: what odd customs, what peculiar rituals. In the morning you pledged allegiance to the flag, but I didn't know the words, and was regarded with suspicion: was I some sort of communist? Sometimes there were drills in case of atomic bomb attack, but if you hid under your desk the fall-out wouldn't get you. Otherwise you sat behind the desk all day with about thirty (silent!) kids, while Miss Saul talked, and you wrote down what she said.

The class was studying Babylon, which I knew to be a town somewhere on Long Island. It sounded an interesting place. Apparently they had a lot of wars there, masses of treasures, and a king whom everybody worshipped, or else. I raised my hand:

'Please, Miss Saul. How long does it take to get there?'

I am not sure whether an entire class can guffaw, but I think that is what happened. They already knew I was different, and thus peculiar and not to be trusted. I was too good at maths, had read an awful lot of books, but didn't know anything about science, or, it was clear, history. After class, Miss Saul gave me a book entitled *Ancient Babylon*. I didn't read much of it, but it was annoying that they had to give it the same name as our local town.

We moved into a block of new apartments, where Ruthie and I shared a bedroom, but within a year, once dad's practice had begun and a few clients rolled up, we bought a new house (for $20,000, which was such a *lot*) on Brookside Drive. Only well-off kids lived in *new* houses; you could tell which kids were poor just by looking where they lived. My fourth-grade classmate Judy Hackstaff lived in an enormous really old house, with a wrap-around front porch and peeling white paint, and funny towers like a haunted castle. It looked spooky and dirty to me, and I felt sorry for her and invited her up to see our new house, so she could tell her parents how rich people lived.

Ruthie and I had separate bedrooms, there was a den and two

living rooms, and a garden where mom could plant stocks and phlox – she loved bright and strongly perfumed flowers. All of the other houses on the road were exactly the same – that was nice – only in different colours. But only ours had a cherry tree in the front, with yellowy-red cherries that weren't too bitter once you got used to the taste.

Ruthie and I fought over colours for our bedrooms: of the hundreds of choices we both wanted the same blue. (I wanted it first, of course.) There were tears, and she got the best blue, while I settled for the next best. Somehow she also got the biggest bedroom, which I resented without coming to the conclusion, quite, that she was the favoured child. All it proved was that if you made a big fuss you could get your way. We both got new beds with real foam rubber pillows, new desks, and got to choose prints for the walls from a museum shop. New, everything new. It was like starting all over again. Mom and dad treated themselves, in the master bedroom, to a built-in unit behind the bed, which had a long bookshelf with louvred doors which, when closed, you could prop your pillow against. It was painted the same colour (not blue, taupe) as their room, and looked, we all felt, distinctly ritzy. I admired it very much – asked if I could have one too – but it hardly occurred to me, in those pleasure-hazed first months, to look at the books in it. Anyway, they didn't look very interesting. They were fat blue and brown volumes, without even any dust jackets to make them fit in with all that newness, hardly worth a glance.

One day, though, I paused in my envious contemplation of this exclusive piece of furniture, and noticed the titles. It was a day – I must have been twelve – when my reading life was to change forever, a day after which reading was to become my major source of excitement and delight. The titles of those dull looking books, once focused on, though admittedly puzzling and obscure, had something to recommend them: *Psychopathia Sexualis* by Krafft-Ebing,

Sexual Anomalies and Perversions by Magnus Hirschfeld, *Sexual Aberrations* by Wilhelm Stekel, MD. Sex, all sex! Anomalies (I looked it up) *and* Perversions? Bliss.

A chirpy '*Can I borrow this, dad, it looks pretty interesting?*' was not likely to withdraw these books from their appointed shelf. If I wanted to read them I would have to be sneaky. That, it was to turn out, was part of the fun. Reading them was going to be exciting *and* dangerous, like a Hardy Boys adventure with nefarious foreigners. The entry of these books into my life coincided with the onset of puberty – indeed, they probably caused it – and they were to fuel my imagination for the next few years. I was so intensely stimulated that it was embarrassing just to be me. Surely, anyone would be able to tell? Mom would be able to tell. She would know. I was in a cringingly explosive cycle of lust, shame, delight and abandon. Nothing could better exemplify Carlyle's dictum that 'the best effect of any book is that it excites the reader to self activity.'

I liked Hirschfeld the best. The plots certainly weren't up to much, there was too much medical jargon, and a deeply frustrating amount of the text dropped into Latin at key moments, but there was plenty to hold my attention. The characters were distinctly interesting, and each had a little story to tell. Not enough detail, of course: the stories were reprehensibly succinct, but there was sufficient to fire the imagination. Anyway I only wanted the dirty bits.

Rereading the texts, fifty years later, I was astonished how much I *remembered*. Oh my God, it's her! It's him! It's *that*!

His first spontaneous sexual excitement occurred when, at the beginning of puberty, he saw himself for the first time full length in a mirror . . . There was an instantaneous erection and he grew excited. Excusing himself he pressed his lips to the mirror and covered his mirrored lips with kisses . . .

He made the following statement in writing: *my sexual appetite is directed towards myself and to lick my own member would give me the greatest pleasure.*

There were further reports of an American girls' boarding school where there was 'a veritable epidemic of lesbianism', an account of a thirty-year-old doctor much given to bottom kissing, a Parisian inventor of an electrical flagellating machine, and a serious and stern woman given to 'punishing and cherishing' her male lovers, while riding them about the bedroom. Though chapters on masturbation reassured me that it was *not* proven that it led to 'softening of the brain', nevertheless Hirschfeld did not recommend that one lathered one's penis (like one of his masturbators) and carried on gaily. No, 'the principal effect of masturbation is depression which may change to melancholia, leading to thoughts of suicide or even actual suicide.' That didn't scare me: as long as my brain stayed unsoftened so could my penis, lathered or unlathered.

Though unimaginably distant in time and place, Hirschfeld's people were not, by-and-large, freaks or monsters. A few were distinctly to be avoided – chapters on Sadism and Sexual Murder required quick skipping over (who'd want to read about *that*?) – but many of these obscure mittel-Europeans became exemplars of human possibility. Who would have supposed human life so richly peculiar, so various in possibility, or imagined that adults – those distant, intimidating, over-dressed and other-worldly creatures – could have been so rude? For some time I lived the overheated inward life of a Viennese petit bourgeois. I scoured Huntington for ladies dressed exotically in furs, with nothing but corsets on underneath. I wasn't sure what a corset was, but according to my sources it could elicit astonishing homage. Ladies with big breasts and protuberant bottoms were enticing, until I noted with dismay that my Granny Pearl pretty much fitted that bill.

The discovery of my father's erotically charged books signalled the beginning of that period when mere proximity to a lockable space was sufficient to cause an erection. Obsessed though I was with reading and rereading my father's secret library, it wasn't long before I had internalized the most exciting bits, refined and extended them according to what I began to find were my own needs and desires. An internal catalogue of fantasies began to emerge, and they were every bit as satisfactory, inside those lockable spaces, as the books were. Better, even: no book to hide (try putting the two volumes of *Psychopathia Sexualis* under your shirt). No book to balance precariously whilst otherwise pressingly engaged. Fantasies were prompted by books, but they were better than books.

My bedroom had a rudimentary lock on the door, but it was hard to justify why one needed to be locked in there so often. Bathrooms – at home or away – were the best, because no one could question why you were in there, though they might well wonder why you needed to be there quite so frequently. I must have seemed to be suffering from chronic diarrhoea. And there is nothing that piques the interest and concern of Jewish parents and grandparents as thoroughly as trouble in the lavatory. *Was I all right?* I was asked, returning from a third trip to the bathroom in two hours. *Oh, fine, yeah, all right*, I'd say, hurrying away, ashamed. Did they know?

Granny Pearl did, I was sure of it. In her tiny apartment in the Hotel Brewster on Manhattan's West 86th Street, there was a glass-fronted bookcase in the living room, with an assortment of books, each bearing poppa's book plate STOLEN FROM THE LIBRARY OF NORMAN KORNBLUEH. There was one that I wanted to steal for sure, but presumably its absence would have been observed, and (worse) remarked upon. Written by two Danish psychologists called Kronhausen, its unassuming yellow and orange paperback covers announced the title *Pornography and the Law: The Psychology of Erotic Realism and 'Hard Core' Pornography*. There was nothing lurid about the book, but the promise of the title was sufficient to

ensure that it sold in large numbers to a readership ostensibly interested in its liberal agenda.

To me though, and I suspect to most of its readers, the allure
was simple: because the work was a serious intellectual enterprise
it could, in the service of argument and analysis, quote from a vast
range of dirty books which were otherwise unavailable through
the normal American outlets of the 1950s. There were excerpts
from Victorian pornographic classics like *The Lascivious Hypocrite*,
The Autobiography of a Flea, or *The Oxford Professor* by L. Erectus
Mentulus, which were then unfavourably contrasted to their apparently 'higher' counterparts, those novels that are erotically realistic
rather than pornographic, and which need clear criteria to distinguish them as worthy of general release: books like *Ulysses*, *Lady
Chatterley's Lover*, *Memoirs of Hecate County*. My dad had some
of these – I'd even pawed my way through a few – but I liked the
proper dirty ones better. I was not interested in redeeming artistic
quality, it got in the way of the sexy scenes, or diminished their
impact. I wanted unadulterated smut. Who cared what the various
characters thought, where they came from, what their aspirations
outside the bedroom might have consisted of?

Not that the smut *was* unadulterated, even the Kronhausens
weren't allowed that. They could quote from the most salacious
passages, but a frustrating semantic propriety pertained: *no* dirty
words. Thus we have the ludicrously censored scene from *The
Strange Cult*:

> . . . on that nice little bed down there I'm going to give you
> a wonderful [vernacular for coitus]. After that, if you're real
> nice, of course, I'm going to teach you [vernacular for fellatio].
> Then I'm going to [vernacular for cunnilingus] till you [vernac-
> ular for orgasm], and then after that we'll [vernacular for
> coitus] some more!

Even I skipped over this [vernacular for risible persiflage]. But there were sufficient passages to keep one's pecker up. I spent hours with the book cradled in my lap, in a chair in the living room of the apartment, so that neither the cover nor my excitement would show, recurrently half hobbling back and forth to the bathroom. When mom or dad came to pick me up, granny would say, 'Oh, Ricky's been shpritzing over the books all day,' which I was guiltily certain had a wry knowingness. (The Yiddish verb to shpritz usually means to add a dash of seltzer, but it also means to squirt or to spray.)

These early experiences of reading stolen erotica from family sources transformed the act of reading for me entirely. It would be catastrophic to be caught reading such books, for not only were they clearly not for me, but my excitement at reading them would mark me as a pervert of the class of those chronicled in the texts. (Though it did not signal my father or grandfather as similarly deviant, of course. They were intellectuals. I wondered how they kept mom and granny from looking at the books.)

Farewell, Hardy Boys. From now on, I would seek better and more exciting things to read, forbidden ones. I learned how to skim a page and instantly pick out the key words: breasts, nipples, vagina, buttocks, anus. My father's whole library of fiction loomed. I began to skim it, book by book. Some piqued my immediate interest, only to disappoint. There was a copy of Van de Velde's *Ideal Marriage*: *Its Physiology and Technique*, which even I recognized as a peculiarly evasive title. I scoured the pages for illustrations and examples sufficient to ignite sexual fantasies, though this research was retarded by the inscription on the front end-paper, from my mother to my father: 'For Bernie, in the hope that ours will be.' I tried desperately to block that out, its implications unthinkable, and skipped through the pages in search of something to get my fingers round. I ignored all that detail – bit yucky – about periods and pregnancy. I skipped all of the stuff about something called the clitoris, and about female orgasm. I didn't have one of those, and I had boy orgasms. This lack of curiosity was a mistake, and my first girlfriends (and I) would pay for it.

When, for my Bar Mitzvah, I asked for a subscription to the Book of the Month Club, it was mistaken for a precocious academic request, and honoured accordingly. What I was looking for, of course, was a new source of books with dirty bits. MacKinlay Kantor's *Andersonville* had a couple of choice moments, but they were hardly worth the trouble of finding, and more frequently monthly offers were feel-good cutesy books like *The Snake Has All the Lines*, or *Cheaper by the Dozen*.

Anyway, I had already assimilated whatever fantasy material our family erotica could prompt, and there was no further supply of such books. The fever didn't go away – it never does – but it abated, and left room for something more substantial than the Hardy Boys. It was time, at last, to start reading some proper books. It was time for literature.

3

CATCHING AND HOWLING

My boyhood was very much the same as that of the
boy in the book, and it was a great relief telling people
about it.

     J.D. Salinger, talking about *The Catcher in the Rye*

Holy the supernatural extra brilliant intelligent kind-
ness of the soul!

     Allen Ginsberg, footnote to *Howl*

'High school.' To this day the very words provoke in me the kind
of anxious repulsion occasioned by terms like 'ethnic cleansing',
'root canal', or 'George W. Bush'. I loathed being in high school,
loathed it so utterly and viscerally that I was hardly aware of the
cause of my discontent. I seethed with a restless unhappiness wildly
in excess of the usual teenage surliness and sense of entitlement.

    The recently constructed Huntington High was much admired
by all save those who had to use it. A low brick building with
endless corridors along the sides of which were austere, vaguely
ominous, metal lockers, painted in institutional greys and greens,
with linoleum floors, fluorescent lighting and an overactive boiler,
the place looked like a film set of a laboratory where sadistic psychological experiments were performed. At the start and close of the
day, and between classes, these aisles would be crammed with
rushing, gossiping, overheated students, but during classes, they

were transformed into a bleak no-go zone, patrolled by monitors and hawk-eyed teachers anxious to corral truants of any kind. You needed a pass even to go to the bathroom. The message was simple: this place was hard to break out of. You'd better knuckle under.

There was a dress code – no jeans, no sneakers, no shorts, dresses and skirts at an 'appropriate' length. Hair fell under opposite injunction: it *had* to be short, crew cut if possible, and I remember my mother, observing a trace of curling at my neckline, warning me, censoriously, of the consequences if it were allowed to fester. I cut it off, brutally, and whatever festering went on thereafter was purely internal.

Oddly, there were touches of great satisfaction: I was leading the life that most of the other kids aspired to. I captained a tennis team that won 110 straight matches. I was dating an exceptionally pretty and loveable girl, and having amazing fun with her. Nor were the classes unstimulating, though I proved curiously intractable in my post-Burgundy Farm ignorance, like the hero of Sam Cooke's 'Wonderful World', who didn't know much about history, biology or the French he took.

I was regarded as bright, but like Mr Cooke's hero, I was not an 'A-student', which allowed my teachers enthusiastically to describe me as an 'under-achiever'. I was nevertheless put in the top stream (called 'XX', as if a coded form of obscenity), which had the happy effect of giving one a bonus at the end of the year, whereby a 'C' would count as a 'B' in one's grade-point average. Riding the back of this benefit, I finally managed an exact 3.0 average (straight B) which just allowed me to slip into the top 10 per cent of my graduating class. My transcript, if you looked at it even without this enhancement, was undistinguished. My grades in English classes were particularly disappointing.

The teaching was enthusiastic and competent, but the set texts were unstimulating. There were the thumping rhythms of Vachel Lindsay's *The Congo: A Study of the Negro Race*:

THEN I SAW THE CONGO, CREEPING THROUGH THE BLACK,
CUTTING THROUGH THE JUNGLE WITH A GOLDEN TRACK.

which even I, in the ninety-nine per cent white Huntington High
School, could tell was total tosh. Then there was some pappy stuff
from Stephen Vincent Benét, and lashings of homespun wisdom
from Robert Frost, who liked choosing between different tracks
in the woods, or building walls, and then making a fuss about it.

But XX English with Miss Wyeth, in my senior year, was a different
kettle of literary fish. Relentlessly high-minded in the way bright
and frustrated high school teachers can be, Miss Wyeth had composed
a year-long crash course in Western Literature and Philosophy,
beginning with Homer, through Plato, Aristotle and the Greek
tragedians, and ending, via a commodious vicus of recirculation,
with *Finnegans Wake*. Miss Wyeth was a moony fan of my father's
(who was president of the local Arts Council) and had decided that
I should be the star of her show. She would pick me up from the
back of class, where I sat slouched over my desk doing the *New York
Times* crossword, to ask the most trenchant questions.

'And what do you think, Rick, of the quality of this translation
by Dudley Fitts?' (This to a class illiterate in Greek, having read
no other translations, and based simply on a sheet outlining a few
possible alternatives for the Greek phrase in question.)

'It seems to me admirably to exemplify the old phrase . . .' Miss
Wyeth gave me an anticipatory glare. '. . . if the Dudley Fitts, wear
it.'

'Out!' she said, pointing to the door.

I knew the way to the principal's office by then: word of mouth
had led me there frequently enough. He looked up wearily as I
entered.

'What is it this time?'

'Well, sir,' I said, as contritely as possible, 'I insulted Dudley Fitts
in Miss Wyeth's class.'

The principal was no classicist.

'What did you say to him?'

'I was teasing him about his name, sir.'

'Well,' he said firmly, 'I want you to go back to class immediately and apologize to Dudley. You know our Honour Code requires courtesy between students!'

'I'll be extremely happy to do that, sir.'

Retelling the story over dinner, I thought my dad would rather admire my wit, though he was getting tired of coming to school to apologize for my behaviour, which I was generally unwilling to do on my own behalf.

'She had it coming,' I would say steadfastly, though I felt a little guilty. Miss Wyeth wasn't a moron or a phoney, like many of the other teachers. This unpleasant dismissive language I had learned from my contemporary, a seventeen-year-old named Holden Caulfield, who was one of my closest confidants. You will remember him as the hero and narrator of J.D. Salinger's *The Catcher in the Rye*, which was much my favourite book at the time.

Holden is a drop-out from a series of posh prep schools, but unlike me was no smart-aleck. Unfailingly polite, and inclined in public to take the blame for his many academic shortcomings – he too only liked English – Holden is internally scathingly dismissive of almost everyone who has taught him. He is a veritable walking crap detector, unfailingly sensitive to every cliché, insincerity, and bit of educational jargon. Counselled by yet another of his disappointed English teachers 'to learn how to play the game', Holden isn't buying: 'Game, my ass. Some game. If you get on the side where all the hot-shots are, then it's a game all right – I'll admit that, but if you get on the *other* side, where there aren't any hot-shots, then what's a game about it? Nothing. No game.'

I, too, was on the other side, wherever that was. Holden and I, we were in opposition, unreceptive to second-hand wisdom, unwilling to take counsel from self-appointed betters. I took Holden's example literally, mistook intensity for fairness of feeling. Teenagers do this, though it is a sign of retarded development in adults.

But there were two things I failed to learn from him. First, was how to keep my mouth shut, though that didn't matter much. But second, and significantly, was how to fail. Holden will not do what he doesn't believe in, study what doesn't interest him, take advice where it doesn't resonate with what he needs. If this means that he drops out of one school after another, he feels no shame. His father, kid sister Phoebe says, will 'kill' him for his latest failure, but he fails nonetheless. There is some integrity in this: the more good-willed educators praise the value of what he is being offered, the more he rejects it. In his inchoate way he knows that it is a characteristic of narcissistic forms of life that they generate lashings of self-praise. Phoneys, this is what Holden means by phoniness. But what is *not* phoney? He doesn't know yet, save for the clear knowledge that *he* isn't. And his unwillingness to play the proffered game confirms something intransigent and authentic in him.

The psychotherapist Alice Miller observes that for children who are being pressured by ambitious parents, failure may be the only way to assert independence: 'it may come about that something inside refuses to produce good grades. They are unwilling to take part in a cover-up of a lack of love, and they use their bad grades to protest hypocrisy and to defend the truth.'

Holden chooses to fail, and it provokes no anxiety in him, though he has some (admittedly mild) regret at the distress it causes others. He doesn't fear failure, he does it, chooses it. Failure is a confirmation of his integrity.

But Holden Caulfield was in a situation radically different from my own. We may both have been surly high school kids, but Holden had adequate reason for his disaffection, what Eliot calls an 'objective correlative'. He is profoundly and admittedly depressed, his only attachments being to his younger sister Phoebe, and to the memory of Allie, his adored kid brother who died when Holden was thirteen. The day that Allie died, Holden broke his hand smashing windows in the garage. Three years later his hand still hurts, and he is still angry, but the anger has twisted and turned inward. At the end of the book Holden is an in-patient in a psychiatric institution, and has written this account of himself as a kind of therapeutic self-explanation.

He is grieving, still. What had I experienced that I should have found his situation so sympathetic? If I had a sense of loss it was only obscurely: a product of a child-centred environment, I had fallen from an egocentric state of innocence into a world that expected *me* to centre on *it*. Yet if my reasons for grief, if you can call it that, bore little comparison to those of Holden Caulfield, they certainly produced similar symptoms.

Catcher is a protracted moan, but what Holden really needs to do is to howl. His sense of loss – so unlike my own – is sympathetic, conscious and overwhelming. He is filled with numb rage and unshed tears. No one seems to have helped him properly: in the course of the narrative not one of his many well-wishing adults, no teacher, no parent, no friend, sees fit to mention Allie's death. (Only Phoebe does that.) Holden needed better, wiser, more psychologically and culturally radical counsel.

Perhaps he needed Allen Ginsberg? Holden couldn't have read *Howl* (which was published five years after *Catcher in the Rye*) but I was lucky enough, in 1960, to read both books, and in the right order. *Howl* begins where *Catcher* ends: in a mental hospital, where a tormented and intensely bright inmate is trying and failing to make peace in and with the world. Though it is often referred to as *Howl*, Ginsberg's book was originally titled *Howl for Carl Solomon*. A lament for his mad friend, it begins:

I saw the best minds of my generation destroyed by
    madness, starving, hysterical naked,
dragging themselves through the negro streets at dawn,
    looking for an angry fix . . .

and continues:

. . . who were expelled from academies for crazy &
    publishing obscene odes on the windows of the
    skull,
who cowered in unshaven rooms in underwear . . .

Who was this stylistic hooligan? I'd never read anything like
this before, words stomping about the page without discernible
rhythms, much less rhymes, lawless and free. It was strident, rep-
etitious, shockingly outspoken. (It was also bombastic and not
entirely accurate: Carl Solomon later claimed to be mystified by
the whole business: 'Why he wrote the poem, I don't understand.
I was seeking only a rest and attempting to give up smoking. I
don't understand all this grand opera.')

Whatever this was, it certainly wasn't poetry. It was better than
poetry. Poetry was the clanking Mr Lindsay (student of the Negro
Race) and the homespun Mr Frost. Poetry was as fluent and as
memorable as that contemporary hit by the Shirelles: 'Will You
Still Love Me Tomorrow?' But no one could feel cosy with this
Mr Ginsberg, or quote more than a couple of lines without starting
to hem and haw, eventually grinding to a mid-line halt.

If Ginsberg's verse calls Holden Caulfield to mind – leaving
school, drunk in a seedy New York hotel room, angry and desperate,
dreaming of an escape to the lonely outreaches of the West – they
also transcend him entirely. You could relate to Holden, internalize
him as a friend. Even his creator did that. According to his girlfriend at the time, when Salinger was writing the novel he used to

quote Holden Caulfield enthusiastically and extensively. I did too. 'What would Holden have thought about this bullshit?' I would think, as I sat, superior, in judgement on the inadequacy of my teachers. And my friend Holden would tell me, at length.

But Allen Ginsberg? No, he was neither a friend, nor someone inwardly to consult, and his voice wasn't so easily introjected. If Holden was a comfortable companion, Ginsberg made me both excited and anxious. It was his aim to provoke, and what he provoked in me was a fierce desire for escape, and a reflexive rejection of that impulse so quick that I could hardly remember having felt it. Talk about having a vigilant system of defences. He made me feel both trapped and pathetic, yet the net effect was curiously exhilarating.

Ginsberg and his beat friends – *Howl* is dedicated to Kerouac, Burroughs and Cassady – were, of course, in a long American tradition, exploring the wilderness within and without. We remember Huck Finn, fleeing the forces of convention in the form of his Aunt Sally (who wants 'to adopt me and sivilize me'), getting ready to light out for the territory. It is clear to Huck that there is something preferable and unconstrained in this metaphorical, pre-lapsarian terrain. It was clear to Allen Ginsberg as well, though the nature of the freedoms he envisaged might have surprised even the liberal-minded Huck. They surprised the hell out of me. Ginsberg was omnivorously, rapaciously sexy, hetero- and what we called, with anxious fastidiousness, 'homo': happy it seemed to be on the giving or receiving end of whatever was coming or going. William Carlos Williams, speaking of *Howl*, put this perfectly: 'He avoids nothing but experiences it to the hilt. He contains it. Claims it as his own – and, we believe, laughs at it and has the time and effrontery to love a fellow of his choice and record that love in a well-made poem.'

The major antecedents of *Howl*, which seems a quintessentially modern poem, lie in the nineteenth century: in James Fenimore

Cooper and *Huckleberry Finn*, and particularly in Walt Whitman's *Song of Myself*, which Ginsberg had read while at high school in New Jersey. Walt's dictum: 'I am huge I contain multitudes,' became the young Ginsberg's mantra. The panoptically loving *Howl* embraces (*takes in*) the outlawed and outcast, the rejected, the poor, the black, the downtrodden. More than accepts but embraces (*celebrates*) that which tests boundaries, attacks prejudices, transgresses. In those great words of Whitman's:

> 'love the earth and sun, and animals, despise riches . . . stand up for the stupid and crazy, devote your income and labor to others, hate tyrants, argue not concerning God, have patience and indulgence towards the people . . . re-examine all you have been told at school or church, or in any books, and dismiss whatever insults your soul.'

I wasn't sure, contemplating this lofty sentiment at the age of seventeen, quite what insulting one's 'soul' might consist of, as compared to, say, insulting one's self. I had certainly heard of souls, but was unsure whether I had, or indeed, whether I wanted one. They sounded pesky things, these souls, a bit like puppies: endlessly importuning, hungry for sustenance, altogether too demanding.

Soul or no soul, the arrival of Allen signalled the end of my identification with Holden. He and I had not yet got past a negative version of 'dismissing', were ruthlessly without charity. Ginsberg pointed the way to something larger, more generous and more dangerous. That's what happens when you wish to say YES, unconditionally, to the world, which is what Ginsberg recommended and exemplified.

Having been so moved by Whitman in his teens, Ginsberg was simply waiting for Blake to happen. In 1948, he did. In a vision that was to shape his life, the poet Blake appeared before the twenty-six-year-old Ginsberg, who, transported, emerged from the experience clear that he had been visited by God. Much later, I was lucky enough to hear him singing, with his partner Peter Orlovsky, from his settings of *Songs of Innocence and Experience*. I had always been sceptical about the idea of the poet as bard, or (worse) shaman. Those are easy cloaks to put on, easy to abuse, altogether too self-aggrandizing. Yet Ginsberg was wholly convincing, his audience rapt. It was one of the most moving experiences of my life. I'd never understood or appreciated Blake properly before, or Ginsberg, or (I supposed) myself.

It made me wish I had made more of myself. I was at the time teaching English at the University of Warwick, at which Ginsberg's reading took place. After the reading, still deeply moved, I found myself standing next to him as we peed at the urinals. It was my chance, my only chance, to acknowledge what I owed him. What words would be adequate?

'Thanks,' I said.

'Sure,' he said, smiling.

I felt blessed, and went home glowing to tell Barbara about the experience. She immediately sensed something dangerous in my response: she had once observed that it wouldn't have surprised her entirely, if one day she found a note from me saying that I was off. Not off as in off with another woman, or to a different flat, but really off. Not off somewhere, but to nowhere, to anywhere. And that she might not then hear from me for a very long time. It was an acute reading of a fantasy of mine – not to abandon her, but in some unexamined way to find myself – but she knew, as I knew even better, that I was far too dutiful, too conventional, finally too frightened, to do more than contemplate such a thing. I had an inner lexicon of sad and attenuated fantasies of life on the road, which involved moving from one stereotype to another: open-topped cars on endless roads to nowhere, vast Western landscapes with critters and varmints howling in the night, bars with drunken and available women, lonely motels . . . All the stale tropes of noir fiction. Nothing too difficult, highly charged, or genuinely imagined. Nothing exotic, nothing foreign. It was a by-product of the genius of Allen Ginsberg that, in reanimating these clichés, he made me feel more alive.

Allen and Holden had become guides, though eventually their voices merged with whatever was developing as my own. They engendered loyalty, and that kind of naive identification where we find ourselves unconsciously mimicking not merely our friends' attitudes, but also their habits, likes and dislikes, voices and postures. For a time I could recognize an inner Holden and an inner Allen Ginsberg, but eventually they got assimilated, increasingly mixed up with the myriad other voices I was to make my own, to make myself.

Philip Roth's protagonist Nathan Zuckerman puts this perfectly, in the novel *Exit Ghost*: 'All I can tell you with certainty is that I . . . have no self, and that I am unwilling or unable to perpetrate upon myself the joke of a self. What I have instead is a variety of impersonations I can do . . .'

So Zuckerman, ironically, while disallowing the very concept of the self, also uses it, because he has to: it is built into the psycholinguistic structures we are stuck with: 'I am unwilling or unable to perpetrate upon my*self* the joke of a self.' There's no way round it – a process that Jacques Derrida calls using concepts 'under erasure' – at the very moment at which we disallow a concept we may be obliged to employ it.

Charles Lamb, in a much quoted phrase, claimed that he loved to 'lose himself in other men's minds', and that is what I did, though not in the sense that Lamb intended. He thinks there is something comfortable about the process, something seamlessly enhancing. But my assimilation of the Caulfield and Ginsberg voices had something spurious about it – I didn't simply learn from them, I appropriated a whole series of attitudes and beliefs which were neither warranted nor engendered by my own experience: I despised phonies! I wanted to be lawless and to embrace all!

Perhaps, though, that is the point, and what poor frustrated Miss Wyeth was trying to teach us. That literature offers us foreign voices, and enables, even urges, us to assimilate them. How we do that, of course, is up to us. You have to be careful whose company you keep, and how. Matthew Arnold recommended 'the best that has been known and thought' as internal models, without remarking, too, the concomitant danger of what Jung calls psychic inflation. I suspect that he thought the process would make one humble, but identifying with and appropriating views of the world that one might not have come to on one's own does not necessarily lead to humility.

Therein lies the paradox: we cannot form our views of the world without exposure to 'other men's minds', yet in doing so we risk something second-hand, inauthentic. Literature becomes both our experience and our substitute for experience. There is, after all, a crucial distinction between actually being on the road, being Kerouac and Cassady, and reading about it, identifying with them, and regarding oneself as, similarly, an outlaw. To be outside the law you must be as honest as Jack or Neal, and not like their many admirers and wannabes.

Allen Ginsberg's valuation of spontaneity, his desire for sexual freedom and loathing of the conventions of the political process and of petit bourgeois life, moved and convinced me, and I have never entirely freed myself of these attitudes, nor entirely wished to. But they have left me with a lifetime disposition to seem to be, to pretend to be larger, more interesting and important than I really am. Like Philip Roth's Zuckerman, without a self that is anything more than a vast echo chamber, with resonating voices, intertwined, from any variety of sources. Is this why we sense, in people who are steeped in literature, a kind of intractable pomposity, as if they are swollen by voices not legitimately their own? 'As Charles Lamb was fond of remarking,' they say, remarking it themselves. Charles Lamb, *c'est moi*.

I cite therefore I am? There is something compellingly ridiculous about the process. Even in its most distinguished examples, compulsive quoting always suggests something second-hand to me. Take Joan Didion's moving account of her response to the sudden death of her adored husband, John Gregory Dunne, *The Year of Magical Thinking*. The text is littered with references to those writers Didion most admires, and who may be able to offer insight or consolation. And, reading, I was irritated by this: can't she grieve, even, without this plethora of literary citation? But there is nothing second-hand about the process, not to Joan Didion: these voices, these authorities, these friends are part of what and who she is. What is this, this chamber of citations, but the self?

Whatever self I was beginning to form in high school sought eagerly, if not for a genuine escape, at least for some radical way of marking my difference and disaffection. It would have to be subtle, this protest, no failing, no dropping out, no confrontations beyond the normal wise-crackery, no locks flowing over the collar. At last I found an ideal gesture: every day during my senior year I would wear a sports jacket and a tie! Unlike the other boys in their chinos, checked shirts and v-necked sweaters, I would set myself apart, formal and superior, and never indicate why I was doing so.

It wasn't easy. I only had the one (green and gold threaded) jacket, a couple of white button-down cotton shirts, and three thin ties, each with bright horizontal stripes. But I persevered. My fellow students were puzzled, but my teachers thought I looked nice. They didn't realize that I was dressing ironically, but Allen Ginsberg would have. I liked to think he would have been proud of me.

In the summer after I graduated, I got to do a different sort of dressing up, while employed as a campus guard by Burns Detective Agency, stationed at the local C.W. Post College, at the time a deeply undistinguished campus largely for the graduates of the local high schools. I was issued with a peaked cap, and a badge that I pinned on my khaki shirt. My role was to make sure that nobody except the administration officers parked in the car parks outside the administration offices. This entailed standing on the broiling tarmac from 7.30 in the morning until 3.30 in the afternoon, with half an hour for lunch at midday. It was exhausting, and the sun gave me headaches until I bought a pair of aviator sun glasses.

I have never been so bored. I would check my watch every few minutes, certain that an hour had passed. It was intolerable, and I took to bringing a novel with me, from the suggested reading list that the University of Pennsylvania had sent prior to my matriculating in the autumn. I found I could read a book a day, and was beginning to rather enjoy it, wishing only that they had issued me with a chair, when the President of the College approached me sternly.

'What are you doing?'

'Guarding the car park, sir.'

'No, you're not. You're reading!'

'Believe it or not, sir, I can do both at the same time.'

'It doesn't make the right impression. I want you to stop this reading immediately!'

I put my copy of *On The Road* into my pocket wearily.

'If I might say so, sir, it seems to me I am the only person on this campus who actually reads books. Could you not regard me as setting a good example?'

He couldn't, and wasn't amused. I spent the rest of the summer standing at my post, broiling in the sun, guarding my little heart out, turning away the occasional student brave or stupid enough to try to swipe one of the prohibited places.

To make some extra money to take to college I also worked in the evenings that summer, in the sporting goods department at Macy's in the local mall. My specialty was drilling bowling balls, and I got sufficiently good at it that customers would return to tell me that they'd bowled an especially good game. During the occasional lulls, I'd chat with my colleagues, who measured golf clubs, or sold sneakers and tennis rackets.

It turned out that one of them was a summer school student at C.W. Post.

'C.W. Post! Do you know the car park by the president's office?' I asked eagerly.

'Oh yeah, sure, I tried to park there last week, but there was this really tough-looking cop, and I got scared away.'

It was the high point of my summer.

4

LEARNING TO READ

The first step in education is not a love of literature, but a passionate admiration for one writer; and probably most of us, recalling our intellectual pubescence, can confess that it was an unexpected contact with some one writer which first, by apparent accident, revealed to us our capacities for enjoyment of literature.

T.S. Eliot, 'The Education of Taste'

'Let's begin here,' our instructor in Introduction to English said. 'You have read *The Waste Land* for today's assignment. Can you recite the opening line? Not *lines*, just the one. You should be able to, it's famous enough, almost a cliché by now.'

He was regarded by most of the class with incredulity, and by me with contempt. That was obvious, wasn't it? What was the catch? We all knew it, and recited it almost as if it were a nursery rhyme: *'April is the cruellest month . . .'*

'Wrong!' (You won't believe this. We didn't.) 'Think again.'

We did, and we wouldn't back down. What was this guy: stupid?

'Have a look in your book.' And sure enough the first line reads:

April is the cruellest month, breeding

'Why does it start like that?' he asked. 'How is that different from the line you remember? Why does he do it like that – what is the effect?'

We read the next line:

Lilacs out of the dead land, mixing

which repeats the pattern of the first line – doesn't it? – with the active hanging verb suggesting fertility and hinting at sexuality. (Lines three, five and six will do the same.) Why is it that 'lilacs' are what is bred? There is no appended note by Eliot, and our first association was with Whitman's 'When Lilacs Last in the Dooryard Bloomed', the elegy on the death of Abraham Lincoln. Thus new life in the springtime brings with it a hint of the destruction of the best and brightest? That is – is it? – why April is cruel? Is there some later association with the 'hyacinth girl' – hyacinths being visually similar to lilacs, similarly strongly perfumed – and the moment of epiphany associated with her?

I can't remember when I first read T.S. Eliot. This may account for my feeling that he has always been with me, for Eliot, more than any other writer, has been a constant reference point: read and reread, reconsidered, rethought, reimagined, indeed, re-sounded, for the poem can be recited in many ways and voices. For almost fifty years he has been a constant but shifting part of my self-definition, as if what I made of Eliot, at any given period of my reading life, were essential to what I made of myself. And, equally, as my sense of myself has evolved, my responses to Eliot have shifted.

Perhaps – (if this isn't true nevertheless it carries the weight of truth for me) – it was my father who introduced me to Eliot? His heavily annotated copy of the poet's *Collected Poems* was in a prominent place on his shelves, and in everyday conversation he was likely to interject a phrase or image of Eliot's: at a party the 'women come and go, talking of Michelangelo', and we could not enter spring without being reminded that April was 'the cruellest month', which to my mind it so obviously wasn't. (That, dad observed, was exactly the point.)

I like the notion that he introduced me to Eliot, because my nature and ambitions so closely mirrored his as a teenager. In 1930, the eighteen-year-old Bernie Gekoski, recently graduated from high school, adored eldest child and the hero of his younger sister, a well-read, earnest young man and aspiring writer, entered the freshman class at the University of Pennsylvania. He had already read some Freud, and had hopes that he might one day train as a psychoanalyst, but (aware that you needed to be a doctor or a psychology graduate to do this) contemplated instead a career as a professor of English. And if that didn't work out, he recognized, you could always train as a lawyer, a perfectly respectable profession for a young man with a conscience.

Change the date to 1962, and 'Bernie' to 'Rick', and all the rest stands. I was aware of the parallels without having considered them, and had no sense of pursuing, as it were, a carbon copy of my father's life. But the University of Pennsylvania he attended and the one I did, if they had the continuities of genteel Philadelphian propriety and Ivy League architecture, nevertheless were substantially different places in which to major in English. The very act and nature of reading had redefined itself since my father's time. He had been schooled by historicist and belle-lettriste professors (and gentlemen, and Gentiles) for whom understanding a text consisted of placing it squarely in the historical, cultural and intellectual milieu from which it emerged, and which it might be claimed to represent. To read Shakespeare without knowing about the great chain of being, or to approach Pope lacking an understanding of the premises of the Enlightenment, were activities associated with amateurishness, of reading for the mere fun of it. Indeed, properly understood, such pleasure was a thin and unreliable product in the absence of its background.

It was hardly a sympathetic milieu in which to read Eliot. *The*

Waste Land was widely reviled by contemporary American critics, and more so by American academics of the Penn sort. In 1930, of course the poem was still avant-garde in a way that, by 1962, it no longer was. My father would recall, with a smile and shake of the head that carried, still, an aura of astonishment, what an impact the poem had upon him, how exciting it was to read something like *that*. Modern? That was the naturalist novels of Dreiser and Sinclair Lewis, the mid-Western twang of Carl Sandburg, the fine discriminations of Edith Wharton and Henry James. *The Waste Land* was something else, and required a new concept: 'modern*ist*', that would do it. Though the term first appears as early as 1879, its use to refer to the early twentieth century's explosion of creative innovation in literature, painting and music, is more or less contemporaneous with the publication of *The Waste Land*. When you wrote or painted, when you *composed* in this new way, you redefined not only what art was, but how it had to be described and discussed.

A key figure in this shift of readerly perspective was I.A. Richards, the Cambridge don whose *Practical Criticism: A Study of Literary Judgment* defined the aesthetic of this new ahistoric approach to the reading of poetry. Richards would distribute to his classes the texts of poems (which he called 'protocols') without divulging the author or the period in which they were written. There were only the words on the page, and it was the job of each student to produce as detailed a 'reading' of them as possible. Under such tutelage, that extraordinary undergraduate William Empson was soon to publish *Seven Types of Ambiguity*, still one of the great examples of what close reading can accomplish.

In America, the term 'new criticism' (after the title of a book by Allen Tate) came to be preferred to 'practical criticism', though they were largely the same thing. Exegesis and formal analysis became the modes. Just as Picasso and Braque required of their critics a fresh eye, and an accompanying new vocabulary and conceptual apparatus, so too did Joyce, Pound and Eliot necessitate a different set of lenses and critical tools. To understand them required that one re-schooled oneself in the very art of reading. And to do that you had to learn, too, how not to read.

When I first read *The Waste Land* my response was some literary version of an anxiety attack, accompanied by an enormous exhilaration. As Eliot was to remark, 'genuine poetry can communicate before it is understood.' The poem tugged at my mind fore and aft, the images recurring and reigniting as if from a bad dream, or what Eliot called 'the octopus or angel' with which the poet, and the reader, struggles. The poem was like a crossword puzzle or literary quiz, which was rather fun, but the real difficulty lay in assimilating it emotionally. It had emanated from the immense collapse that followed the First War, as well as Eliot's own nervous breakdown, leaving that 'heap of broken images' that its poetic voices struggle to preserve: jagged shards, partially apprehended echoes, scenes glimpsed but hardly comprehended, the past confused with the present, mind, body and spirit in collision.

The Waste Land neither demanded nor allowed paraphrase. Neither did it have a philosophy, a single voice (like a poem by Whitman or Ginsberg), or a clear structure. Though we were supposed to confine ourselves to the words on the page, we snuck off to the Van Pelt Library nonetheless. It was one of my haunts in my first semester as a freshman, a refuge from that lonely disorientation that accompanies leaving home for the first time. I had located a comfy chair in a quiet alcove, which I began to regard as my own, and would repair there most days to read: first the novels of Camus, then all of Kafka, then the major novels of Sartre. Existentialism – in high school I thought the term was 'existentionalism,' which I used with embarrassing frequency – was current and sexy, and I wanted to know more.

My enthusiasm for the new philosophy occasioned one of my very few arguments with my father, who liked plain speaking and caught a whiff of cant in my advocacy of the existential.

'What does it mean, exactly?' he asked in a voice I suspect he used for cross-examinations.

'It's from Jean-Paul Sartre,' I explained, 'it's a form of French philosophy.'

'I know that perfectly well. Tell me about this philosophy.'

'The key is that existence precedes essence, that you choose who you are, you don't have any nature. You are entirely free to make yourself. If you make the wrong choices it's called bad faith, and the responsibility is entirely your own.'

He considered this for a moment.

'Tell it to the Jews who died in the concentration camps,' he said tartly. 'Did they choose that? Do Negroes choose segregation? Have they got this "freedom" to make themselves whatever they wish?' A member of the American Civil Liberties Union, he had done pro bono work on cases involving discrimination, was entirely on the side of the underdog, and had little time for 'philosophy' abstracted from the reality of daily engagement with the world.

'I'm not so sure Sartre is interested in that,' I said. 'He's more concerned with the French bourgeoisie . . .'

'He should be interested! He lived through the war, didn't he? But I am more interested in why *you* are so concerned with the French middle classes. Surely there are more pressing things to worry about right here, and now.'

He was genuinely cross, and we agreed to drop the subject. I'd rarely encountered him in such an unforgiving mood, though it was to recur a few years later, when I wrote from Oxford to say that I was contemplating a trip to Poland to find members of our family. I got a sharp letter by return, asking why I supposed that any of them had survived, and why it was that I wished to visit a country from whose barbarous anti-Semitism my grandparents had narrowly escaped? I made other plans.

I suppose my reading in the library during my freshman year was partly designed to frame a rebuttal of my father's argument, but instead it confirmed it: Sartre had recanted his original position, for the very reasons my father had given. (I never told him this, and began to suspect he'd read the relevant texts.)

Better to join him in our mutual regard for T.S. Eliot whose palpable anti-semitism my father was curiously able to forgive, I became obsessed with *The Waste Land*, with trying to figure it out. There were a lot of books about Eliot, confirming how difficult he was, but no *Collected Letters*. His essays were studiedly impersonal, and left his personality a matter of conjecture. A starchy young man from the mid-West, who had assimilated seamlessly into English social and intellectual life, Eliot evolved into a high church, high table sort of chap: formal, conventional, retiring. That was the prevailing impression anyway. There were no biographies to be found; indeed, on his death in 1965 he left express instructions that no such were to be attempted. When Peter Ackroyd published his, in 1984, the Eliot estate refused the author permission to quote from his works, ostensibly on the grounds that Eliot had not wished for a biography to be written. (The book nevertheless won the Heinemann and Whitbread awards.)

But the pattern of withholding permissions goes deeper than this, and it is a sanitized Eliot that we still read today. The Eliot estate, run by his still enraptured widow Valerie, has offered us a version of the poet as saint, resisting publication of Eliot's early King Bolo verses (which are charmingly obscene) and often refusing permission for quotation from his works. I recently did a BBC Radio 4 programme about the Hogarth Press, and applied to the estate for permission to read the short poem 'The Hippopotamus'. It was denied. I was cross and bemused, and demanded that the BBC confront Mrs Eliot.

'You've got to be kidding!' said my producer. 'We need Mrs Eliot a lot more than we need you!'

I didn't know, reading *The Waste Land* in my freshman year, that the poet was a more amusing character than one might have supposed. A devotee of music hall, a lover of the Marx brothers, and an inveterate practical joker, he was a constant source of amusement to his publishing colleagues at Faber's. He was known to return from his morning visit to the Gents with pieces of that old-fashioned, virtually grease-proof toilet paper, on which he had written something silly. Examples were distributed at board meetings: 'Mr T. S. Eliot salutes the Directors of Faber and Faber.' (I owned one once, and sold it for £100.) At Christmas parties he would have a few drinks and regale his colleagues with a variety of English accents so stupendously off key that people would sneak out of the room when they thought he wasn't looking.

It turns out he was rather fun, this Eliot, but you sure wouldn't have known it in Introduction to English in 1962. Looking up from the page, bewildered, we begged for help. 'Ah,' our instructor told us archly (quoting Archibald Macleish's dictum), 'a poem should not mean, but be.' That wasn't much help. It wasn't at all clear what *The Waste Land* meant, we agreed on that. But what help was it to remind us that it *was*? If it wasn't, then we could get the hell out of there, but if it *be'd*, what kind of being did it have?

We canvassed various opinions as to the essence of poetry. Housman reminded us that unless a poem made our skin prickle with delight, so that we cut ourselves while shaving, it lacked poetic quality. (The girls rather objected to this.) And Wordsworth, evidencing the fatal attraction aesthetic theorists have for the verb to be, claimed that 'poetry is the spontaneous overflow of powerful feelings'. There was plenty of powerful feeling in *The Waste Land*, but not much evidence that it was spontaneous, or that it had overflowed. Indeed, much of it seemed crimped and desperate.

The 'spontaneous overflow of powerful feelings', surely, is what you get when you find your neighbour in bed with your wife? Even if this emotion is later, as Wordsworth was hastily to insist, 'recollected in tranquillity', it is hard to see how memory can inject the necessary poetic elements. Eliot is ruthless on the subject, observing that Wordsworth, like some sloppy undergraduate, has got *everything* wrong:

> '. . . emotion recollected in tranquillity' is an inexact formula. For it is neither emotion, nor recollection, nor, without distortion of meaning, tranquillity. It is a concentration, and a new thing resulting from the concentration, of a very great number of experiences . . . These experiences are not 'recollected' and they finally unite in an atmosphere which is 'tranquil' only in that it is a passive attending upon the event.

That showed him. And Mr Eliot was prepared to help us as well. When the poem was first published in England in 1923, by Leonard and Virginia Woolf's Hogarth Press, Eliot accompanied it with a set of notes, of limited explanatory value, partly in order to bulk up the slim volume. Curiously, we get a clearer personal voice from these notes than from the poem itself. Whereas *The Waste Land* is a palimpsest of persons, voice and languages, images, references, and places, and cannot be reduced to a personal statement, its notes, recondite and wry, reveal an Eliot who takes himself seriously but not too seriously, and is happy to acknowledge how much of the poem is, indeed, personal. The note about tarot cards is a perfect example:

> I am not familiar with the exact constitution of the Tarot pack of cards, from which I have obviously departed to suit my own convenience . . . The Man with Three Staves (an authentic member of the Tarot pack) I associate, quite arbitrarily, with the Fisher King himself.

When he was later to describe his masterpiece as 'just a piece of rhythmical grumbling', we recognize the tone from the notes, not the poem itself. And, like the notes, the comment misguides as much as it shows the way. If the grinding, abiding misery of *The Waste Land* is a form of grumbling, it is hard to imagine how Eliot might have sounded when he was really unhappy.

At Eliot's suggestion I read Jessie Weston's *From Ritual to Romance*, consulted Frazer's *The Golden Bough*, stuffed myself with references to the Fisher King and associated myths of maiming and regeneration. Coming back to the poem I found I could talk knowledgeably about its structure and cultural references, as if I had constructed an internal version of what was later to be called a hypertext.

The Waste Land had thrown down a challenge, and continues to do so. I made of the poem a lifetime companion. Some five or six years later, rereading *The Waste Land* while doing my BPhil at Oxford, I was surprised to find how much it had changed. I suppose I had too. Texts alter their meaning as readers change their situations, as Eliot argues so cogently in 'Tradition and the Individual Talent'. I had been reading Freud and Jung compulsively while Barbara and I were both in therapy, and much given to regarding all utterance as symptomatic of an internal state. Though himself undergoing psychoanalysis during the composition of *The Waste Land*, Eliot maintained that the poem was not a symptom of mere personal distress, that its ravaged landscape was an 'objective correlative' of a state of mind that was hardly his alone.

In fact, the bad poet is usually unconscious where he ought to be conscious, and conscious where he ought to be unconscious. Both errors tend to make him 'personal'. Poetry is not a turning loose of emotion, but an escape from emotion; it is not the expression of personality, but an escape from personality. But, of course, only those who have personality and emotions know what it means to want to escape from these things.

When I hear Eliot in this magisterial frame of mind I often suspect he has something to hide. There is something wonderfully perceived here, yet also egregiously wrong. Who is it, what sort of deformed being, who has *no* personality and *no* emotions?

The new Mrs Eliot had plenty of both. Eliot had married the charming, highly intelligent and distinctly unstable Vivienne Haigh-Wood in 1915. (He didn't tell his parents.) A period of his poetic production ends at this point, as the languid melancholy of *Prufrock* (1915) is increasingly replaced by, and culminates in, the sustained misery of *The Waste Land*. Vivienne was an acute reader of, and occasional contributor to, the manuscript of the poem as it evolved – it was she who wrote 'WONDERFUL' in the margin of the poem's section *A Game of Chess*, with its harrowing failure of communication between two lovers, whom it is difficult not to imagine as the poet and his wife.

Indeed, *The Waste Land* is shadowed by her presence. Most of the poem's women are her: she is the remembered hyacinth girl, the languidly miserable chess player, the sexually inert typist. *The Waste Land* was written during the poet's nervous collapse, and its references to Margate Sands (where 'I can connect Nothing with nothing') and Lake Leman (where 'I sat down and wept') correlate to his visits to those places in 1921. The 'I' in these sections feels more personal than at any other point in the poem. In Geneva he was consulting a psychotherapist, and there is a powerful temptation, even without knowing this, to read the poem as documentation of extreme, if generalized, personal suffering.

It would be impertinent to speculate on exactly what had gone wrong between the couple, but it is widely conjectured that sexual relations between them had broken down catastrophically. Do the recurring images of this sere, sterile and implacably inhuman landscape invite the reader to imagine a dry and impenetrable vagina? And surely Eliot's therapist might have inquired about the location of the horrifying 'rats' alley, where the dead men lost their bones'?

What is one to make of the Fisher King – the sexually maimed figure whose presence haunts the text – 'fishing in the dull canal'? Anyone with a grounding in psychological interpretation would have a field day with this.

The poem is filled with the echoes and cadences of what Eliot had read and been moved by, and its view of the self – that it is inhabited by fragments and broken images derived from reading and thinking – was wholly recognizable, and increasingly my own. I felt a curious kinship with this unhappy Eliot, *mon semblable, mon frère*. And so T.S. joined Holden, Allen, and Walt – add Albert, and Franz, and Jean-Paul, add a lot of new other voices, not just 'existentionalists' – in the echo chamber of my emerging sense of myself. It was no wonder I responded to the poem so intensely, felt invaded by its multitude of influences, voices and cadences, by its confusion regarding stable identity: for that exciting brief period, *The Waste Land* was me.

As I write this in my office, opposite me sits my most recent purchase: the Jacob Epstein bust, in green patinated bronze, of T.S. Eliot. Created in 1951, in an edition of six, it is a wonderful work of art, without the brutalism of many Epstein bronzes, with a delicate and moving serenity as the poet bends his head slightly forward, as if listening intently. His tie is heavily knotted, and stands out like a lump in his throat. He reminds me, in his almost beatific dignity, of my father.

When Eliot's bust first arrived, I would pat him on the cheeks in the morning to say hello, but it soon felt impertinent. Only Mrs Eliot – owner of one of the other five busts – should be allowed such an intimacy. She was once asked by Colin St John Wilson, architect of the new British Library, if he might borrow the bust in order to have a copy made, to sit in the foyer of the library.

'I could never allow that!' said Valerie.

'It wouldn't take long,' said the urbane and persuasive Wilson. 'I'd have it back to you in a couple of days, and he would sit in pride of place as you enter the library. What better tribute could there be?'

'It's quite impossible! I need him. I talk to him during the day, and I kiss him goodnight before I go to bed.'

Wilson retreated, knowing when he was beaten. I understood Mrs Eliot's impulse. For a time I considered kissing my bust of the poet goodnight when I closed my office, but I was too embarrassed, and now I settle for a little wave of farewell. He reigns quietly on the shelf in the corner. Sometimes when people come in to the shop they notice him, but usually they don't. I find this surprising, and am rather shocked by it.

5

DESCARTES, HUME AND THE MIRACLE OF LOVE

I will suppose, then, not that Deity, who is sovereignly good and the fountain of truth, but that some malignant demon, who is at once exceedingly potent and deceitful, has employed all his artifice to deceive me; I will suppose that the sky, the air, the earth, colours, figures, sounds, and all external things, are nothing better than the illusions of dreams, by means of which this being has laid snares for my credulity.

René Descartes, *Meditations*, Book I

It was one of the hits of 1961, and caught perfectly yet discreetly the prevailing sexual mores. In the Shirelles' 'Will You Still Love Me Tomorrow?' the singer seems to be contemplating sex with a boyfriend, and wishes reassurance that she is loved for herself and not just for her body. The song ends:

Tonight with words unspoken
You say that I'm the only one
But will my heart be broken
When the night meets the morning sun?

I'd like to know that your love

Is love I can be sure of
So tell me now, and I won't ask again
Will you still love me tomorrow?

She knows not to nag, but is aware that men can feel differently in the morning. I know it was always thus, but it was more so in 1961: girls gave themselves for love, and boys fell in love in order to be given girls.

We recognize in the Shirelles' plaintive cry a version of that need for reassurance sought by the philosophers: how can we be sure that the future will resemble the past? Can we be entirely confident that the sun will rise tomorrow? The Shirelles knew that it would (I love 'when the night meets the morning sun'), but their emotional and epistemological angst moves me in a way that mere philosophy never could.

Of course, none of this had occurred to me in my final year of high school. 'Will You Still Love Me Tomorrow?' was just one of a number of good songs, slow and smoochy, that made life sweet. No, I didn't start to think like this until 1962, during that freshman year at the University of Pennsylvania, as a student of Philosophy 101: Rationalism and Empiricism.

I'd done some philosophy with dear Miss Wyeth, read the ancients, some Montaigne and Erasmus, monkeyed about with the major philosophical questions regarding goodness, or the existence of God. So, unlike many of the first-year philosophy students, I was neither in search of the meaning of life, nor signing up to study a set of works through which I hoped to improve myself. No, I knew that philosophy was abstract, logical and impersonal, and would contrast sharply with my courses in English. Reading literature sounded your feelings as well as your intelligence and discrimination, while philosophy rigorously and impersonally interrogated the way you understood the world. There seemed no strong reason to choose between them – at least until my third year, when one would become my major, the other my minor.

Our sparkly and inspiring teaching assistant Mr Varnedoe, who was to become a mentor and lifetime friend, opened the course with the admonition that unless we 'cultivated' discipline as readers, we were unlikely to 'till any philosophical potatoes'. We began by reading Spinoza's *Ethics*, which I wanted to admire because my father did, but didn't, and Leibniz, who seemed to believe the world consisted of monads, likened by commentators to building blocks which could be imagined as ping-pong balls. This seemed improbable until Mr Varnedoe suggested one think instead of atoms. That made sense, but it still wasn't very interesting.

It was only when we read the *Meditations* that I got excited. Descartes began by suggesting that nothing be taken as knowledge unless it was beyond any imaginable doubt. He would – he suggested one joined him – doubt universally. Not only would we do that, we would also imagine that an omnipotent being, malign rather than beneficent, had made it his project to make us believe what was not the case.

I'm eating an orange? How do I know that? Could my senses deceive me? Might I be dreaming? Might that miserable imp, the malevolent demon, be fooling me in some way, perhaps with an apple that looks and tastes like an orange? Anyway, was there really any 'me' that could feel, and taste, and come to a conclusion? Perhaps I was not dreaming myself, perhaps I was a phantom in someone else's dream? Nevertheless, Descartes maintains, there is something left, even in this miasma of doubt, and that is the fact that some thinking is going on, and the 'I' who is thinking is myself. The fact that I am thinking means that I must exist. In the classical formulation: 'I think, therefore I am.'

Now that was fun, that was terrific. It didn't matter that there was clearly something wrong in the argument – (all that the perceived 'thinking' can really establish is the conclusion that 'thinking is going on', and not that there is some 'I', much less *me*, who is doing it) – because I liked the method every bit as much as the conclusion. I loved doubting in the way that fanatical believers adore God. I felt the spirit of Holden Caulfield stirring, newly animated, as if he had come to college with me. We both felt free at last. Now it wasn't people that were phoney, but ideas and beliefs. I found myself moving from the kinetic, balky opposition of my high school attitudes to something more powerful and satisfying: a capacity to doubt based on reason rather than emotion.

But if I had been stimulated by Descartes, I was bowled over by first reading Hume's *An Enquiry Concerning Human Understanding*, which took Cartesian doubt to a new level by applying it empirically to what we think we know of the external world, by holding up our unconsidered basic truths to sceptical analysis. Bertrand Russell describes the method clearly, in *The Philosophy of Logical Atomism*: 'The point of philosophy is to start with something so simple as not to seem worth stating, and to end with something so paradoxical that no one will believe it.' Thus Hume begins with the unarresting observation that if you hit the white billiard ball into the red, the red will carom away, and ends with the startling conclusion that there is nothing incontrovertibly necessary about this effect:

For the effect is totally different from the cause, and consequently can never be discovered in it. Motion in the second billiard ball is a quite distinct event from the motion in the first, nor is there anything in the one to suggest the smallest hint of the other.

It is no overstatement to say that such arguments and considerations radically altered the way in which I saw, engaged with, and described the world. I walked about campus lost in a fug of speculation like a reincarnated medieval cleric. What if a woman were to give birth to a fish, or an apple ascend after leaving the tree? Why should they not do so?

This had inevitable emotional consequences. One Saturday afternoon, after my girlfriend and I had enjoyed ourselves in bed, she nestled her head into my shoulder to ask if I would always love her. At that very moment it seemed inconceivable that I would not, but I nevertheless gave the question the due consideration that it was so obviously not expected to prompt.

'I don't see how I could say that,' I said.

Her head popped up, tears pooling in her eyes.

'Why not, what's the matter?'

'It simply isn't the sort of thing you can be certain of, is it?' I asked, in that irritating, pompous voice I was starting to adopt for academic disputation (and still do).

'Is there somebody else?' she asked.

'Certainly not!' What a misunderstanding!

I explained Hume's arguments on induction to her, certain that this would clarify why it was that I could not, with any philosophical integrity, promise that which could not be guaranteed.

She listened carefully, and at the end of my disquisition stood up and started to dress.

'I think we should go to dinner now,' she said. 'I'm getting hungry.'

The subject was never mentioned again, nor did she again inquire if I would still love her tomorrow. A girl raised on the Shirelles knows not to nag. She was a bit standoffish for a while, but I knew women could be irrational. No wonder there were no women philosophers.

But if this was an emotional disaster – though I did not recognize it as such at the time – there were further humiliations attendant on my Humean discipleship. In my sophomore year I took a course on The Philosophy of Religion, with a philosophical cleric by the name of Evans.

We ran through the traditional arguments for and against the existence of God, read widely in the ancients and medievals, and ended with Hume's essay 'Of Miracles'. The argument went like this: what is more likely, that a miracle has occurred, or that the human testimony on its behalf is faulty? Given that no instance of a miracle has been adequately proven, is it not foolish to believe them possible? To believe that a break in the laws of nature has occurred seems to depend on the credulousness of those who witness the supposed 'miracle', and of those who credit their testimony.

These arguments seemed sensible if unexceptional; what interested me more, though, was the manner in which they were presented. Unlike, say, Locke, whose prose is lumpy, utilitarian and consistently unremarkable, Hume is sprightly, accessible, and always anxious to please. There is something almost boyish about his eagerness to enter into direct contact with his readers. He enlists the evidence of our natural responses, and solicits agreement through the commonality of human experience. He begins the essay 'Of Miracles' by citing Dr Tillotson's argument against 'real presence', before going on to add: 'I flatter myself, that I have discovered an argument of a like nature, which, if just, will, with the wise and learned, be an everlasting check to all kinds of superstitious delusion, and consequently will be useful as long as the world endures.'

The slow accumulation of clauses beckons the reader into agreement, inviting him to share the exploration, not merely to concur with its conclusions, so much as coming to them himself, with Hume as his guide.

But, however engaging the tone and satisfying the arguments, there was something odd about the essay, which (given that it is published as part of *An Enquiry*) seemed curiously to miss the point.

I raised my hand.

'I don't quite understand this,' I said.

'What's the problem?'

'I can't figure out why Hume needs all of these ancillary arguments, when it is obvious from his epistemological position that there can be no such thing as a miracle . . .'

Mr Evans looked puzzled.

'Although he refers to a miracle as a break in "the laws of nature", all that a law of nature can be, if you follow his reasoning, is a long and unbroken series of spatial and temporal connections between two events. After sustained experience, we assume that seas do not part, nor will the sun cease to rise. But if one day either were to happen, this might only mean that we had had insufficient experience to see it coming, as an astronomically unsophisticated audience might regard a solar eclipse as miraculous. There can thus be no miracles, because the miraculous would seem to involve a break in the connection between things, and no such connection can be shown to be necessary.'

I exhaled mightily.

'I think you are right,' he said after a moment. 'That is a really interesting line of thought.' (He was wrong, as I was, for Hume is neither so lax nor so foolish as to have no answer to my objection.)

When, some weeks later, the final exam came round, I was very confident. I'd loved the course, done the reading obsessionally, revised the probable exam topics. But I was rather surprised to see, as question six (you had to do three of nine): *Describe why Hume's arguments about miracles are unnecessary in the light of his epistemology.*' I could do at least seven of the questions perfectly well, but, having been offered this treat, I chose to take it. I reaffirmed and added to my original classroom arguments, did two other questions, and was rewarded with an 'A' in the course. What a dope. It would have been more stylish to have ignored the bone proffered to the good little doggy. I would have been proud to take such an attitude, had it occurred to me, but sadly it did not. I gobbled up my freebie, unaware of something unseemly in the process. It still rather embarrasses me.

I think I fell for this generously offered titbit because I was already recognizing that philosophy was too hard for me. Once I had read the major philosophers it was clear that they were a *lot* smarter than me, and that I could hardly even follow some of their thinking. (Test case: Kant's *Critique of Pure Reason*.) Philosophy, like maths or physics, tests and defines the limits of our understanding and intelligence. You know what you can't do when you study philosophy.

Such self-knowledge is by no means a wholly positive thing. If philosophy has the capacity to make you humble, it can also supply you with the tools to mask your shortcomings with extraordinary aggression. I did further courses in symbolic logic, ethics and aesthetics, metaphysics, and the philosophy of science. I read widely in both the primary and secondary literature. I honed my analytic skills. Honing is a dangerous metaphor here, for in general we are rightly anxious about immature people with knives. You can sharpen a scalpel or a butcher's knife, and achieve marvels of accurate surgery upon the living or the dead. But offer a knife – even worse a badly honed one – to someone without the skills or the sense to know how to use it, and a lot of misdirected slashing is likely to result.

I became even more pedantic and argumentative, scorned sloppy reasoning and crass induction, demanded that my interlocutors define their terms. Your average person, I was fond of remarking, is quite incapable of distinguishing an argument from an assertion. And since it must be the case, empirically and philosophically, that some people are right more often than others, I happily assimilated myself to this first category, and waged a kind of tacit war on those in the latter. (My ex-wife and children will testify to the effects of this, and the kind of everyday bullying that it can engender.)

In short, I was quickly becoming the sort of person who wants to be a university teacher. But not a teacher of philosophy. Though urged to major in the subject by my new friend Mr Varnedoe, and enlivened by my readings in it, I was clear from the start that philosophy was not the field for me. I wasn't clever enough to do original work and, in any case, there struck me as something arid and inconsequential in much philosophical discourse. Albert Einstein remarked that 'when I study philosophical works I feel I am swallowing something which I don't have in my mouth.' I could not imagine feeling this way about the reading of literature, and it was eventually an easy decision to major in English rather than philosophy.

If one could imagine a mindset antithetical to Allen Ginsberg's inclusiveness and generosity, academic philosophy was it. I could see, already, that there was something of a conflict between the two disciplines, between scepticism and imagination, which I had initially experienced as the Holden voice versus the Allen voice. Yet the fields had more in common than the easy academic distinctions between them might lead one to believe. Philosophers as well as imaginative writers have to find just the right language to convince their readers, both attempt to locate and uncover the nature of what is most important, be it goodness, truth or beauty.

I did my English Honours thesis under the joint guidance of members of the English and philosophy departments, which was, at the time, an unusual arrangement designed to accommodate the fact that I had interdisciplinary interests. As my subject I tried to unravel what it was that Keats's Grecian urn *meant* when it said that:

> 'Beauty is truth, truth beauty', – that is all
>   Ye know on earth, and all ye need to know.

The poet obviously believes something important is at stake here – the urn is 'a friend to man' – but what exactly that friend is claiming is not entirely clear.

I read through the available critical literature on the subject, and began by dividing it into categories. There were two major questions to be asked: was the utterance true? And did it matter, in the sense of having consequences? (After all, what is true for Grecian urns – for immortal art – may not be true for mortal humans.) Thus there were four possible positions: true and with consequences, true but without, false but with, false but without. I found critics who occupied each of the four points of view, and tried to mediate between them.

If there is something clunky about this, my aesthetics tutor nevertheless found the resulting analysis palatable, but when it was handed over to the English Department the Honours Committee hated it, rightly feeling it lacking in literary analysis. This meant that I was to graduate with neither honour nor Honours in my chosen subject, which was presumably intended as a signal that I had no future in the field. I certainly took it to be one. Given that I had spent my final year applying to do post-graduate work in English, this came as something of a shock.

I imprecated, I supplicated, I appealed, I pointed out my many virtues. I demanded a reread. The department treated me with a courtesy that my aggression hardly deserved, got reports from each of the readers of the thesis, commissioned a new one, and confirmed its original judgement: this philosophical Gekoski was not of sufficient standard to be awarded Honours in English. Which left me in the odd – indeed, I think it was unique – position of graduating *summa cum laude*, at the very top of my class, but without Honours.

I pointed out to the chairman of my department that as various universities and foundations had offered me PhD places and scholarships, perhaps it was the Penn English Department that was out of line here, and not me? He (a kindly man) assured me that he had every confidence that I would do well, perhaps even better if I confined myself to proper English studies.

I didn't tell him, in listing my achievements and prospects, that I had been turned down to do a PhD by Yale, for reasons that would have confirmed his doubts about me. The Yale application form demanded both that one send in a sustained essay on a literary topic – I submitted one of my better course papers – and write a further essay of 'up to a thousand words' assessing one's prospects as a graduate student at Yale.

This seemed to me an idiotic requirement. They already had my transcript of grades and courses taken, three recommendations from tutors, and the course essay. Was one supposed to be honest in writing such self-description, citing one's strengths and weaknesses like a penitent on a pilgrimage? No thanks. My eventual submission (of up to a thousand words) read as follows: 'My prospects as a graduate student at Yale University are uniformly excellent.' Given a choice between affirming the sensibleness of their requirements, and accepting this renegade candidate, the Yale Graduate Admissions Department chose the former, and rejected the latter. I never much wanted to go there anyway – too preppy – and went to Oxford instead, to 'read' the newly fashionable BPhil degree in English.

I loved that word 'read', which came from the Delegacy of English's handbook, and was reiterated in the literature from Merton College, which also advised that 'gentlemen are responsible for bringing their own tea crockery.' My mother adored the phrase, and used it repeatedly over the months before I left for Oxford.

'He's responsible for bringing his own tea crockery, you know,' she told her friends.

'What's tea crockery?'

'I don't know,' she admitted, 'but I bought him a mug.'

I took it with me to Oxford, and it came in handy when my next door neighbour in the college graduate house at 21 Merton Street, Vijaya Samaraweera, arrived from Ceylon with an entire chest full of (who would have supposed it?) tea. I showed him my mug. We became instant friends.

Going to Oxford was the right decision: great Philosophy Department, and reasonable enough in English. I bought a Harris tweed jacket, a Merton scarf and tie, and had a three-piece pin-striped suit made by Hall Brothers in the High. I had tea and apple crumble with custard at George's in the covered market, used 'jolly' as an adjective, took afternoon tea in the Middle Common Room, learned to call my tutor by his first name, went to evensong in the chapel, and joined the varsity tennis club (during the fixtures you stopped for tea between matches). My fiancée Rachel, who still had a year to finish at college, would join me in Oxford the next year, after our forthcoming marriage in June of 1967. What a great plan. You could count on love, whatever those sceptical Shirelles and that Mr Hume suggested.

6

YOUNG AND OLD
WITH W.B. YEATS

And I though never of Ledaean kind
Had pretty plumage once – enough of that,
Better to smile on all that smile, and show
There is a comfortable kind of old scarecrow.
W.B. Yeats, 'Among School Children'

When I remember my first love, my mind often turns to W.B. Yeats. She would probably be mystified to hear this, all these years later, and I'm a little puzzled by it myself. I suppose it must be because my copy of Yeats's poems is all that I have left of her. It is a blue cloth volume stamped in gilt, as many of the early editions of the poet's works were, though it lacks the elegance of their original design. I purchased this unprepossessing book in 1963, in my second year at the University of Pennsylvania, and subsequently used it at Oxford, and later while teaching at Warwick. It has been constantly in my possession, then, for some forty-six years, save the one during which I lent it to Rachel, who was reading Yeats in one of her college courses.

My memory of her – what she looked like, how she moved, what her voice sounded like – has largely faded, and I threw out all her letters when she left me, forlorn in Oxford, for her college English teacher in April of 1967. Her *Yeats* teacher. Her Yeats teacher with whom she used *my* book. There seemed to me something bibliographically perfidious in this treachery, some unaccountable wickedness. Surely if you are going to have an affair with your English teacher you don't use your fiancé's book as the medium? It would be like using his bed, only worse: this left permanent stains. Because, on many pages of the *Collected Poems* there were annotations in her hand that, had I been granted an early glimpse at them, might have enabled me to foresee what was coming.

In themselves her notes are slight and fundamentally uninteresting. I had annotated the book copiously as well, and my notes, too, are hardly enough now to divert one's emotional or intellectual attention. They were, I suspect, largely transcriptions from a teacher's voice on to the page. But viewed suspiciously, hers gave implicit testimony, if not to the forthcoming infidelity, at least of some overheating of her imagination in the presence of her ardent teacher.

Her note to 'Leda and the Swan', that tale of the overcoming of innocence by male lust, seemed in retrospect positively prescient: 'Zeus – passionate. Leda – helpless and terrified.' So my loved one was overcome by a God-like teacher (the animal!), but it wasn't her fault. That was some consolation, though her notes stressing the purification that comes from the flames of passion in the margin to 'Byzantium' seemed to indicate that much good could, and had, come out of it for them both, if not for me.

Risible nonsense, of course: merely a nice example of how badly we read if our feelings obtrude unduly. But in comparison my own annotations seem sexless, impersonal, and banal: 'Wit!' I say here, 'Symbolism!' there, make references to Shelley, Keats and Arnold, paraphrase this or that, add a reference to gyres, or to Fergus and Cuchulain, those supremely uninteresting figures from Celtic mythology. What a boring little pedant I was, how bloodless in contrast to my winsome, passionate lost love.

We met in 1961, during my senior year at Huntington High

School (her junior year), and were welded together until I left for Oxford in 1966. I thought her quite the most beautiful girl ever, dimpled, wavy-haired, easy-smiling. When I said so to my father, who liked to be accurate, he agreed that she was 'rather pretty'. I was so furious that I hardly talked to him for days.

This unformed, infinitely agreeable girl – I hardly recall an angry word between us, and I am the sort of man who makes women cross on a regular basis – may have seemed to him an unprepossessing object to occasion such an intense attachment. I was drunk with the intensity of my desire for her, though the opposite possibility (of *hers* for me?) never seemed plausible. In that period young women didn't have sexual desires, they responded to them. If you were lucky. Love needed to be involved: kisses, troths, going steady, having 'our song', rings, charm bracelets and anklets, professions of fidelity, plans for the future. But when the regulations had been negotiated and obeyed, the erotic possibilities were surprisingly varied and exciting.

My pre-pubescent reading in my father's library had led me to the exhausting supposition that sexual love consisted of a geometrically expanding series of *activities*. Having done this, might it not be exciting to do this, and that, and that? The sexual mores of the time were obsessed with drawing lines and establishing boundaries, but it began to seem as if the purpose of all these prohibitions – kissing but no tongues, above the waist but not below the waist, below the waist but no penetration – was to multiply the possibilities of daring, guilty transgression, and satisfaction. Lines were drawn and breathlessly crossed, redrawn, recrossed. The months passed in a haze of yearning and erotic exploration.

Not that there was a lot else to do on Long Island in 1961. We watched Elvis on The Ed Sullivan Show and hardly knew whether to laugh or cry. We were too square for any of that, all that shimmying and shaking. I couldn't and wouldn't do the jitterbug, and was utterly humiliated trying to do the twist in front of my bedroom mirror. (I still cringe at the memory of my mother grinding away desperately to my Chubby Checker record: 'That's it, isn't it!' she'd cry. 'I think I've got it now!') Our other tastes and pleasures were equally suburban: we had rounds of miniature golf, ate at that quirky new eatery McDonald's (you couldn't even eat a dollar's worth!), played family tennis at the racquet club, hung out at the beach, begged the car to go to a drive-in movie in the evening. 'What did you see?' my mother would ask, disapproving yet slyly animated by the thought of what we might have been doing in the back seat of the car. We made it a point to remember a scene, or at least the title. Sometimes someone would give a party, after long negotiations with parents, and we would try to wangle some beer, making regular trips to the car to consume a can, before returning to swoon to Johnny Mathis and Pat Boone. Later, when we were more than making-out, when we were actually doing it in our own college rooms and apartments, in came a new wave of music, as if in confirmation of our sense that the times were indeed a changin': Dylan, the Beatles, the Stones. Sometimes, smugly, I felt as if we'd fucked the new decade into life, ignited it. A lot of people felt like that then, and they were pretty much right.

It was intoxicating. I spent years drugged by sex, by the memory and anticipation of sex, indifferent to the creeping certainty that it would be right for both of us to move on. The physical fervour was not accompanied by an equal emotional intensity and curiosity – I had encountered no equivalent to Hirschfeld regarding the inward life. We were both stuck, and bored, without recognizing it, enacting the same old postures and rituals, both physical and emotional. Fortunately she saw this before I did, and had the courage to break our engagement just before we were due to get married in the summer of 1967.

I soon discovered (though I can't remember how) that Rachel's teacher had courted her by sending her a copy of Yeats's early poem, 'Brown Penny', which opens like this:

I whispered 'I am too young,'
And then 'I am old enough';
Wherefore I threw a penny
To find out if I might love.
'Go and love, go and love, young man,
    If the lady be young and fair.'
Ah, penny, brown penny, brown penny,
I am looped in the loops of her hair.

I was horrified by this bit of pretentious loopiness, so typical of the worst of Yeats, with a characteristic build-up to a pseudo-climax where sound overwhelms sense. It seemed to me breathtakingly banal, the final repetition serving only to suggest that the would-be lover (read: her teacher) was the sort of fanciful dope who would seek, and follow, such advice. It was obvious that Rachel was in trouble, and should tell her undiscriminating suitor to get lost. He must, I concluded, be both an emotional and a literary retard.

Unlike me. Outraged that my loved one should be courted so ineptly, I responded by sending her another, and palpably better, Yeats poem, 'The Song of Wandering Aengus', which ends with an exalted crescendo of feeling:

Though I am old with wandering
Through hollow lands and hilly lands,
I will find out where she has gone,
And kiss her lips and take her hands;
And walk among long dappled grass,
And pluck till time and times are done
The silver apples of the moon,
The golden apples of the sun.

That would do it! When I regained my lost one – and how could I not, sending her such a wonderful poem? – then we would enjoy the fruits of those countless nights and days. We'd be reunited, and I would have freed her from the momentary blindness that had caused her to choose (and to read) so clumsily.

Actually it was me who was reading badly. At least 'Brown Penny' is in the voice of a young man, full of desire, while 'The Song of Wandering Aengus' is that of an old man full of regret for what has been lost. We do not believe, reading it, that Wandering Aengus will reunite with his love, only that it is characteristic of age to yearn for lost vitality. Why would I have sent Rachel such a poem? Was I unconsciously acknowledging and accepting her decision? And in so doing, acknowledging, too, that she was right?

Months went by as I waited despondently for her answer. Surely, someone as sensitive as me had to be preferable to this surrogate, this seducer foolishly chosen while I was away at Oxford. Surely no woman could prefer the prosaic twerp who sent her 'Brown Penny' to a man with the passionate intensity to choose 'The Song of Wandering Aengus'? And if my dear one – here was a startling and terrible thought – could make such a choice, perhaps she wasn't the girl for me after all? I was in a vulnerable state, sleepless and emotionally wrought, and informed my Oxford supervisor not to expect any essays 'for at least a term', owing to my broken heart.

It was just as well. Literary criticism was hardly my strong point at the time. In any case, I've always had my reservations about Yeats, who is the most irritating poet since Blake, whom he revered, and whom he edited (with Edwin Ellis) in 1893. Blake invents a cosmology and cast of characters for his prophetic books which are allegorical – there is, loosely, a one-to-one correspondence between a named 'character' and the force(s) that are represented. This seems oddly at variance with his insistence on the goodness of 'minute particulars', and his credo 'to generalize is to be an Idiot', which is my favourite generalization. You can see why Yeats was drawn to this, though there seems something oddly unimaginative in the project, which is why, I suspect, people who claim to admire Blake are really only delighted – as I am – by the *Songs of Innocence and Experience*, and *The Marriage of Heaven and Hell*. The later works are deeply obscure, and read largely by nerds, or Blakeans, as they call themselves.

Yeats is never this prolix, and begins from a different starting point. Amongst his earliest works he edited collections like *Fairy and Folk Tales of the Irish Peasantry* (1888) and *Irish Fairy Tales* (1891), and steeped himself in Celtic lore. He wrote a considerable number of plays based on these subjects, which are (thankfully) rarely performed, even at the Abbey Theatre. This obsession with the world of druids and mythological Celtic figures can cause a softening of the brain, and has been known to lead to the compulsive singing of songs, and even (in extreme cases) to vegetarianism.

When I took my course on Yeats at the University of Pennsylvania, I can remember mugging up this material, being furiously engaged with it, in the way that characterizes ambitious undergraduates, anxious to master and to stand out. But none of it stuck. The mere thought of such folkloric subjects now fills me with a kind of agitated vacancy, as if I were listening to a prolonged weather report in Esperanto.

Yeats's later, and even more boring, reading in eastern religion and philosophy, as well as Christian mysticism, was driven by the desire not so much to master these traditions, as to root about within them for new metaphors and sources of poetic inspiration. The process through which the material was filtered did not ask 'is this true?' but 'how might it be useful?'

The effect of this rage for abstract thought, which Yeats allied to a 'longing . . . to be full of images', has curious effects on the poetry. So intense is his desire to see the world whole, that he rarely sees it clearly, or, to put this more carefully, he rarely registers it in its particularities. I can remember few characters, moments, or voices from individual poems by Yeats (as one does from, say,

The Waste Land). He strains for, and reaches, a kind of pitched intensity that has archetypal – he occasionally uses the term 'ceremonial' – radiance, but he frequently lacks a way to locate that visionary quality in the ordinariness of everyday life.

And hence, I think, why I reach for my Yeats when something large is at stake, as one might reach for the Bible. Since that time in Oxford, perhaps semi-consciously prompted by memory of Yeats's role in my life when I was twenty-two, I have increasingly turned to his poetry, not for solace, exactly, but for that assured magisterial understanding that characterizes his later poems.

I now feel uneasy with most of early Yeats, even 'The Song of the Wandering Aengus', which strikes me as suffering from a number of the same flaws that characterize 'Brown Penny'. I have had enough of those poems. (I *hate* the much anthologized 'The Lake Isle of Innisfree'.) Perhaps it would be a sign of retardation if I hadn't, at my age.

Of course, most great romantic poetry has been written either by those who died young (Byron, Keats, Shelley) or those who, having written poetry while young, later wrote less (and less well) and turned instead to criticism (Coleridge, Wordsworth, Arnold) – as if, no longer able to produce great poems, one could at least reflect upon the nature of what one had done. Yeats is a great exception here. He not only maintains the intensity of his early thinking and feeling, but enriches, deepens and widens it in his later work: instead of turning to prose to reflect upon his early sources of inspiration, he allows such reflection to become part of the poetic process.

He is no less, though differently, moved and inspired by the fact of growing old than of having been young. Yeats provides, of course, many of our most haunting images of physical decay. My favourite of all his poems, 'Sailing to Byzantium', puts this squarely. It begins with a most wonderful evocation of the urgent flow of universal life:

That is no country for old men. The young
In one another's arms, birds in the trees
–Those dying generations – at their song,
The salmon-falls, the mackerel-crowded seas,
Fish, flesh, or fowl, commend all summer long
Whatever is begotten, born, and dies.
Caught in that sensual music all neglect
Monuments of unageing intellect.

But this flood of procreative activity, this swell of comings and
goings, hardly takes account of, or makes a place for, the consciousness of those who – having experienced the tides of youth – have
time enough, also, to reflect upon their withdrawal. And thus the
second stanza immediately, almost necessarily, begins:

An aged man is but a paltry thing,
A tattered coat upon a stick

You get a stick when you detach a piece of wood from a branch,
when it dies and the sap dries up, when the organic connection to
its tree of life is severed. So too, and yet more poignantly, can a
man apprehend his own slow detachment from his vital sources:

. . . sick with desire
And fastened to a dying animal

It is a harrowing, unforgettable image: one of those phrases that
attaches itself to one's consciousness, defines and refines it. For
desire is never shed, neither is it overcome. It is remembered, and
unless transformed by the spirit, or the imagination – by the power
of poetry – it torments us with what we have lost without putting
anything in its place. Yeats's answer to this, in the fourth stanza of
'Sailing to Byzantium', is not entirely satisfactory – the poet imagines

himself immortalized as a Byzantine golden bird, singing 'of what is past, or passing, or to come'. This final artistic incarnation feels impotent and trivial, hardly enough 'to keep a drowsy Emperor awake'.

But the poet does not insist upon the need for transcendence. There is an inalienable conflict between flesh and spirit, youth and age, the transient and the immortal, the world of sensual experience and the world of art. You can't wish away this tension, nor can you solve it: all that you can hope is that the transforming powers of the imagination can use such conflicts as sources of art – however inadequate the process may sometimes seem – and hence be of some consolation. T.S. Eliot, who regarded Yeats as the greatest poet of the century, makes this point perfectly:

> one feels that the most lively and desirable emotions of youth have been preserved to receive their full and due expression in retrospect. For the interesting feelings of age are not just different feelings; they are feelings into which the feelings of youth are integrated.

It's not an easy process, not as I experience it, this mixing (as Eliot put it) of memory and desire.

Much of what I remember of Rachel is so intense and so vivid that it seems as if it were played by some inward video, recalling the delights of first love. All of forty-odd years later this – might one call it emotion recollected in senility? – is so fresh, and very occasionally so stimulating, that it rather embarrasses me to admit it, though it is testimony to the unfolding of time, to its radiant refulgence, its pathos and inevitability.

First love is only infrequently revisited, when the right catalyst occurs. It might be hearing that significant song, or talking to an old friend, or looking through those old photos. Or reading W.B. Yeats. Perhaps I've had it wrong: it is not Rachel that makes me think of Yeats but the other way round. Yeats makes us all think about first love, the flushes of youth: what we never cease to regret the loss of. This is, he came to feel, the essential task of the poet: to become that golden bird which sings forever of 'what is past, or passing, or to come'. There is no consolation in art, only formulation: the pain of our inevitable loss of vitality is not slowed by the intercessions of the artist, but in listening attentively we may smile, and remember for a moment what it was to be vibrantly alive, to have been young and in love.

First love is better remembered than continued, and Rachel was right to leave it when she did. The irony – I was too young to expect it – is that pain releases energy, just as pleasure often retards it. I indulged myself with a few months of operatic grief, in which I wrote a two hundred-page account of my travails, and then threw it away. Soon enough I was seeing other women, had a romantic idyll in Ischia with an attractive classmate of Rachel's who'd decided I was just the right sort to serve as her first lover, and returned to Oxford happy and refreshed. In my overstuffed pigeonhole at Merton, amongst the usual college notices and invitations to join various societies, was a letter from Rachel. I carried it back to my flat in my breast pocket, and put it on my desk, where it sat for a few minutes before I was ready to open it. What might it say? What did I want it to say?

She had ended her relationship with her teacher, which had been a mistake, but a necessary one. We'd had a 'very young' relationship, she acknowledged, but the pause might be good for us. Could we not try to get to know one another again, in a better way? It was the letter I had yearned for, the letter that Wandering Aengus was designed to prompt, it had a tentative delicacy that hurt my heart, but it was too late. I thought for a few days, and composed a letter of thanks, and of regret, to say good-bye. It was florid and self-regarding – April was our cruellest month, but I was breeding lilacs out of the dead land – which rather confirmed her sense of how immature the relationship had been.

I still was. At the time I got her letter we would have been married for three months. I presume it wouldn't have lasted. Better the lifetime pleasure of first love, remembered. Better, too, that sadness, that loss.

7

SWEET AND SOUR

Yet we in Oxford, brought up amidst the beauty and sweetness of that beautiful place, have not failed to seize on truth: – the truth that beauty and sweetness are essential characters of a complete human perfection.

Matthew Arnold, Culture and Anarchy

If it had to be Wordsworth or Arnold, then it would have to be Arnold. The Oxford BPhil in English made you choose one or the other as a special subject, and I'd had enough of Wordsworth in my undergraduate Romantic Poetry course. I did not share his reverence for 'nature', and had no desire to be improved by its beggars, leech gatherers, and other drooling rustics. To my sort of Jewish American, nature is dangerous, where you are more likely to be eaten by a bear than improved by neo-Platonic contemplation. I'm rather fond of scenery, though, as long as you don't step in it. You need to be protected from it by a pane of glass.

Not that I knew much about Matthew Arnold. I think I'd read 'Dover Beach', and was aware that Lionel Trilling's PhD thesis and first book had been on Arnold, which was some recommendation. Having made my choice, I threw on my rather dashing magenta-and-cream striped Merton College scarf, and headed to Blackwell's Book Shop, on the Broad, where I had opened an account: 'R.A. Gekoski, Merton' was enough – you didn't even need to prove it

– to allow you a full term's credit. Take a book, take armfuls of books, sign: 'R.A. Gekoski, Merton'. It was a good game. My shelves filled right up. Arnold's *Collected Poems* and *Culture and Anarchy* on the top shelf.

My tutor for the term, Hugo Dyson, had suggested I do an essay on Arnold as a critic. I was anxious to impress him: he'd been a member of the Inklings, was a noted (if not exactly prolific) scholar and bon viveur, and had recently had a walk-on role as a professor in the movie *Darling*, with that super Julie Christie. I worked hard on the paper, and sent it to him a few days in advance of the tutorial. On the day, I popped on the scrappy, distinctly humiliating black rags called a Commoner's Gown – the Scholar's Gowns were capacious enough to flap about like Gandalf – hoisted my umbrella, and made my way down the slippery cobbles of Merton Street for my tutorial.

The essay attempted a demolition of one of Arnold's central critical ideals, concerning the use of touchstones, or memorized lines of poetry of such quality that mere comparison with them would indicate the merit of any other bit of verse. I'd read his two essential essays, 'The Function of Criticism at the Present Time' and 'The Study of Poetry', and been mystified by the combination of extreme self-confidence and methodological laxness that they seemed to display. The following was typical, and typically irritating:

> Indeed there can be no more useful help for discovering what poetry belongs to the class of the truly excellent, and can therefore do us most good, than to have always in one's mind lines and expressions of the great masters, and to apply them as a touchstone to other poetry. Of course we are not to require this other poetry to resemble them; it may be very dissimilar. But if we have any tact we shall find them, when we have lodged them well in our minds, an infallible touchstone for detecting the presence or absence of high poetic quality . . .

What lines did he have in mind? There are eleven examples: three each from Homer, Dante and Milton, and two from Shakespeare. They are 'lines and expressions of the great masters', of the utmost gravitas, and include Hamlet's dying words to Horatio, and Milton's lament on the death of Persephone, as well as his injunction:

And courage never to submit or yield,
And what is else not to be overcome . . .

which is perfectly designed to appeal to high-Victorian sensibility, as well as to scout troops, Sumo wrestlers and American Marines.

Tuck these lines away, add a few dashes of Dante, and 'if you have tact' they will be adequate 'even of themselves' to guide us to a proper understanding and evaluation of poetry. Clearly a lot is being built into the term 'tact', which pretty obviously means 'sensibility'. But if you have such sensibility, surely, you don't need a carrier bag of touchstones to help you on your way? You will have your own standards of quality, your own comparators, your own understanding of the nature of the poetic.

'Poetry,' Arnold informed me, consisted of 'a criticism of life', a remarkably airy notion, accompanied by no definition, as if delivered to an audience that would know what he meant. I didn't. When I went back to Arnold's formulation, seeking further guidance, things only got worse: 'a criticism of life *under the conditions fixed for such a criticism by the laws of poetic truth and poetic beauty*'. It was enough to make you squeal, and I did, for twelve closely argued polemical pages. I sent them to Dyson, expecting approbation.

His rooms were messy and apparently unloved – I'd not yet encountered the concept of the shabby genteel – but there was a comfy chair and the inevitable glass of dry sherry, an astringent drink about which no one had warned me, and of which I'd drunk too much during my college induction meetings. It made me feel sophisticated: Amontillado, or better yet Fino. *Not* Bristol Cream.

My essay was sitting amongst a pile of papers on the table next to the bottle of sherry. I craned my neck, but couldn't see a mark or any comments on the front page.

'Now, dear boy, shall we look at the Marguerite poems?'

I opened my *Collected Poems*.

'Which one?'

'Why don't you read 'To Marguerite'?

YES! in the sea of life enisled,
With echoing straits between us thrown.
Dotting the shoreless watery wild,
We mortal millions live *alone*.
The islands feel the enclasping flow,
And then their endless bounds they know.

But when the moon their hollows lights,
And they are swept by balms of spring,
And in their glens, on starry nights,
The nightingales divinely sing;
And lovely notes, from shore to shore,
Across the sounds and channels pour;

O then a longing like despair
Is to their farthest caverns sent!
For surely once, they feel, we were
Parts of a single continent.
Now round us spreads the watery plain—
O might our marges meet again!

Who order'd that their longing's fire
Should be, as soon as kindled, cool'd?

Who renders vain their deep desire?—
A God, a God their severance rul'd;
And bade betwixt their shores to be
The unplumb'd, salt, estranging sea.

I read the poem, then reread it, and looked up.

'There is only one line of genuine poetry in the entire poem,' he said. He paused while I looked back through the poem anxiously. 'Which is it?'

I peered at the text. Surely it couldn't be the opening line – 'enisled' was awful! I could feel my mind closing down.

What kind of a tutorial was this anyway? I'd never been asked such a question before, and had no idea where to start. Presumably I was supposed to *classify* the lines – both Arnold and Oxford were obsessed by class – give them a First, or an Alpha – both new categories to me, and distinctly foreign. Was this how you read poetry in Oxford?

Dyson looked at me steadily, as if willing me to find the answer – or, perhaps, to fail? My attack on Arnold had been intemperate and show-offy, and Arnold was revered in Oxford, 'that city of dreaming spires' as he had christened it: 'home of lost causes, and forsaken beliefs, and unpopular names, and impossible loyalties'. I drank some sherry – I *needed* some sherry – and looked at the text again. I fidgeted, I sipped, I stalled. I was fast becoming another of Oxford's 'lost causes'.

'Surely,' he said, crisply: '"*The unplumb'd, salt, estranging sea.*" Pure poetry, lovely.'

We spent the rest of the hour – it was intimidatingly intimate, this one-to-one tutorial format, its apparent gentility really just a stage for jousting, testing, competing, probing – in similarly amateurish pursuit. It was a 'tact' test, and I was failing it. I was furious. By the time Dyson had walked me through the other poems seeking lines worthy of touchstone status (though I didn't see what he was up to), I couldn't wait to collect my essay and get the hell out of there. I rose as the college bells tolled the hour, and Hugo handed me my essay.

'Quite interesting, thank you,' he said mildly. I was quite pleased. I didn't know that the English use 'quite' to mean 'not particularly', rather than the American usage, in which it is frequently used to add approving emphasis. I had a similar linguistic embarrassment, though with a better result, in attempting to join the varsity tennis 'club', which had a 'secretary', one Tony Billington, himself a member of the team. I dropped him a note, and by return received his suggestion that I have a game with a fresher called Ian Hewitt, who was 'a useful player'. A few days later Ian and I had a match on grass, on which I had little experience, but rather enjoyed. I didn't expect much from him, given that he was only 'useful', and I won relatively easily. I was immediately invited to join the varsity squad, and soon learned that Ian was a junior Wimbledon player, and played for Hampshire. 'Useful' meant 'bloody good'. He eventually captained the team, and played First Singles in the Varsity Match. I played Sixth, and never took another set off him.

Two countries divided by a common language? It wasn't just a question of different accent, usage and vocabulary – you could pick that up – but what was more complex, and harder to read, were the tonal differences between American English and English English. I'd never read anyone who wrote like Matthew Arnold, never encountered that curious mixture of playfulness and gravitas that make for his particular urbanity. Though committed to 'the best that has been known and thought' – to 'culture' – Arnold rarely has the earnestness that one finds in, say, Trilling; instead he is poised, playful, teasing, disarming potential opposition through the effortless felicity of his manner. Take the opening of Chapter 3 of *Culture and Anarchy*:

From a man without a philosophy no one can expect philosophical completeness. Therefore I may observe without
shame, that in trying to get a distinct notion of our aristo-
cratic, our middle, and our working class, with a view of testing
the claims of each of these classes to become a centre of
authority, I have omitted, I find, to complete the old-fashioned analysis which I had the fancy of applying . . .

Arnold's views of the nature of 'culture', and its relation to
England's class structure, had been criticized as lacking in clarity
and rigour, without an adequate basis in systematic reflection. He
was also accused, again with some justification, of having too little
regard for the alleviation of the suffering of the masses. His response
to such criticism was invariably to smother his antagonist with
approbation, and an apparent show of contrition:

> While, finally, Mr Frederic Harrison, in a very good-tempered
> and witty satire, gets moved to an almost stern moral im-
> patience, to behold, as he says, 'Death, sin, cruelty stalk among
> us, filling their maws with innocence and youth,' and me, in
> the midst of the general tribulation, handing out my pouncet-
> box.

I immediately suspected that Mr Arnold had the greatest
contempt for Mr Harrison, whom he must have classed amongst
his Philistines, and dismissed with a shrug and a smile. Quite the
opposite: Arnold confessed to shrieking with laughter at Harrison's
parody of him, and his riposte has real fondness in it. Though he
was given to playful teasing, and occasionally to ridicule, the sweetness and light that he recommends are most frequently encountered in his attitudes and in his style, as if the very mode and
tonality of discourse established the truth of what he was saying.
One doesn't, finally, learn much from Matthew Arnold.

Understanding of particular poets is rarely enhanced by his readings, while his analysis of the English class system is crass, risible
really. But none of this matters; you get inhabited by his voice, his
temper and his tones. You enjoy Arnold because you are charmed
by him, find his company instructive and congenial, and wish to
recommend him as if he were a new friend. His distinctive and
immediately recognizable voice is worth assimilating, his demeanour
wholly his own. The key is that his terms are basically inter-
changeable: culture, sweetness, light, the best that has been known
and thought, disinterestedness. Same thing, really. The style works
by repetition of these terms and phrases until they have a certain
inevitability, as if it were impossible not to think like this, using
these concepts and ideas. His antipathy to systematic thinking was
entirely congenial to me.

But if Arnold was greatly admired in Oxford, his major follower
in the twentieth century, F.R. Leavis, certainly was not. This was
no surprise to me, because I had never heard of F.R. Leavis, which
occasioned as much astonishment amongst my tutors as my ignorance about the World Cup (which England had just won) caused
amongst my fellow students. Was there no end to the cultural insu-
larity of Americans? Leavis's work was only occasionally discussed
in Oxford, usually slightingly, but he was a potent, if absent, presence. He was consistently referred to, with a curious edge of
contempt, as *Dr* Leavis. In Oxford, even wishing to have a doctorate
(DPhil) was a symptom of self-aggrandizement and second-
rateness, frequently to be found in Americans. Traditionally, a
genuinely clever graduate was offered a college teaching post after
getting a brilliant First; if insufficiently bright to achieve that, then
a BLitt (a lesser thesis degree) was regarded as quite enough by
way of research.

Leavis was not only one of those doctors, he taught at Cambridge,
and there was – to the Oxford mind – something both unsavoury
and unsound about him. He was an occasional speaker to Oxford

societies, but his visits always had something clandestine about them: scheduled in obscure places at odd times like secret assignations, barely advertised, they seemed open only to the cognoscenti and the adventurous: *Dr F.R. Leavis will be Speaking in the Under Crypt of Keble College. Time to be Announced.* Leavis was, by our mild academic standards, dangerous. He seemed always to be arguing with someone, disparaging someone else. The *Guardian's* obituary of Leavis, in 1978, put this squarely: 'His most murderous and underestimated weapon was ridicule, which he deployed in lectures with the virtuosity of a music-hall star and with an insensitivity verging on paranoia.' Had he chomped on one of his antagonists' legs, no one would have been surprised. He was a bite waiting to happen.

He had a reputation for clannishness, and his students revered him with an intensity that was almost alarming. (No one felt this way about Hugo Dyson.) Though in print Leavis could be ponderous, in tutorials and lectures he was provocative, impish, and irreverent to an unexpected degree, even towards his most revered authors. T.S. Eliot, he was known to say, while pointing towards his groin, had 'something missing in the cellar', Milton was 'as mechanical as a bricklayer', Othello, Antony and Cleopatra were derided as 'great babies'. This irreverence was wonderfully bracing, and left me, once I had heard the many stories about it, feeling freer to make personal judgements, and to be less guided by academic pieties.

It was particularly freeing with regard to Matthew Arnold, the occasion of my tutorial humiliation. I'd been caught in the pieties of practical criticism: a finished text is regarded as somehow perfected, and the job of the critic is exegetical, to show how the poem works. But some poems don't. 'To Marguerite' palpably doesn't: it's rubbish, full of rotten poetic diction, and if you abandon the reflex of respect, you can use your critical tools to indicate why. There are very few really successful poems by Arnold, and it can be just as much fun dismantling the bad ones as explicating the good.

Leavis had learned from Arnold, and extended his lesson: instead of using single lines of poetry as touchstones – how silly! how limiting! – he used whole *authors*. How did *this* writer compare to the standards of serious engagement with life set by Jane Austen, George Eliot, Joseph Conrad, D.H. Lawrence? And there is, surely, something both wrongheaded and something sensible here. Wrongheaded in the pedestrian sense that my essay for Dyson had located, but sensible in the obvious sense that in saying that something is good we inevitably imply 'better than *that*, but not great, like *this*'. We are implicitly pointing, comparing, ranking in some implicit hierarchy.

Though his reputation for sour ferocity was not entirely unearned, when I actually began to read Leavis there was a great deal to admire and to learn from. If he generated less sweetness than Arnold, there was, in compensation, rather more light. I was particularly taken by a marvellous essay called 'Literary Criticism and Philosophy' (from *The Common Pursuit*) in which Leavis puckishly reacts to a review of one of his books by René Wellek, whom he is delighted to label 'a philosopher', a category for which he has an amused contempt. (Actually Wellek was a seminal figure in 'new criticism', and wished to provide for it some theoretical ground.) Leavis uses him, as Arnold had used Mr Frederic Harrison, as a figure of fun: the grindingly theoretical practitioner, wholly lacking in tact, or as Leavis would have it, sensibility.

Wellek had requested that Leavis, before making his literary judgements, elucidate and defend the premises on which they were based. (C.S. Lewis has made a similar demand, accusing Leavis of smuggling in a value system, based on 'relevance' and 'maturity', which he was unwilling to state or defend.) But Wellek's statement of this criticism is utterly pedestrian: Leavis has an implicit 'norm', he suggests, with which he judges every poet. 'I would wish,' said the exasperated Wellek, 'that you had made your assumptions more explicitly and defended them systematically.' It might have been tempting to play skittles with such critical cack-handedness, but Leavis uses the occasion to make a subtle statement of his critical practice that became, for me, a sort of touchstone in itself.

> Words in poetry invite us, not to 'think about' and judge, but to 'feel into' or 'become'– to realise a complex experi-ence that is given in the words... My whole effort was to work in terms of concrete judgements and particular analyses: 'This – doesn't it? – bears such a relation to that; this kind of thing – don't you find it so? – wears better than that,' etc.

Criticism, so viewed, is a communal search for shared – for 'true' – judgement. Critical assumptions are undoubtedly lurking some-where in the background, which is where they should stay. Foolishly, Leavis almost immediately goes on, following this memorable state-ment about critical practice, to sketch his underlying belief:

> traditions, or prevailing conventions or habits, that tend to cut poetry in general off from direct vulgar living and the actual, or to make it difficult for the poet to bring into poetry his most serious interests as an adult living in his own time, have a devitalizing effect.

This is so ponderous, so murky, so ill-framed, that it is no wonder that Leavis had resisted saying it: what is poetry *in general*? Why need *living* be described as *vulgar*? Whose *actual* life? A *devitalizing* effect on what, or whom? Raised in a middle-class Cambridge family, privately educated, and a university don for his entire life, his knowledge of the (vulgar?) working classes was derived largely from D.H. Lawrence, who couldn't get away from them fast enough.

Leavis loved to provoke, and to provide something to argue against. He must have been scarily fun to study with, more stimulating for sure than the elegant and superior Dyson, with his lines of true poetry. But it was impossible for me, a twenty-two-year-old immigrant fresh from the distant shores of American suburbia, to make much of this: to navigate between the urbanity of Arnold and the ferocity of Leavis, to make anything substantial of these quintessentially English goings-on. Better to go back to the tennis courts, try to beat Ian Hewitt again, and confront the milder but still patronizing attitudes of a set of English public school boys: 'you don't pronounce it *ar*istocrat, it's *ar*istocrat!' At least I could tell them to go to hell, but I didn't. I was too shy.

I wasn't shy, though, with the girl in the downstairs flat on Bardwell Road. As I was leaving the building with my flat-mate Vijaya's fiancée Dineli, just opening the door of the ground floor flat was a ravishing woman, who looked more like Julie Christie than Julie Christie did: fuller lips, slimmer, higher cheekbones. Her clothes – was she wearing a dress with black polka dots on a white background? – draped her with effortless grace.

I made an abrupt volte face, and knocked on the door. Barbara Pettifer, as she was called, answered immediately.

'Sorry to bother you,' I said, 'but I have just moved in. Could you tell me where the rubbish bins are? I've looked everywhere.'

She told me. I introduced myself and Dineli, and made some ingratiating small talk, before we moved off, ostensibly in search of the bins.

'I am going to marry that woman,' I said.

Dineli laughed.

'You're crazy. What do you mean?'

'I want to be able to tell this story to our children, about how I met their mother.'

'You're crazy!'

The next evening I knocked on Barbara's door, mug in hand, to say that I lacked the ingredients for my cup of tea, so could I borrow a cup of water? She sighed but invited me in, boiled a kettle, and we had a companionable cuppa together. That weekend she came to our flat-warming party. (We'd bought a case of Mateus Rosé, and I was reprimanded by a friend who thought it ostentatious to serve 'fine wine' at a party.) Barbara arrived in a newly fashionable short skirt, greatly enhanced by a red garter belt which looked both saucy and demure simultaneously, had a few drinks and a dance, and talked captivatingly and intelligently about this and that.

The next Sunday morning she asked if I would like to go for a walk.

'Sure,' I said. 'Where to?'

'The Parks.'

'What's there?'

'What do you mean? Trees, and the river. It's lovely.'

'What will we do there?'

'You don't do anything, you just go for a walk.'

What a romantic notion! I'd never gone for a walk before. I'd walked round golf courses, malls, campuses and cities, walked home from school or to the tennis club, but always in pursuit of some end. It had never occurred to me that you might do such a thing just for the sake of it.

It was quite pleasant, in a desultory sort of way. I kept looking for somewhere to have coffee, but it was just a park. Mildly disappointing really, save for Barbara's good company. Like me, she'd only recently ended a serious relationship, and we shared details of the pain and loss. She had hastened to assure me from the very start that she had promised herself 'never to liaise with another American', her previous boyfriend having been (like me) an American post-graduate, a tennis blue, and the driver of a new sports car. (Sometimes on her way out to work in the morning – she was secretary to the principal probation officer of Oxford – she would give my blue Morgan a kick. 'Bloody spoiled Americans,' you could hear her thinking.) I had reassured her that it was far too early to consider 'liaising', and that my intentions were honourable. They weren't. How could they be with a creature so luminously attractive?

As we strolled along, I was accosted by a hideous yappy dog, small and furious as a miniature Leavisite, who looked ever so keen to bite me on the ankle. His owner, a dowdy and upright dowager of the kind that have virtually occupied North Oxford, followed shortly.

'You must excuse him,' she said, 'he's very nervous.'

'I'm nervous too,' I said crossly, 'and I haven't tried to bite him.'

The lady glared, Barbara smiled, and we carried on.

8

FORMS OF LANGUAGE
AND FORMS OF LIFE

Everybody's life becomes more fabulous, every minute,
than the most fabulous books. It's phony, goddam it . . .
but *mysto* . . . and after a while it starts to infect you,
like an itch, the roseola.
Tom Wolfe, The Electric Kool-Aid Acid Test

If a lion could talk, we could not understand him.
Ludwig Wittgenstein, Philosophical Investigations

I'd worked hard, and now it was time to have fun. I finished my
BPhil exams in the early summer of 1968, and headed back to the
States for a holiday, my head humming with passages from Matthew
Arnold, Lewis Carroll, Arthur Conan Doyle, and other Victorian
luminaries. It was then easy for me, over a short term, to mem-
orize large chunks of text, and to use them where appropriate in
exams. After the results were announced one of the examiners asked
me, with a mixture of incredulity and respect, whether I had a
photographic memory. I did, sort of – I could actually see chunks
of text and inwardly read them – but the photographs faded quickly,
so that by the time summer had blossomed, and the muggy Long
Island heat set in, I could hardly recall more than occasional phrases.

I was glad of it, because Matthew Arnold didn't go down very well in that second summer of love.

It is a major premise of *Culture and Anarchy* that a belief in 'the prime right and blessedness of doing as one likes' was the besetting error of Victorian liberalism, and that this disposition towards the merely personal had to be combated by the full force of culture. One must follow what 'right reason' and disinterestedness ordain, or else anarchy would surely prevail. And in that drug-hazed musical summer it did. It was great, 'doing your own thing', unswayed by the force of Arnold's hundred-year-old disapproval.

I lounged about smoking dope, reading book after book, listening to Dylan's 'Blonde on Blonde', Jefferson Airplane, the Grateful Dead and Country Joe and the Fish, who did a gig on Long Island that summer. We drove to it down the Expressway passing a joint back and forth through the window, at sixty miles an hour, with the amiable folks in a car in the adjoining lane.

Best of all was the Doors, whose song 'The End', while palpably about death, was also a metaphor for entry into a new way of being. In 1967 the group had appeared live on the show of the ghoulish and shockingly talentless Ed Sullivan, an accolade also offered to the Rolling Stones, having been firmly instructed to alter the line 'Girl we couldn't get much higher', from 'Light My Fire', lest it suggest – gosh! – indulging in drugs. Jim Morrison sang it anyway – unlike Mick Jagger, who had agreed to change 'let's spend the night together' to 'let's spend some time together'. Sullivan was furious, and vowed that the Doors would never return. They didn't want to anyway. Presumably the Stones did.

The new literature was as good as the music, and explained it to those of us too remote to understand, quite, what was going on. There was a crazy new spirit in the air, and we learned about it through a remarkable series of books written in the style called 'new journalism', in which the writer becomes a participant in the pageant, observing both it and himself as the story. I adored Hunter

S. Thompson's creepily fascinated book on the 'strange and terrible saga' of *The Hell's Angels*, and the equally chilling *In Cold Blood*, Truman Capote's novelized version of the murder of a family of mid-Westerners, both of which came out in 1966. Then there was Norman Mailer, whose evocation of the march on the Pentagon in *The Armies of the Night* caught the wild energy of the time.

Joan Didion's *Slouching Towards Bethlehem*, a dry-eyed account of hippy California, served as a useful antidote to Mailer's enthusiasm for the encroaching new forms of life. Less forensically, and with more verve, Tom Wolfe's take on the same place and period focused on Ken Kesey and his band of Merry Pranksters. Entitled *The Electric Kool-Aid Acid Test*, I first heard of it in the *New York Times* Magazine in August of 1968, in which Wolfe described his experience writing the piece on which the book was based: 'I had a terrible time writing the article . . . the weird fourth dimension I kept sensing in the Prankster adventure. I wrote most of it at such a burst that to this day I have no perspective on the book.'

I'd read Kesey's *One Flew Over the Cuckoo's Nest* – who hadn't? – but these Pranksters were new to me. Contemporary incarnations of the archetypes of the Trickster and the Fool, they had traversed America in 1964 in a psychedelically enhanced, Day-Glo school bus, blaring music, totally spaced out on hallucinogens, doing their thing, blowing people's minds. It was sheer mania, there were *no* rules. It made *On the Road* seem as exciting as a picnic at the local Elks Club, though synchronistically, at the controls – no, call it at the wheel – of the bus was Kerouac's old muse and travelling companion Neal Cassady. And who should show up at Kesey's house in the woods but Neal's old friend Allen Ginsberg, and his new pals, the Hell's Angels. Everything seemed to be coming together, though the principles of connection were obscure. Jung was cited: *synchronicity, an acausal connecting principle*. That was it!

I rolled my joints, and read and read, putting the book down only to change LPs, have a beer and a sandwich, substitute a pipe full of Balkan Sobranie for the dope. Wolfe was a revelation. The book was captivatingly fresh, like hearing Bob Dylan for the first time: totally authentic, creating a new sound, making you wish you could think and talk – sing! – like that. Form, sound and content in perfect harmony. Finding the right language to convey this curious new form of life was a problem that exercised Kesey too. The acknowledged guru of the group, he denied that he was in any way the 'Chief', and in so doing confirmed that he was. He was uncertain about how to convey the being-experiment of the Pranksters, with their crazed bus-ride across America, their clanging devotion to the machinery of sound, their incessant desire to – as the Doors put it – 'break on through to the other side'. How could you make the Acid experience more widely available, convey its visionary and spiritual nature?

> Christ! How many movements before them had run into this self same problem. Every vision, every insight of the . . . original . . . circle always came out of the *new experience . . . the kairos* . . . and how to tell it! How to get it across to the multitudes who have never had the experience themselves? You couldn't *put it into words.*

Kesey had stopped writing. Though acknowledged as one of America's great young novelists, what he was now experiencing was so powerful that it seemed to leave language behind. He had no further desire, he said, to be 'trapped by artificial rules . . . trapped in syntax . . . ruled by an imaginary teacher with a red ball-point pen who will brand us with an A-minus for the slightest infraction of the rules'.

But if Kesey couldn't or wouldn't find a new way of writing, and keeping his finger on the pulse, Tom Wolfe could. To do so he had to reanimate the available language: he practically reinvents the exclamation mark, uses extended runs of full stops . . . not to indicate some omission from the text . . . not *that* . . . but to enact the rhythms of the mind, thinking and experiencing, pausing as it reflects . . . moving forwards in staccato movements of perception . . . repeating itself. And how frequently such perception seems to demand *italics*, or CAPITALS! He invents a line through which the apprehensions buzz across neural synapses – *electric prose*, you can hear the hum! – and the staccato rhythms seem to re-enact the activities of the stoned mind as it goes about its business of apprehending, and *making*, the world.

Just as Kesey was bent on extending the range of how we can think and feel, so too Wolfe had to find a language that not merely conveyed this, but caused an analogous excitement and dislocation, leaving the reader feeling exhilarated, even transported.

> You had to put them into ecstasy . . . Buddhist monks immersing themselves in cosmic love through fasting and contemplation. Hindus zonked out in Bhakti, which is fervent love in the possession of God, ecstatic flooding themselves with Krishna through sexual orgies or plunging into the dinners of the Bacchanalia, Christians off in Edge City through Gnostic onanism or the Heart of Jesus or the Child Jesus with its running sore, – or – THE ACID TESTS.

This was way further out than Dylan's recommendation that 'everybody must get stoned'. That was easy, we were all doing that. But dropping acid? Or, as happened in the first Acid Test – a large public party with strobe lights, thumping music, Pranksters galore, everyone zonked – having it dropped on you, unawares. The freely available, apparently harmless, Kool-Aid was spiked with LSD – that was why they called it *electric* – and a lot of unsuspecting people had their first trip, some of them damagingly. It created a terrifying precedent: these Pranksters were capable of anything!

No one was safe! The anxiously privileged citizens of Piedmont, California, just next to Berkeley, were so alarmed that they built a cover for the town reservoir, at enormous cost, lest some crazed freak put LSD in their drinking water.

Tripping was scary, even if one chose to do it with that nice intellectual Professor Timothy Leary, and a lot more so if you gave yourself to the Keseyan way, abandoned what you knew and had been: gave up the sanctuary of your inner Piedmont, opened the doors of perception. How do you know, asked William Blake – in a line much quoted at the time – 'but every bird that cuts the airy way, is an immense world of delight, closed by your senses five'? How *do* you know?

I thought I knew quite a lot about that. I'd read about it, thought and written about it, followed my Blake through Whitman, Yeats and Ginsberg, but I found it difficult to understand what Kesey was up to. Lots of people did. A film editor called Norman Hartweg drove up from LA to see if he might help the Pranksters edit the monumentally confused film that they had made of their journey on the bus, some forty-five hours of psychedelically mashed material. In Wolfe's account:

> Then he realizes that what it really is is that they are inter-
> ested in none of the common intellectual currency ... the
> standard topics, books, movies, new political movements –
> For years he and all his friends had been talking about nothing
> but intellectual products, ideas, concoctions, brain candy,
> shadows of life, as a substitute for living: yes. They don't even
> use the intellectual words here – mostly it is just *thing*.

We were a long way from Merton College, Oxford, from college scarves and tutorials with sherry, from Matthew Arnold. In only a few months I'd smoked a tub of dope, changed into jeans and work shirts, begun growing the Ginsberg-like beard that was to flourish in the next few months. I soon looked the part, almost. But I was just following a half-apprehended fashion, like so many straight middle-class kids who dressed a little like hippies, but palpably were not. They – we – I – were unprepared to take the risks, to turn on and drop out. To take the ACID TEST. To find a new form of life, a new language.

It was so beguiling, this new psychedelic utopia, partly because spending that summer at my mother's was so stressful, and I was so grateful to find a way to avoid the daily conflict. My parents had separated, and dad was now to be found in a modest apartment block a mile from the family home, where he professed himself 'content', and had donned a beret, love beads, and a new, strikingly contemporary, set of attitudes. My mother seethed in our old house, ill with cancer, frightened, brittle, and increasingly irrational. She maintained she'd had 'a royal screwing', by my father, a phrase that she insisted that Ruthie and I not merely acknowledge, but parrot: *a royal screwing*! When we refused, she attacked us venomously, claiming that our professed neutrality sanctioned our father's abandonment of her, and insisting desperately that we make him come back.

It was hard for me, but it was murder for Ruthie. I was only an occasional visitor to America, and honoured accordingly, whereas my sister bore the full force of my mother's cancer and post-separation distress. She insisted that her daughter ought to *relieve* her unhappiness, ameliorating her sufferings through the balm of constant unconditional love and support, which was cruel and unrealistic to ask of a young woman of nineteen, and impossible to deliver. Ruthie had transformed from the gawky girl called Tarzan by her sixth grade classmates into a considerable beauty, often compared to the actress Natalie Wood, but not a confident one. Her mother's incessant hysterical demands undermined her self-confidence, and she had retreated into a quietude which was regarded by strangers, particularly male ones, as pleasingly enigmatic.

Ruthie and I trooped to our father's apartment, and put our mother's case, however half-heartedly. He looked pained, took care not to criticize us for the weaklings that we were, and said that he was sorry we had to go through this. Of course he was not going back. We knew that, we believed he was right not to, we'd done our duty, and could again enjoy our visits with him.

We'd put on some music – he loved 'Sergeant Pepper' – and one night he, Ruthie and her boyfriend Bobby dropped acid together while I smoked some dope. I didn't want my mind blown, just fuzzed about a little. My dad showed me the notes he'd taken during his last trip – he was always very well organized – and they were total gibberish.

'You have to be tripping to understand,' he said.

I didn't. I'd sectioned off the new alternative lifestyle, the music, the language, the drugs, and turned them into leisure pursuits. You could put on your hippy gear, as well as your Commoner's Gown. You could turn on, sure, but you could also turn off: partake, or not. In short, I was tempted, I had fun, and I hardly learned a thing.

Not then, anyway. What Tom Wolfe eventually taught me was something about Ludwig Wittgenstein, when I came to read him ten years later. And Wittgenstein helped me, retrospectively, to grasp why Tom Wolfe wrote as he did. This instance of the Law of Unexpected Consequences may strike you as no big deal, but at the time, and even in retrospect, I am as grateful to both of them as I am to, well, the Grateful Dead. This insight gleaned from my days as a pseudo-hippy is confirmation, no doubt, of the fact that I am not – and never was, even in those heady days – much of a psychotropic risk-taker. I had no real desire for a new kind of life, nor to talk and think like one of the Haight-Ashbury types. I just about managed to incorporate 'cool' into my vocabulary (it's still there) but as for 'groovy', 'far-out', 'good vibrations', the many variations of having one's mind 'blown', none of these stuck. I just don't talk like that, and I don't live the sort of life that makes it necessary to do so.

That kind of language was largely reserved for teenage wannabes and their (uncomprehending) parents, bad pop songs (as well as a few good ones), and crappy journalists – it was the homogenized and commercial form of the real thing. The new language was used – all those groovies and far-outs – by the characters satirized in the 'head comics' of the time, by Mr Natural and Flakey Foont, Honeybunch Kaminsky (who wanted some more orgasms), and the Fabulous Furry Freak Brothers. No, to hear the language that was really generated by the psychedelic experience, you had to have been there, and done that. Failing that, you needed a good journalist. You needed Tom Wolfe. 'I have tried,' Wolfe tells us, 'not only to tell what the Pranksters did, but to recreate the mental atmosphere or subjective reality of it. I don't think their adventure can be understood without that.' That is, starkly: you can only understand the inner reality of people who are zonked out of their minds on LSD if you find the right language to convey it. Because what you experience determines what you can say, and likewise what you can say determines what you may experience.

In *The Philosophical Investigations*, a work filled with memorable poetic perception, Wittgenstein remarks that 'if a lion could talk, we could not understand him'. It is never entirely clear what this means: like most poetic language it both demands and resists explication, and is diminished by commentary that makes this wonderfully suggestive metaphor into some prosaic paraphrase. Wittgenstein made his intentions clear: 'philosophy,' he says, 'ought really to be written only as a form of poetry.' He means *exactly* what he says: 'if a lion could talk, we could not understand him,' but not *only* what he says.

Imagine, if you will, a talking lion. Try to have a conversation with him. Where and how might such a conversation occur? What might you have in common? What sort of experiences might a lion have, what sort of life might he lead, what might he wish or need to say? What might you wish to say to him? Would he understand?

It doesn't matter how hard you try. You *cannot* understand him: he's a lion and you're not. (Or, as the Pranksters put it: 'either you're on the bus or you're not on the bus.') We might be reading a poem by Blake, or a story by Oscar Wilde, or Richard Brautigan Or . . . perhaps . . . a song by Jefferson Airplane? Peter, Paul and Mary? The Incredible String Band? Far out.

But I *can* imagine a talking lion: he would talk like any of the myriad creatures who 'people' children's literature, and speak to us in the language we use and understand ourselves. The tortoise, the hare, the White Rabbit, Peter Rabbit, Pooh. Who couldn't understand them? They convey their animalness by denying it through the very language that is imposed upon them. If a lion were to sidle up to me and say, 'I say, old bean, you're looking rather delicious today,' I would certainly understand him. At the same time, I would presume that I was not about to be eaten, because no *lion* could talk like that. That's why children aren't terrified by their talking animals, no matter how gruff. They're people, really, in animal drag.

So Wittgenstein's lion must talk real lion-language, call it Lionish, which is not like, say, Latvian, which is incomprehensible to most of us until a translator helps us, and then we can understand. When a lion says *growl!* we may assume his appetite and infer his intention – I say it too when offered a hamburger – but the ancillary meanings would be entirely lost on us.

Lionish is an example of what Wittgenstein calls a 'language game', which 'is meant to bring into prominence the fact that the *speaking* of language is part of an activity, or of a form of life'. What is a lion's form of life? Does he have any ethical problems with killing a helpless animal? Why does he choose one rather than another? When he kills, does he take pleasure in it? Is the new meal delicious, even better than the last? Does he feel he should share? Is he scared of elephants? When he says *growl!* or *roar!* it would be inappropriate for us to claim that we know what he means. We can't empathize with a lion, we have too little in common. You can't understand Lionish unless you have lion-experience: forms of language, Wittgenstein insists, are inextricable from forms of life. Meaning is a matter of context.

I don't wish to suggest that Pranksters and other acid heads were lions, and thus incomprehensible, though they sometimes insisted that their experience was not shareable unless one dropped acid as well: as if, to understand a lion, you had to join the pack, drink from a watering hole, stalk wildebeest, and roar in the night. You *can* just about imagine that, even if you can't do it. Kesey eventually came to feel that ecstatic and boundary-breaking experience was possible without the drugs, and that this should be the goal. And though he was not interested in conveying the experience in words – 'I'd rather be a lightning rod than a seismograph' – he never quite denied that this was possible. It just didn't interest him. Like Neal Cassady, he didn't want to *think* anymore.

It was Wolfe's task to find 'the right language to convey this curious new form of life'. The line of thought is derived entirely from Wittgenstein. When puzzling over my first reading of *The Philosophical Investigations*, trying to find examples of what Wittgenstein was driving at, my mind went back to Tom Wolfe, and the solution he had found to making us understand the apparently foreign, distant and incomprehensible. That is the job of the writer, of course, and I wonder if Wittgenstein underestimated somewhat what great writing is and can do? We can't understand what a lion might say because we do not know how and what he feels. Read D.H. Lawrence's animal poems, or Ted Hughes', and you get at least the impression of some vivid understanding of what a cow might feel and be, or a bear, or a crow.

That's what writers try to do. Not tell us how animals feel, but how other people do. After all, what is claimed about the lion – that he has a form of life too foreign for us to understand what he might have to say – was being claimed also, in 1968, by women, say, and blacks, anxious to reclaim their own territory, power and language. How could a white male begin to understand the experience of someone with a womb and menstrual cycle, or with dark skin? Both groups have been discriminated against. What effrontery, even to try to understand. Leave that to women writers, and to black ones.

This is neither a sympathetic position nor a defensible one, but it has some truth in it. Did Freud not admit that women were lions to him, that he could not understand, after years of observation, what it was that they wanted? There is some general truth lurking here. If lions, women and blacks cannot be understood from outside the group, why is it not also true of men, or whites? After all, what woman could fully comprehend the gloopy mixture of aggression, competitiveness, insecurity and lust that drives most men?

The implications are clear: how do I understand you? Or you, me? We all roam our internal savannahs, bask in our own sun, hunt our own zebra. Even in our most intimate relationships we are frequently struck by the sheer distance that separates one mind – one person – from another. In those days we would say, exasperatedly, 'you don't know where I'm coming from,' as if by an effort of will our partner or friend might be able to bridge the chasm between one mind and another. If a *person* could talk, we could not understand them?

Unless, perhaps, we were reading a novel. What is so addictive about fiction is that it is the one reliable place in which we can apprehend and participate in – fully understand – the inward world of another person. To get the connection between the form of life they are placed in, and the language that they speak. In this sense

– a limited one, but satisfying – I know Leopold Bloom better than I know my wife. There is nothing unknown about him, his motives are revealed to the extent that he has them, everything that he feels is displayed. This is satisfying, but it's not enough. That is of course why one prefers life to literature: because knowing is less exciting and less satisfying than *not* knowing.

The implication is ironic and amusing. Wolfe invents his electric prose to deal with the extremities of a form of life – the acid experience – that is so foreign that we can't seem to apprehend it. Yet in so doing, he stumbles across a general truth. Acid heads are alien to us, and seem to operate from a lion-like distance from ordinary life, *but there is no ordinary life*. We are all irremediably foreign and separate. And so you can write like that, you need to write like that, not merely about Pranksters, but about anyone and everybody. Wolfe's later books use similar prose to describe much less outrageous characters, to describe 'ordinary' people who, once you start to get them, are almost as zappy, as other, as those Pranksters were.

So vivid was the experience of reading Tom Wolfe, that his readers wanted to become Pranksters: *to be on the bus*. To hop on to what the Beatles were to call, in their derivative and commercially watered-down version, the 'Magical Mystery Tour'. Great writing does that to and for you. It was a terrific fantasy, to use one of Kesey's favourite words. To be that *free*, to push all boundaries, demand the ecstatic rather than the everyday, to do one's own thing entirely, pass that acid test.

> The Acid Tests were one of those outrages, one of those *scandals*, that create a new style or a new world view. Everyone clucks, fumes, grinds their teeth over the bad taste, the bad morals, the insolence, the vulgarity, the childishness, the lunacy, the cruelty, the irresponsibility, the fraudulence and, in fact, gets worked up into such a state of excitement, such a slaver, they can't turn it loose. It becomes a perfect obsession.

But all these reasons for disapproving were, finally, persuasive, though I indulged my fascination. I knew my inner Prankster was purely a fantasy figure, not something to live by, but something to contemplate, and perhaps to learn from. Learn about what I could and could not do, who I was, and wasn't.

No, what I really wished, wished fervently but without hope of success (as one would wish to play golf like Tiger Woods) was to write like Tom Wolfe. To give myself fully to experience, and to learn from it. To empathize without losing separateness of judgement: if there is plenty of the enthusiasm of Allen Ginsberg in his project, Holden Caulfield is there as well, as evidenced by the occasional fastidious use of the term *phoney*. Though I realized perfectly clearly that I would never be able to write like *that*, even so there was plenty to learn from Tom Wolfe: participate – give yourself to – what you see and write about. Be both in and out of it. Find the right language, the inevitable language, to capture the form of life you are observing and participating in. Take some risks. Listen to the lions. And above all: *Make it fun.*

It was a great lesson, and I forgot it almost immediately. Indeed, I have had to continually remind myself of it for the rest of my life, for the pressure to regard reading and writing as forms of work – which is endemic to the form of life, and its associated language, that academics have chosen – is inexorable. I went back to Oxford at the end of the summer of 1968, grew my beard, and began work on a DPhil on Joseph Conrad's moral vision. There's nothing obviously playful about such a project. If there was fun to be had in it – and there might well be, to someone more free-spirited than I was then – I never found it, never established any synergy between being serious and having fun. You had to choose. Oxford is the setting, after all, for the mournful poetry of Matthew Arnold, not the electric effusiveness of Tom Wolfe.

9

A DIVIDED SELF IN OXFORD

The range of what we think and do
Is limited by what we fail to notice.
And because we fail to notice
That we fail to notice
There is little we can do
To change
Until we notice
How failing to notice
Shapes our thoughts and deeds.

R.D. Laing, *Knots*

The Abysmal (*Water*). It was apparently an uncommon reading, and potentially a disastrous one. Barbara and I had thrown the *I Ching* sticks, seeking guidance as to whether we should get married. *We* couldn't decide, perhaps the ancient wisdom of the Orient might point us in the right direction? The text seemed to issue a clear warning to us, and particularly to me:

Danger comes because one is too ambitious . . . A man when in danger has only to proceed along the line of least resistance; thus he reaches the goal. A man who in the extremity of danger has lost the right way and is irremediably entangled in his sins has no prospect of escape.

That sounded terrible, but the remedy was obvious. There must have been some inscrutable oriental mistake. We threw the sticks again: *The Abysmal (Water)*. The odds against this reading coming up twice in a row are huge. But surely the text was open to interpretation? What does 'abysmal water' suggest? Our first associations, as if we were interpreting a dream, were *dank, polluted, stagnant, filthy, dangerous to life*. Or perhaps a torrent was envisaged, like a tsunami that would drown all those in its path? What could we salvage from that?

We were both fully aware that the archetype of the journey into the underworld, the descent into the murky symbolism – the abysmal waters – of the unconscious, presented one with trials and dangers. That didn't mean it wasn't worth the effort. Surely if we could plumb or navigate those waters we would be strengthened by the process? The *I Ching* was offering us a challenge, and an opportunity:

> if one is sincere when confronted with difficulties, the heart can penetrate the meaning of the situation. And once we have gained inner mastery of a problem, it will come about naturally that the action we take will succeed.

We were married in the Oxford Registry Office on 11 October 1969. It had been a tumultuous courtship, was going to become an even more unsettling marriage, and it wasn't an unambiguously happy moment. Barbara looked both stunned and stunning in a flowing, dreamy silk dress in reds and blacks bought at a shop near Harrods, and subsequently worn by her Auntie Nancy on cruises. My three-piece pinstriped blue business suit made me look like a trainee lawyer in need of a decent haircut.

Her parents welcomed me into the family gracefully and with, I suspect, some relief. She was twenty-six by then – and if she didn't marry me, her father said anxiously to her mother, she would be 'damaged goods'. Catherine characteristically repeated the comment to Bar, who chortled, and remarked that she'd been damaged goods before she met me. The first time I visited the parents, in their semi on a modest little road in Kenilworth, a bastion of Tory petit bourgeois life, I arrived in the Morgan convertible dressed in a red Arab djelaba, with a long bushy beard, and an overstuffed meerschaum pipe filled with some noxious tobacco that made me into a walking bush fire. (Some time later, teaching a seminar at Warwick – students kept asking if I could please open the window – my beard caught fire from a stray ember. It didn't smell all that different from the reeking Latakia tobacco, and I burbled on regardless, until the flames became visible beneath my nose. I snuffed it out one-handed, barely missing a phrase. Nobody laughed, but there was a general sense in the room that it served me right.)

We were cloistered together in the hothouse of a tiny flat in Stanley Road: she emerging only to go to her newly located analyst. Her anxieties, while severe and debilitating, struck me as somehow not personal, more a function of her life situation. She was a changeling, placed in the wrong family and environment, too curious, finely tuned and thoughtful to feel comfortable in the provincial life she had, inappropriately, been given. She'd educated herself as an adolescent, reading her way through the Kenilworth Library stock of books on the history of art, and through a selection of writers including Sartre and Camus, many of the English poets, and a run of contemporary novelists, while studying shorthand and other secretarial skills. She yearned for something larger and freer, left home for London at the age of sixteen, later moved to Oxford, tried to make relationships that were challenging and sustaining. The price she paid for entering the world she should have been given in the first place was too high and too cruel.

Getting her back, well and functioning, became our joint project, more important than anything else. We ceased to go out, lost touch with our best friends, engulfed by the psychoanalytic miasma, claustrophobic and ingrown. The rituals of everyday life became an essential point of stability, but even these were delicately poised. We would wander off companionably in the mornings to do the shopping, perhaps have a coffee at the local café. But this progress was retarded by the intercession of the neighbour's dog, an Alsatian of malign disposition, like the Hound of the Baskervilles on steroids, who would hide behind a tree until passers-by got to the garden gate, and then come charging towards them, barking ferociously, jumping upon the gate in an attempt to scale it and eat the terrified pedestrians. The first time it happened I almost fainted from fright. Then I got furious.

'I know,' I said to Barbara, plotting revenge that evening. 'I'll buy a huge rump steak and put rat poison all over it, and chuck it in their garden.'

'You can't do that!' said Bar, genuinely disapproving. (She liked dogs enough, even, not to want to kill this one.)

'I guess you're right. How about lashings of Tabasco sauce?'

'No,' she said, 'I can think of something much worse. When the dog is inside one evening' (we'd noticed he was often in the house for a couple of hours at night – perhaps they fed him one of their many cats) 'we can sneak into the garden and snip their daffs!'

'Snip their daffs?'

'That'd do it!' she said.

We never visited our neighbour with this quintessentially English form of retribution, alas, nor my archetypal American one, and learned to walk down the other side of Stanley Road instead. The dog still tried to get us, but it was less frightening at a distance.

In the flat, we read together the essential works of Freud, Jung and A.S. Neill, and for a period we were both entranced by R.D. Laing, who all of a sudden had become a cult figure. His first book, *The Divided Self*, had been published in 1960, way before all the sixties shenanigans began. It was not so much ahead of its time; in part, at least, it caused it. It became an extraordinarily influential book. Laing argued that even the most extreme cases of schizophrenia

– psychoanalytically regarded as untreatable – were capable of being both understood and treated therapeutically. Schizophrenics were not mad, insane, or deranged – categories that merely demonstrated the observer's incomprehension – rather, the individual schizophrenic was to be understood as someone who had creatively tried to accommodate sets of radically conflicting demands. Using Gregory Bateson's double-bind theory, Laing and his early colleagues were working towards an understanding of the reasonableness of the schizophrenic world, however apparently incomprehensible the symptoms manifested by any given schizophrenic might seem.

To this set of ideas was aligned a bias towards phenomenology which claimed that no response or set of responses to the world, if sincere and accurately reported, could be given privilege over any other. The schizophrenic's inner voices and inward experience were real to him or her. That's what real is: reality is what is generated by an act of perception.

You might wonder why the emerging hip generation of the sixties should have cared about schizophrenia, and how it should or should not be regarded and treated. And we didn't, really; the reason *The Divided Self* had such an impact was that it posited radical alternatives to received wisdom, that it was so stringently anti-establishment. It allowed people their own voices, however deviant: it seemed to extend a remarkably generous form of fellowship.

It sounded great to us. Authentic self-realization seemed an admirable goal; after all, I regarded myself as a student of the results of inspiration, a romantic not a classicist. Barbara was determinedly trying to find a way to escape the various mixed messages and double binds of her upbringing. Laing, without denying the stresses of the internal life, made it sound *exciting*. Listen to your inner voices! Be inhabited by spirits! Hadn't Blake told us that the road of excess leads to the palace of wisdom? Though my reading at the time was dominated by Freud, and my life by the Freudian, Laing seemed to take more risks than Freud, and to point in less conventional directions.

Barbara, coming home from a session with her Freudian analyst one afternoon, quoted him as saying that she should be more like his wife, who was 'a good, sensible woman'. I'd seen the frumpy figure thus alluded too, and was certain I would prefer Barbara as she was.

But therapy helped her. After a lot of time, and a brave internal effort, the boundaries of life began to expand: we went out more, and more people came round. We were friends with a number of people ranging from the eccentric to the downright dangerous. John lived off vegetables discarded in the bins at the Oxford market, and never washed his hair, ever; Reg, a brilliant but schizoid potter, had served time at Broadmoor Hospital for a murder committed in a pub, and became a founding member of the Oxford Arts Lab; John Preston, a frustrated painter, woodcarver, husband and spirit, ran a contemporary ceramics gallery on North Parade. He was the sort of person that North Oxford sub-culture was made for: talented, but not talented enough, unhappy, something of a fantasist.

From the moment Barbara first came into his shop, beautiful, enthusiastic, approachable, he fell in love with her. She hardly had the income to indulge her excellent taste, but bought things anyway, even if it meant eating less: a beautiful yellow Lucie Rie bowl, a larger brown one by Gwen Hanson. Sometimes John would offer a lovingly cooked dinner, a bottle of wine, and a lot of talk about himself. He carved a wooden figure of her in a piece of gnarly fruit wood, about four inches high mounted on a plinth, that was an unsettlingly accurate image of her in the nude. He frequently came round to our flat to visit her, and to complain about the constraints of his marriage, and how much his children sided with their mother against him.

One weekend John came round after closing his shop. He was in a lot of pain with headaches, which had increased in severity over the last month, and which he described – and we agreed – as a symptom of the unhappiness that his marriage caused him.

'You know,' he said, 'sometimes I don't think I can stand it any more. I feel like I'm going mad.'

We listened sympathetically. Mad didn't scare us.

'Sometimes I have these thoughts, I keep having them, that one day I'll just get a gun and kill us all . . .' He held his head in his hands. I went to make tea while Barbara comforted him.

'I know,' she said, 'people often have fantasies like that, I'm glad you can talk about it. You're not mad. You mustn't feel guilty.'

He shook his head. 'I can actually see myself doing it. I go upstairs and get the shotgun . . .'

'Don't!' Barbara said. 'Don't dwell on it. It isn't good for you.'

He cheered up a little after dinner, stayed the night, and headed back to his house in the country in the morning.

Later that week, I found Barbara waiting for me tearfully, clutching a copy of the *Guardian*, outside St Clare's College, where I had been teaching a course on modern English Literature to a group of American junior year abroad students. On the front page was the story. John had, indeed, shot his wife and children, then himself after setting the house on fire.

'We should have taken him more seriously,' she said, 'we should have helped him.' Although the autopsy revealed a brain tumour, which was held by the coroner to be an explanation for the tragedy, we couldn't help but feel responsible. Our problem hadn't been lack of seriousness, we'd been serious in the wrong way. The obvious and appropriate response – *are you sure you're getting the right medical advice about these headaches?* – was disabled by the times. Doctors were not to be trusted: purveyors of mother's little helpers like valium, barbaric imposers of ECT, doctors treated symptoms rather than causes, believed in suppression rather than expression.

The example of John Preston might have shaken my faith in my psychological premises, but it didn't destroy it. Only a few years later – some time in 1973 – I resolved to quit university teaching to begin training as an analyst, and drove down to London for an interview with a member of the Philadelphia Association, which had been founded under Laing's aegis in 1965.

Haya Oakley was an Israeli therapist with the requisite phenomenological biases. Sympathetic though I was to the practical effects of such a position, however useful it might be in talking with patients mired in some alternative reality, I expressed some scepticism about whether she actually *believed* in what she was professing?

'Absolutely,' she said.

'If a patient believes he is accompanied into your consulting room by a pink elephant, then that pink elephant is actually there?'

'For him, it is.'

'Or Manchester United football team? The Royal Philharmonic Orchestra? The hunchback of Notre Dame? Cliff Richard?'

'Yes, in all cases,' she responded, a little tartly. 'If that is what he perceives, then that is what is there.'

'For him,' I acknowledged. 'But he is wrong.'

'Not at all,' she said. 'For him there is an elephant, or whatever. For me there is not. Neither of us is wrong. Or right.'

'But surely it is your job as a therapist to banish the pink elephants of your patients' imaginings?'

'Quite the opposite,' she said firmly. 'It is not up to me to judge what my clients perceive.'

'What about dreams then? If I dream that I am in a relationship with the hunchback of Notre Dame, that doesn't mean it is actually true, does it?'

She looked at me with a sudden new interest, and I had a feeling she was about to ask me about my marriage.

'These are just philosophical cavils, and smart counter-examples. Perhaps you haven't read enough, and need some clinical experience? I think you'd better talk to Ronnie,' she said. That would sort me out.

Though this extreme phenomenology still seems to me wrong, her position was appealing, and useful, in two distinct ways. First, it succeeded in crediting the inward world of the schizophrenic, and hence welcomed such people back into the world of potential discourse. They were not to be regarded as mad, or deluded, or wrong. They weren't allowed their own reality, which would be patronizing, they simply had it.

Laing makes the point explicitly, and strikingly, in *The Divided Self*, when he remarks that understanding a patient's 'existential position' is not a purely intellectual process: 'For "understanding" one might say love,' and that such love is impossible without crediting the way in which the patient experiences himself and the world. Though deviant inward realities can be resistant to conventional forms of therapeutic intervention, individuals could be helped to accommodate that reality to the competing claims of the world.

And secondly, of course, it was a period in which wayward and extreme acts of imagination – some of them prompted by drugs of various types and potencies – had entered as close to the mainstream of middle-class culture as had ever been the case. Formerly the prerogative of bards, poets and seers to seek the extremes of vision, now swathes of middle-class kids were doing their heads in, taking trips, challenging the boundaries of what could be said, and seen, and thought, and felt, and experienced. Taking the Acid Test. Schizophrenics were mad? Mad was out there, mad was cool.

In his 1965 Preface to the paperback edition of *The Divided Self*, Laing observes that psychiatry does not have to be repressive, it need not deny the validity of unusual acts of perception or deviant lines of thought: it can be 'and some psychiatrists are, on the side of transcendence, of genuine freedom, and of true human growth . . . Thus I would wish to emphasise that our normal "adjusted" state is too often the abdication of ecstasy, the betrayal of our true potentialities, that many of us are only too successful in acquiring a false self to adjust to false realities.'

So he was no mere relativist, Laing, arguing for seeing the other chap's point of view, however loopy it might seem. No, there is constant iteration distinguishing the 'true' or 'genuine' from the 'false'. What is radical here is the change of criteria by which the one is distinguished from the other: criteria which involve existential notions of authenticity and good faith, and which credit the individual's will towards self-expression and the search for transcendence and delight.

It took some time to get an appointment with Laing, but when we met in his consulting rooms in Belsize Park, he made it abundantly clear that I had his full attention. He sat me in a comfortable chair only a couple of feet in front of his, because he sat next to his desk, not behind it.

'Tell me about yourself,' he said.

I had done so, formally, in my letter of application to the Philadelphia Association, which I could see on his desk. I was anxious that I wouldn't interest him. His business was with psychotics, whereas I was a pure-bred neurotic, and afraid that my symptoms – writer's block, uncertain relations with women, failure to commit to work – would be uninteresting to someone usually engaged with the seriously mad. I had resolved – I was very excited at the prospect of meeting him – that I would be as honest and as accurate as possible in talking about myself. No bullshit, nothing *academic*: that was, after all, what I was trying to escape.

'I'm not sure I know what I'm doing,' I said. 'I've made a lot of bad choices. Dubious ones anyway . . .'

He raised his eyebrows, his unblinking eyes (can they really have been black?) never leaving mine, preternaturally calm, unwaveringly attentive. He had the quiet dignity and demeanour of a wise man.

He was publicly candid about himself: he had learned a new way of being, taught himself how to breathe properly, meditated, rebirthed, taken every imaginable prohibited substance, sought new models. The result was impressive: I had rarely encountered such a compelling self-contained stillness, though I had the feeling, too, that it was designed, a little, to impress. That he wasn't merely seeking some inward wisdom, he wanted to lead. He wanted you to believe in him. (His son Adrian referred to him, ironically, as the Guru from Glasgow, though his view mellowed, and he was later to say that he got on with his father much better once he had died.)

'. . . I shouldn't have done a PhD, shouldn't have finished it. If I'd had more strength I would have given it up. Maybe gone back to the States? And Barbara – my wife. It isn't working.'

'Why?'

'I'm jealous of her analyst, and want to take over his place. I want to be everything for her: therapist, protector, mentor, lover. Yet the more I try to support and love her the less it works.'

'Does she love you?'

Curiously, I hadn't thought much about that. She *needed* me, which was something different. But loved? She said she did, some-times.

He stayed silent, and motionless.

'I know, I know,' I said. 'It will lead to trouble. It already has. I can't seem to learn anything about love.'

'What are you reading?' he asked.

'Nothing that helps. The more I read things designed to help, or to explain, the worse it gets. I'm sick of serious reading. I hate wisdom. It makes me feel ill, and I can feel my mind closing down. What am I reading? Agatha Christie, mostly. They're badly written, but I really like Hercule Poirot.'

He smiled. 'I like him too.'

'My problem is that I need to find a way both to employ the little grey cells, and to give them a rest. I don't know how to do it. Can I ask you a question?'

'Of course.'

'What does your training programme actually consists of? The literature isn't clear about that. I would be uneasy about anything simply academic . . .'

'That's because there is no set programme. Everyone has to go to the weekly training seminars, but after that it depends on the individual – on who you are and what you need – and that can range from deep analytic therapy to Chinese dancing . . .'

Chinese dancing? Me? I had a quick, harrowing image of myself in a mandarin's gown, doing some sort of courtly, balletic movements in front of an emperor.

He paused for a moment. 'If you decide to join us' – such a lovely way to put it, that I hardly registered that I had just been accepted to train with the Association – 'I think you can be seeing clients within six months.'

Six months! And after that, over the next few years I could begin to build a practice, cut down the teaching to part-time, and eventually make my escape from academic life. I left Laing grateful and delighted, and began to attend the weekly seminars led by his colleagues Hugh Crawford and John Heaton.

I didn't enjoy them much. I was an outsider joining an on-going process and group, and there was no social time to get to know people: we all struggled to fit the weekly seminar into already crowded lives, and no one (including me) had time or the desire for a drink before or after the seminars. Or perhaps some of them went off and didn't invite me?

But my unease wasn't primarily social. I had walked into a group of people comfortably employing a language heavily dependent on the usual sources of Merleau-Ponty and Husserl, with which I was familiar but which I didn't speak, and which sounded unconvincing and clunky to my ears. But the deference paid by the group to these phenomenological mentors was as nothing compared to the deference they paid to Laing. Not in person – he rarely attended the training seminars, being far too busy – but in absentia. He was quoted extensively and uncritically; it was taken as a fact that any sentence beginning: 'Ronnie says . . .' was about to enumerate a truth. I suppose the early Freudians, too, acted like disciples. It is hard to imagine one of them saying, 'Herr Professor Freud believes this or that, but he is wrong.' You can imagine the silence, the reports back to Freud, the potential ostracism.

After a few months, we had a seminar in which we discussed A.R. Luria's *The Man with a Shattered World*, an account of a man with appalling brain damage suffered in the First World War, trying to regain some sense of himself and the world.

'I have a lot of trouble with this book,' I said. 'I think it is not about a man, but about his brain, and that it never makes the distinction clearly, if it can be made at all . . .'

An earnest fellow-trainee, who was always keenly, and competitively, involved in our discussions, looked at me disapprovingly.

'Ronnie says . . .' he began.

'I don't give a fuck what Ronnie says,' I replied irritably. 'Why don't you tell me what you say.' I suspect Ronnie would have approved of this, but the group didn't. I decided to shut up. They were glad.

I couldn't wait to get home, and fumed all the way up the motorway back to Warwickshire.

'Fuck Ronnie,' I mused, 'but even more fuck the Ronnians! Who needs them?'

And at this point – could one say fortunately? – my mother died. She'd been ill with breast cancer, had a mastectomy, suffered grievously and demandingly, and within a couple of years it had metastasized into her liver. Barbara and I went to Long Island to see her through her last weeks. Our only consolation during the period was six-month-old baby Anna, whom we volubly and visibly and overweaningly adored. Mom said she looked like Winston Churchill, and didn't mean anything flattering by the comparison.

My mother watched us cooing, cuddling and carrying on, looking both bemused and slightly disapproving.

'I never loved you that much,' she said to me.

I don't know, and didn't ask, whether she regretted this. She was in no mood for final truths and tearful Dickensian leave-takings. Occasionally her spirits would rally, and she would ask what we were wearing to her funeral, and suggested that we bury her in that famous paupers' cemetery, Potter's Field. But she was unreconciled to her coming death, furious, beyond consolation.

I couldn't bear it. Sat with her for a few minutes, fidgeted, couldn't find the right thing to say or the right tone, got up, sat down, found an excuse to leave, came back, left again. I was numb with horror and, though she palpably needed me to be there, I simply could not sit and stay. I remember thinking to myself that I had no experience of death, didn't know how to do it: canvassed my reading for succour, solace, even wisdom – tried to Joan Didionize – and found nothing to help me. The Bible, Shakespeare, Donne, Keats, Dickens? Nothing. Nothing but the desire to run away.

Literature didn't help me. Indeed, it was literature that was disabling. (Or perhaps people who are already emotionally disabled manifest this in their love of the secondary enhancements of literature?) When I encountered intense emotion in books, I could empathize and shed the odd tear, laugh and exult occasionally, close the covers and walk away when I chose, feeling morally enhanced. It was no training for sitting at your mother's bedside as she wasted, wept and died. My Mayzie, gone for ever, aged fifty-seven.

Would F.R. Leavis or T.S. Eliot have done better than I did? Worse, I suspect, even worse. Think of *The Waste Land*. I began to feel that too much reading and writing unfits one for the trials of real emotional life, makes one constrained, mental, constipated, lost in words and fictions, selfish, distracted. It's no wonder that the novel is usually a chronicle of human unhappiness. Is an intense immersion in the literary good for you? Does it help you to deal with your emotional trials? Don't ask the practitioners, ask their wives, their children, their parents. Ask my mother.

Barbara, on the other hand, with as little experience of death as I, but less professional reading, found reserves of peaceful energy, and sat chatting with my mother for long periods. What about? Just the normal things: baby Anna, clothes, shopping, what we were doing in the house, who was coming that day, what mom might be willing to eat for supper, whether she'd like a cup of tea.

'She's still your mum,' Barbara said to me gently, 'there's no need to be so frightened. She's frightened enough, and we have to help her.'

She had one dying wish, which was that Ruthie, then aged twenty-five, should marry her boyfriend the medical student: marry him immediately, in our house, *right now*! And Ruthie, who found it almost impossible to resist my mother – she'd been 'guided' into becoming a social worker, against her own disposition – said no, and stuck to it. Various friends and relatives, goaded by my mother, urged her to capitulate. *It would make her so happy! He's such a nice boy! He's going to be a doctor!* No! It was to make the triumphs of her later life possible, this final denial of my mother's will.

When the end came I was sitting downstairs, having spent a few final moments with my mother as she drifted in and out of consciousness. Her final assessment of her time on earth was uncompromising.

'Life is shit,' she said. Within a couple of hours she died, clenched and impassable, her head turned away from us.

After which, I found I had no desire to recommence my training as a therapist, Laingian or not-Laingian. It was, inexplicably, over. I didn't have reasons – in my experience major life changes never occur rationally, in response to reasons and arguments, but unconsciously. I couldn't give an adequate account of what had happened, and why this major change of direction and focus had imposed itself upon me. My description of my change of direction – 'If I have to choose between sitting in a chair and listening to people kvetch, or lying on a couch doing the kvetching, I prefer the latter'

– was evasive, but it was the best I could do. Now, with my mother dead and having become a parent myself, the internal planes shifted.

They did for Ruthie as well, we were both released by it. A couple of years later she married a Hortonishly good man, also a social worker, Roy Greenberg. A few months after the wedding he was diagnosed with Multiple Sclerosis. He was visited, over the twenty years before he died, by a constellation of symptoms of Biblical cruelty, any one of which would have ruined the life of a normal person. He declined into a pitiable state, but he squeezed the available joy from it, never complained, adored Ruthie and his sons Matthew and Jesse, pronounced himself happy.

But if Roy was constitutionally able to cope with his burdens, I wouldn't have predicted Ruthie would be able to deal with hers. *I* certainly couldn't have. Within a few years she became bread-winner, mother, nurse. It was grievously difficult and unrelenting, and she expanded to fill the space that she needed to inhabit. If she fell apart they all would have. I would not have supposed that grace under pressure could involve so many tears, so much mucus, such desperation and bravery. I thought it was something Hemingway's heroes did, with wars or lions or fishing in the sea.

By the time Roy died, some twenty years later, she'd not only survived the fires, but been refined by them. She became more confident, filled the room with laughter and ebullience as well as storms of tears, enlarged and matured in ways that no one could have predicted for the poignantly withdrawn little girl she had been. At Roy's funeral she said she could not have wished for a better husband and family, or a different life.

Anyway, after going through the experience of my mother's death, all of that Laingian stuff seemed fatuous, merely a set of gestures, and I derived no comfort from it in my grief. Pink elephants, rebirthing, Chinese dancing? Give me good old-fashioned 'common unhappiness' any day. Isn't that what Freud considered the result of a successful analysis?

10

WHAT WILL YOU DO?

The key to the strategy of liberation lies in exposing the
situation, and the simplest way to do it is to outrage the
pundits and the experts by sheer impudence of speech
and gesture . . .

Germaine Greer, *The Female Eunuch*

A few weeks after my appointment as lecturer in English at the
University of Warwick, in the autumn of 1970, Professor George
Hunter, the chairman of the department, invited me for a visit and
tour round the university, prior to joining the department in the
new year. Having opened only a few years earlier, Warwick was
still being gouged out of the earth, and didn't so much resemble
a building site, it was one. Our vice-chancellor Jack Butterworth
and his appointed architects York Rosenberg were progressively
revealing a fetishist fascination with white tiling, and the recently
finished Library, in which the Department of English was situ-
ated, was a first class example: it looked like a gigantic urinal.

George's office was at one end of a dreary institutional corridor,
and we had a short and unproductive meeting with my immediate
colleague in the philosophy and literature department, John
Newton. Dressed entirely in black, Newton was a largely silent and
quiveringly sensitive Leavisite, clearly somewhat at a loss outside
Cambridge, where he had previously studied and taught. His

demeanour, in which sentences were haltingly produced in an almost inaudible voice, each word charged with significance, seemed to suggest both how extraordinarily sensitive he was, and (by implication if not intent) how crass his more loquacious interlocutors were. I had rarely met someone so intimidating. I was later told that he had boxed for Cambridge, and that his method was to attack furiously until either he or his opponent was exhausted.

In company like this I tend to babble. The more I talked, the more Newton withdrew, and the more alarmed and disapproving Hunter became. I outlined my opinions about the syllabus, suggested a range of possible new avenues and courses, worried about reading lists, formulated new methods of examination, suggested a variety of innovative forms of assessment, including assessment of teachers, recommended my dad's recipe for turkey tetrazzini (add sherry!), chose the next England football team, and gave a quick account of my position on nuclear proliferation. John gazed at me steadily, as if I were mad. I talked some more. I'm lucky he didn't punch me.

'Perhaps,' George said sternly, 'we might go downstairs for a sandwich?' Newton looked relieved, and said he had work to attend to. I was desperate for anything to put in my mouth to stop it chattering.

It stopped soon enough. It fell open, and stayed open. As we re-entered the corridor heading for the lift, a quite extraordinary figure came striding towards us: a woman of heroic proportions, moving as if carried by the very force of the zeitgeist itself, trousered in purple suede. Gauchos, I think they were called. As she rushed towards us it became clear that she was strikingly attractive in an androgynous way: strong cleft chin, high shoulders, a mass of dark hair cunningly disarranged, hips thrust forward like a figure mysteriously released from some Teutonic myth, or the young Robert Mitchum in drag.

George stepped in front of her, impeding her headlong progress.

'Germaine,' he said firmly, implicitly upbraiding her apparent rudeness, 'may I introduce our new colleague, Rick Gekoski?'

She stopped abruptly.

'Do you realize,' she said, fixing him with a look of such manic intensity that it made me yearn for the return of John Newton, 'I've just shit my pants?'

What is one to say to that? Germaine rushed off. I looked at Hunter, seeking confirmation that this had really happened. He gave a minute shrug of the shoulders.

'That's Germaine,' he said philosophically, as the author of the just published *The Female Eunuch* rushed off to the women's toilets.

I stood there gawping like an idiot. It happened so quickly, and so unexpectedly, that it would have taken considerable reserves of self-confidence and urbanity to handle it, and her, lightly. I had neither. She was clearly out of my league, and even in extremis determined to assert it from the start. I stuttered, looked at the floor, said nothing. The lesson was clear: she, even with her pants full, was a figure of authority, control, audacity. Me? I was a hick.

What a department! Hunter was tougher than me, Newton more sensitive, that Greer person sassier and hipper. Thank God I didn't get introduced to anyone else.

Germaine's remarks were, I was soon to learn, typical of her. She loved to shock, and to play the uncouth Aussie that she so palpably wasn't. She was imposingly sexy, bright and in your face, anxious either to assert dominance or to determine whether she might just be in the presence of one of her (few) equals. She was, likeably and democratically, equally insouciant in the presence of her peers. Shortly after the publication of *The Female Eunuch* she confided to her friends the theatre critic Kenneth Tynan and his wife that she was now so in demand by the newspapers that 'if I peed on the paper, they'd print the stain'.

I may have looked like that hairy hippy, Freewheelin' Franklin of the *Furry Freak Brothers*, but my response would have earned the approval of the local vicar. I was shocked. Not so much by the earnestly playful scatology: as any four-year-old can attest, if you say poo-poo and botty sufficiently loudly in company, you are bound to get a response. No, what shocked me was the context. What was a luminous, foul-mouthed creature like her doing at Warwick University? Why would she say such a thing, not so much to me – I sort of looked the part – but to her starchy, Calvinist head of department? Did she have no restraints?

She had come from Melbourne to do a PhD at Cambridge – one of a generation of brilliantly outrageous, raspberry-blowing Aussies – Barry Humphries, Richard Neville, Clive James, Robert Hughes – who hit London like a fart of fresh air in the mid-sixties. They were jesters, entertainers, thinkers, drinkers and druggies, anxious to subvert and to provoke: 'reverence before authority,' Germaine wrote, 'has never accomplished much in the way of changing things.' Merely trying to describe these Aussies seemed to demand strings of adjectives, buckets of oxymoron.

I had, in fact, come across Germaine without knowing who she was: the 'Dr G' of Neville's *Oz* magazine, and 'Rose Blight' of *Private Eye*, though I didn't know she also had backstage groupie privileges with Led Zeppelin. She clearly regarded sex, drugs and rock 'n' roll as her favoured and natural milieu, but she was also a talented academic, and determined to inhabit both worlds. She regarded herself, she explained to *Rolling Stone* in 1971, as an infiltrator: 'I'm still into converting the straights. That's why I teach. I guess the university doesn't really know about all the things I'm involved in. I don't push it down there.'

That was the rock and roll version of herself, but as an academic she wasn't nearly so subversive as this might suggest. The reverse, rather. Like her equally talented, beautiful, and socially and sexually adventurous colleague Gay Clifford, Germaine was a stickler for the rules of academic discourse: a hard marker, insistent on academic protocol, likely to be on the right wing in any argument about rules, rubrics, or students' rights. Our colleague Bernard Bergonzi memorably observed that Gay 'played Mussolini to Germaine's Hitler'.

But on the publication of *The Female Eunuch* Germaine became something more than an ultra-smart groupie and academic, she became a celebrity. Reporters from the tabloids would camp outside her office, cameras and notebooks at the ready, waiting for her to emerge. All of a sudden she was everywhere: in the papers, on TV and radio, endlessly quoted by a host of people, and most especially by herself.

The basic position of *The Female Eunuch* is relatively straightforward. Women have been remorselessly depotentiated, castrated, by patriarchal culture. They must collectively and individually resist any offers of 'equality' with men, because the model they are being offered is not worth having. Instead they must develop (the key terms of the book) self-reliance, pride, spontaneity, impudence, vociferousness. They must renounce marriage, the consumer society and the claustrophobic atomism of the nuclear family.

The ideal society is based on Greer's experience of southern Italian peasant society:

I think of the filthy two-roomed house in
Calabria where people came and went freely,
where I never heard a child scream except in
pain, where the twelve-year-old aunt sang at
her washing by the well, and the old father walked
in the olive grove with his grandson on his arm.

This romantic idyll is most remarkable for what it leaves out, which is more or less everything: the grinding poverty, the incest, the gossip, the feuds between families and villages, the distrust of outsiders, the hatred of sexuality except in marriage, the baleful effects of the Mafia and the Catholic Church, the relentless exodus of the young people. Other than that it sounds pretty pleasant, though Dr Greer seems not to have stayed for long.

Never mind. The book's strength is in its negative positions, its criticism of women's compliance in the scraps that they are patronizingly offered, and weaker where it suggests some model of culture and society which would be preferable.

Germaine didn't argue, she asserted. Though *The Female Eunuch* had its scholarly elements, it had none of the defensiveness that disfigures and depotentiates academic discourse. It wasn't disinterested, rather the reverse, it was remorselessly interested. It had a case to plead, and every rhetorical excess was employed to its ends. Germaine Greer was a queen of hyperbole, unworried that this or that might be overstated, or even wrong.

Women have little idea of how much men hate them . . . Men do not themselves know the depth of their hatred.

If you think you are emancipated, you might consider the idea of tasting your menstrual blood – if it makes you sick, you've got a long way to go baby.

A clitoral orgasm with a full cunt is nicer than a clitoral orgasm with an empty one (as far as I can tell at least).

The Female Eunuch is an admirably narcissistic book: an object lesson in what it promulgates. Be like me, it suggests. Say what you need to say, live as you wish to live, fuck who you want to fuck, proudly, without shame. And, Greer insists, do this for your own sake, not because I told you to: I don't wish to lead, nor to be regarded as a model. (Nobody believed *that*.) Her position didn't repay attention, it demanded it. *The Female Eunuch* was – those terms so often used to deride women – strident, provocative, attention-seeking self-dramatizing, intense, compulsive, frequently illogical. And *right*, most often, and viewed as a whole, quite right.

That was the hard part. Greer's description of the claustrophobia of the nuclear family, the diminished, thankless and exhausting role of housewife, and the arrogant and sexually domineering role of the average husband – even those of us of benevolent and liberal disposition, *particularly* of those – seemed accurately, if tendentiously, to describe something Barbara and I were experiencing, aged twenty-six, in our isolated cottage outside Leamington Spa.

We were extravagantly unsettled. Barbara was uneasy coming back to Warwickshire, where she'd had dismal experiences at school, and was distinctly ambivalent about living within easy reach of her parents and brothers. I was preparing to teach three new courses (English Poetry, the European Novel and an Introduction to Literature course for first years) and anxious to make a good impression on my colleagues and students. I would leave early in the morning, and come back anxious but exhilarated, needing to spend the evenings reading for the next day and week.

Barbara didn't drive, and the cottage was a ten-minute walk from the nearest corner shop, though there was an intermittent bus service into Leamington. When I got home at night I would find her, agitated and depressed, having passed a day reading and going for walks, cooking something for dinner, watching TV or listening to music. We'd made the decision to take the relatively isolated cottage hastily, beguiled by the pretty garden, and the chance to have a place entirely to ourselves.

It was a bad mistake. One evening, with a gale blowing and the branches of the trees whipping against our bedroom window, I awoke with the perfectly clear and distinct feeling – no, more than a feeling, to the terrifying truth – that aliens were outside, and would soon be trying to get in through the bedroom door. I was far too frightened to cry out, and though I don't recall the hair on my head standing on end, that on my arms most certainly did. I crept out of bed and began to push the enormous mahogany bureau across the floor, to barricade the door. The screeching woke Barbara up.

'What are you doing?' she asked incredulously, turning on her bedside light to reveal me, shoulder to bureau, huffing across the room.

'Shh!' I said, in my loudest whisper. 'They'll hear you!'

Barbara looked round, alarmed.

'Who?'

'Be quiet! They're right outside!'

'Who is? For God's sake, is it burglars?'

'Worse. Shh! From outer space!' I said. 'Help me barricade the door. Quick!'

'C'mon now,' she said kindly and softly, as if talking to an hysterical toddler, 'come back to bed, it's just a nightmare.'

Bureau finally in place, I did. I sat up in bed all night, rigid with anxiety lest the aliens get in. How it was that they could make their way across the universe to get me, only to be thwarted by a blockaded door was unclear, but I watched the bureau intently for any signs of the inward movement that would signal our doom.

In the morning, alien attack successfully averted (they only get you in the dark), I set off for university, fuelled by caffeine, utterly exhausted. As I entered my office Germaine (whose room was just across the hall) looked in, concerned. Propinquity had led us to an easier relationship, and we occasionally popped into each other's offices for a quick natter or a gossip.

'You look like shit,' she said, not unkindly. 'What's the matter?'

I told her everything, even about the aliens. She raised her eyebrows, said nothing, and suggested we had a coffee.

'You need to move,' she said, 'it makes no sense living in such an isolated place. It isn't fair to Barbara.' She was right.

'Come to dinner next Thursday night,' she suggested. 'Can you make it?'

We had absolutely no social life, and had hardly been out save for a stiff evening at Professor Hunter's obligatory greet-the-new-members-of-staff dinner party, so I could accept – sad old me – without looking at my diary.

By this time we'd both read *The Female Eunuch*, Barbara with an excited sense of new possibility, though with some serious reservations. As one with a commitment to psychotherapy, some of Germaine's views seemed misplaced: 'The revolutionary woman must know her enemies, the doctors, psychiatrists, health visitors, priests, marriage counsellors . . . all the authoritarians and dogmatists who flock about her with warning and advice.'

Nevertheless, there was a smell of freedom in the air. Women who had previously described themselves ruefully as 'having problems making relationships with men', freed themselves from this condescending category, and replaced it with the larger and more satisfying notion that such problems were those of women in a dominant and uncongenial male culture. This culture, of course, included me. Barbara joined a woman's group, and was delighted to find that her sisters felt similarly (though not always about me).

I resisted this as best I could. Though numbers of my male friends and colleagues created a *mea culpa* culture in sympathy with the women's movement, I was inclined to regard a men's group as something that met on the first tee, or over a poker table. Happy to avow myself as a sympathetic first-generation feminist (equal rights, equal pay, equal most anything), I regarded the aggression of the new women's libbers, who often presented themselves, shockingly, as victims in the way that blacks had been victims, as morally wrong-headed. My reserves of sympathy for the world's victims, I was often heard (pompously) to claim, had their priority

with the people of the third world, with children dying of star-
vation, with the genuine dispossessed. You can get compassion
fatigue, and I wanted to apportion mine where it best belonged,
and not with a bunch of privileged middle-class women who had
come to regard the term 'man' as one of amusement, exasperation
and abuse. I said so, as frequently as I was allowed. 'Just like a
man to say that,' I was told. I had learned, by then, not to say 'just
like a woman to argue so badly,' but I think my face showed me
thinking it.

Germaine was aware of this problem, though it took her some
time to acknowledge it. In the Foreword to the twenty-first anniver-
sary edition of *The Female Eunuch*, she observes that: '*The Female
Eunuch* does not deal with poor women (for when I wrote it I did
not know them) but with the women of the rich world, whose
oppression is seen by poor women as freedom.' The apparent solip-
sism of this – can you only consider the wretched of the world if
you 'know' them? – is, I assume, caused by sloppy writing, not
mere self-reference.

Germaine lived in a Regency house in Leamington, her flat
exuberantly decorated with Moroccan scarves and artefacts,
colourful and welcoming, with exotic smells of good food, incense
and marijuana. She'd cooked a lamb tagine, and was thoroughly
engaged, amusing, and intently related. It was just the three of us,
and Barbara, warmed by the atmosphere, attention, and a few glasses
of wine, overcame her usual aversion to academic people, and
opened up considerably. By the end of the evening she and Germaine
were chatting away merrily, while I sat back in an absurdly comfy
bucket chair, stoned and happy, a million miles away from my
inward aliens, or they from me.

The next day Germaine popped into my office between classes.
'Thanks so much,' I said. 'That was so generous of you.'
'I've been thinking,' she said, 'and I wonder if you'd like to move
in with me for a while, until you find a flat in Leamington?'

It was an extraordinary, totally unexpected offer. Germaine was given to impulsive acts of high generosity, which were sometimes beyond the boundaries of what she could really manage – and, in this case, well beyond the scope of what her flat could contain. Her second bedroom was small, and the proffered living arrangement would have been quite impossible, even for a short time. I said so to Barbara, a little wistfully, as we sat over a glass of wine that evening. It was tempting, if improbable; it would have been fun, at least for a while.

'Do you think Germaine fancies me?' she asked.

'You seemed to get on pretty well,' I said, rather turned on by the thought. 'Do you fancy her?'

She shook her head. 'I'd be terrified,' she said. 'I think I'd end up as a pile of bones at the bottom of the bed.'

It was a pretty enticing thought, this menstrual-blood-quaffing Valkyrie seducing my Barbara. I could see the headline already: *'Lecturer Watches As Aussie Vampire Eats Wife!'* A few weeks later we found an adequate flat in Leamington, and invited Germaine back to supper. I don't think we ever found a date that suited all of us – her calendar, unlike ours, was always full. Anyway, she'd helped us through a crisis, and after that rather kept her distance. I didn't mind: it had been exceedingly kind of her to intervene, and she had plenty to be getting on with. Within a year she had resigned from Warwick, gone abroad, and moved into a more exciting world. No more English Department, no more white tiles, no more unhappy colleagues. It must have been a considerable relief. It was to take me thirteen more years before I had the nerve to do the same.

Barbara had ironically ended up in a maximally uncomfortable milieu: marooned amongst self-satisfied academics, only five miles from her old home in Kenilworth. She had none of Germaine's swagger, yet *The Female Eunuch* had an effect on her, on both of us, which neither of us would have fully registered at the time.

There are books that produce epiphanies – as Hume had done for me, at eighteen – but *The Female Eunuch* worked on us imperceptibly, in combination with a number of cognate influences. The mature woman that Barbara came to be was, indeed, tougher, sassier, more socially confident, more inclined to seek responsibility on her own terms. She became a good painter, trained as a homeopath and, echoing in her soul somewhere, I expect she would acknowledge the voice of Germaine Greer.

It didn't work that way for me, of course, it couldn't have. But from the time of the publication of *The Female Eunuch* it became a more complex, more embattled, and certainly a more interesting thing to be not a mere male, a penis-toting animal, but a man. *The Female Eunuch* set an unprecedented problem for men of the time: if you disagreed with and opposed it, you found yourself in the company of stodgy, generally right-wing, anti-feminists; if you were generally well disposed, you acceded to a description of yourself which was unbearable.

Germaine knew this was a likely response, of course, and it was part of her rhetorical strategy, as the sentences with which the book ends make clear: 'Privileged women will pluck at your sleeve and seek to enlist you in the "fight" for reforms, but reforms are retrogressive. The old process must be broken, not made new. Bitter women will call you to rebellion, but you have too much to do. What *will* you do?'

The sentence may have been directed primarily towards women readers, but it felt as if it was aimed directly and threateningly at me. Considered thus, *The Female Eunuch* was like a terrorist attack: it was designed to distress, to cause outrage and to provoke just that response which would heighten the tension that it described and bring it to boiling point. I could see this of course – you couldn't miss it – but the book left you with no room to negotiate. I admired the spirit and voice without sharing the analysis or conclusions. I carped, I argued, I quoted selected passages with disdain. It made me defensive, sulky, slightly desperate. I suspect that Germaine would have said that, under the pressure she had imposed, I revealed myself for what I was. It wasn't a comfortable process, and even now I am not sure I would thank her for it.

11

HIGHLY ORCHESTRATED

> You've got very badly to want to get rid of the old,
> before anything new will appear – even in the self.
>
> D.H. Lawrence, *Women in Love*

If you want to understand the difference between sense and sensibility, the following instance, abstracted from one of my Oxford DPhil tutorials, may be instructive. John Bayley and I were talking about Lawrence's *Women in Love*. I don't remember why: might it have had something to do with endings? Or perhaps with the nature of love (his *The Characters of Love* is a remarkable book). I'd inherited John for a year while my thesis supervisor J.I.M. Stewart was on leave, presumably to write another of his Inspector Appleby books. ('*Not* thrillers, dear boy, I think of them as parodies of thrillers.')

Bayley was more fun than Stewart, who had confined our very occasional tutorials to correcting the spelling of my latest chapter, and describing to me the Regius Professor of Greek's erotica collection.

'Can you take me to see it?'

'Certainly not.'

Bayley, though, actually engaged with the words on the page, and I learned a lot from him, if only obliquely. Everything about John was oblique, and one could never predict what he might say next. He was illuminatingly insightful, whimsical and puckish, his premises opaque, his procedures impenetrable. There was a cultivated femininity in his sensitivities. He had a face and demeanour right out of the benign children's books of Edwardian literature, a Bunterish affability which concealed a mind like a velvet trap. It is inconceivable that he might have had followers, as Leavis did. You couldn't become a Bayleian.

His stuttering was not the usual Oxford affectation – they don't do it in Cambridge – but a desperate groping for the next syllable, leaving his listener praying that he would either make it – soon! – or give up trying. You had to be patient, for after a time, as you settled in to the tutorial, he would calm a little, and his performance improve. I remember listening to him lecture at the University of Warwick, some years later, while sitting next to his wife, Iris Murdoch, who was clenched with apprehension as John began, stutteringly.

'He's always much better after the first few minutes,' she said to me, anxiously clutching my hand, and he was, but those moments seemed interminable. In tutorials he had learned to let his students start the talking, and I think it was I who had broached the topic of *Women in Love.*

'I love the ending,' I said. 'You know, when they are talking about love and relations between the sexes? And it ends with a disagreement, when Birkin says he needs two kinds of love, and Ursula disagrees, and he just says "I don't believe that . . ." And that's it, that's the final line. It's a wonderful ending, so shadowy and inconclusive.'

John considered this for a moment.

'I've always th-th-thought it r-rather h-h-highly orch-orch-orchestrated.'

The insight gains from having been stuttered, as if the perception were hard won. But it had the ring of some delicately perceived truth that had been unavailable to me. My reading of the ending was not wrong, it was sensible enough, but it was unremarkable.

It took what was *given*, without grasping the tonality, the latent content, the authorial control.

To think like that, it seemed, you had to have real sensibility, and to be English. I was American: apparently we were bright enough, but earnest, too new world – almost as bad as Australians really – lacking in subtlety of mind, our feelings deep, perhaps, but all in a flow, without rivulets, eddies, or tributaries.

In those days people still took Lawrence seriously, and he had a central place in the canon and syllabus of twentieth-century fiction in a way that, I gather, he no longer does. I suspect he is now seen as dated and more than faintly ridiculous, embarrassing almost. But in the sixties and seventies, he was celebrated as one of the key figures of what Leavis had called *The Great Tradition*.

Lawrence is usually taught alongside Joyce in courses on modernism – *Women in Love* was published only a year before *Ulysses* – but if you were a serious reader of serious literature, Leavis required that you *chose* between Lawrence and Joyce. Joyce may have been technically precocious, but was reprehensibly self-referring, unhealthy, and ultimately solipsistic:

> . . . there is no organic principle determining, informing and controlling into a vital whole, the elaborate analogical structure, the extraordinary variety of technical devices, the attempts at an exhaustive rendering of consciousness, for which *Ulysses* is remarkable . . . It is rather, I think, a dead end, or at least a pointer to disintegration . . .

The terminology explicitly echoes Lawrence: 'vital' lack of the 'organic' is undesirable, 'disintegration' is the process of breaking down into corruption, 'cosmopolitan' is used pejoratively, 'exhaustive . . . consciousness' is a symptom of sickness of being. We might as well be listening to Rupert Birkin, the lead voice of *Women in Love*.

When I announced, in my first year teaching at Warwick, that I intended to offer an 'option' on Lawrence, it was regarded by my colleagues as a worthy choice (if a bit old hat), and a tempting one by the students. So many signed up that the chairman warned me that I wouldn't be given credit for teaching more than two seminar groups. I did three anyway, to accommodate the thirty takers, delighted that so many had chosen Lawrence (and me). We read the major novels, the short stories, essays and travel books, and the *Collected Letters*, went on a visit to Eastwood and Lawrence country, even went down a mine. (I was too frightened and stayed above in the pub, having a pint.)

We agreed with Leavis that, in some fashion worth investigating, Lawrence could be good for you: he had, according to his disciple, 'a vital capacity for experience, a kind of reverent openness before life, and a marked moral intensity'. These very qualities, that now make me recoil with a sceptical fastidiousness that does me no credit, then seemed to me highly desirable, and worth teasing out from the multiple challenges and difficulties of the major Lawrence works. And of these works there seemed little question that *Women in Love* was the key text.

Though published in 1921, the novel is a companion piece to *The Rainbow* (1915) and was originally part of the same project, which was to be titled *The Sisters. Women in Love* is written during the First War, and is apparently set just before it, though the tone of the novel, and its major themes, seem clearly to reflect the chaos and disintegration of that period. How else is one to explain the novel's barrage of reference to dissolution, corruption, disintegration and chaos: 'It's the lie that kills. If we want hate, let us have it – death, murder, torture, violent destruction – let us have it: but not in the name of love . . . I abhor humanity, I wish it was swept away . . . it would be better.'

If it were just Rupert Birkin who felt so, we would presume some individual pathology, but it is a feeling shared variously by his girlfriend Ursula, her sister Gudrun and her lover Gerald Crich, the son of the local colliery owner, and must be assumed to have some general significance. Birkin believes that mankind has reached the end of a stage of being, which is now 'obsolete'. We need to find a way to enter into some new and more satisfactory mode of being, or what he calls 'form of life'. It is by no means clear what any of this means. Birkin says it one way, then another. Tries a formulation, abandons it in disgust, reformulates, re-abandons. He knows something is critically wrong, but can neither describe nor overcome it: indeed the two processes are knotted in such a way that unless he finds the right language he cannot locate the right form of life, and vice versa. So two projects are intertwined for him: to find a new language, *and* a new way of being. If the one fails, so will the other, and yet neither is possible without the other having been accomplished. We are thus 'imprisoned', Birkin insists, within a 'limited, false set of concepts'. It is the archetypal Wittgensteinian conundrum, before Wittgenstein first formu-lated it.

Women in Love is about the yearning for freedom, the struggle and dissatisfaction of sensing the possibility of something wider, larger and more satisfying – something new – and failing either to describe or to find it. It is a chronicle of frustration, and frequently Birkin's attempts to articulate his perceptions are embarrassingly inadequate. Take, for instance, this ludicrous conversation between Birkin and Gerald:

> Birkin watched him narrowly. He saw the perfect good-humoured callousness, even strange, glistening malice, in Gerald, glistening through the plausible ethics of productivity.
> 'Gerald,' he said, 'I rather hate you.'
> 'I know you do,' said Gerald. 'Why do you?'
> Birkin mused inscrutably for some minutes.
> 'I should like to know if you are conscious of hating me,' he

said at last. 'Do you ever consciously detest me – hate me with mystic hate? There are odd moments when I hate you starrily.'

Gerald was rather taken aback, even a little disconcerted. He did not quite know what to say.

One can only sympathize, which is, of course, part of the point. Birkin is working on a metaphor about 'star equilibrium', which he wishes to put in the place of the dead concept 'love', but neither Gerald nor Ursula – nor the reader – trusts him when he attempts 'to drag in the stars'.

He does it anyway. He wants love, surely enough, he yearns for it, but he hates both the idea and the known reality. His desire for a new way of understanding is erotic in its intensity, and it is no surprise that what draws him to Ursula is a recognition that they are using 'the same language'. But it is a frustrating effort, for both the lovers and the readers.

Birkin's effort 'at serious living' is at the centre of the novel, and that effort is a philosophical one. Not merely does he seek a new set of concepts, the progress of the narrative itself attempts, however implicitly, to supply them. *Women in Love* is by design that rarest of things, a genuine novel of ideas, and those ideas are embedded in the very method of telling the story. The effort is, in Lawrence's terms, if not A.J. Ayer's, philosophical. In the essay 'Surgery for the Novel: Or a Bomb?' Lawrence raises this very issue:

Plato's Dialogues . . . are queer little novels. It seems to me the greatest pity in the world, when philosophy and fiction got split. They used to be one, right from the days of myth. Then they went and parted, like a nagging married couple . . . So the novel went sloppy, and philosophy went abstract-dry. The two should come together again, in the novel.

The philosophical effort here, properly understood, is epistemological. Yes, there is a lot of stuff about love, and new concepts, and sociology, and leaders and followers – much of it garnered from Nietzsche and Schopenhauer – which if philosophical at all is only so in a cracker-barrel sense.

The central effort is this: if you have come to believe that knowledge of the self, the world and others is inhibited and distorted when filtered through consciousness, that the 'mind' is an inadequate receptor for knowledge of the world, then what is to take its place? *Women in Love* suggests instead a theory of knowledge based on intuition, quickness of apprehension through 'the blood'. It is surprising, when you leaf through the text, how many paragraphs begin: 'Suddenly he/she realized . . .' Apperception becomes the mode of perception: we know the world through the immediacy of its impact on us, not ours on it.

This is only partially achieved and unsatisfying. What intrigued me more, reading it at the time, was whether the novel's analyses of personal and cultural disintegration might speak directly to my own situation. What could be learned from *Women in Love*? It addressed the questions of men and women, the nature of love and sexual connection, questions of how to be in the world. I wasn't doing very well on any of those fronts. Barbara and I separated for the second time (in only three years of marriage) in 1972, and this time it felt more serious. Her fragility meant we could never capitalize on the early excitement of coming together: have new experiences, travel, make something new and contemplate a spacious future uniquely our own. Our differences in tastes and passions were at first animating, but were beginning to prove, in the language of the law courts, irreconcilable. The discovery and exploration of such differences is a universal experience of new lovers, but after a time the novelty palled, and Barbara began to find me a constant source of pressure, while I came sadly to regard her as retracted and self-absorbed.

We were wedded not to each other, but to ambivalence about

each other: unable to unite or permanently to separate. It was a pattern that was to drag on for many years. She moved back to Oxford, and I took a flat in a Victorian house in Leamington Spa. We'd been trapped in exactly that crimped form of marriage that Birkin so detested: 'each couple in its own little house, watching its own little interests, and stewing in its own little privacy . . .' I had criticized her along Birkinian lines: recoiled from her 'will', accused her of bullying, demanded a simultaneous closeness and separateness. Lawrence made me yearn for a life of passionate intensity, I felt myself coiling within, in readiness and in anticipation.

Yet I experienced *Women in Love*, in spite of its promises, as a source of negative energy: its restlessness and overwrought critical dicta were what affected me, not (as Leavis would have had it) with some purported spiritual intensity, moral seriousness and belief in the deepest sources of being. Lawrence helped me to recognize and to describe how and why things had gone wrong in my life, and made them worse. (Raymond Williams described the novel as 'a masterpiece of loss'.) If *Women in Love* pointed towards richer forms of life, I couldn't avail myself of them, not at all. Reading it made me unbalanced, more dissatisfied, as unrealistically demanding as Rupert Birkin, and, I suspect, just as crazy.

My students, though, responded more generously, curiously and unexpectedly. We discussed the love-making scene between Birkin and Ursula in 'Excurse', which led Rebecca West to complain that Lawrence was incapable of saying exactly what his lovers were *doing* in bed:

> It was a perfect passing away for both of them, and at the same time the most intolerable accession into being, the marvellous fullness of immediate gratification, overwhelming out-flooding from the source of the deepest life force, the darkest, deepest, strangest life-source of the human body, at the back and base of the loins.

You don't need an A.J. Ayer to tell you this is nonsense, but it isn't indecipherable. Lawrence was knowledgeable about tantric sex and Kundalini Buddhism, and there is some opaque reference to such practices here. This becomes (almost) explicit in the chapter 'Continental', when after a night of love-making Ursula reflects to herself: 'Why not be bestial and go the whole round of experience? She exulted in it. She was bestial. How good it was to be really shameful! There would be no shameful thing she had not experienced.' John Sparrow was later to be the first to remark that the 'Night of Shame' chapter of *Lady Chatterley's Lover* involves a scene of anal penetration, and there are similarly described moments both here and between Ursula's parents in *The Rainbow*.

We discussed this, gingerly, in seminars, prompting a hearty woman mature student to expostulate, 'Can't they just be satisfied with a jolly good shag?' Not everyone is. When the course ended an attractive young woman student invited me out for dinner, ostensibly to say thank you for 'teaching her such a lot'. She chose a local bistro, made sure I drank too much, and put her hand on my thigh.

'The problem with you,' she said caressively, 'is that you never do anything you disapprove of. It would be so good for you, it would free you from all that rectitude and conscientiousness. You're so *stiff*.'

By now *that* was certainly true, and the overt appeal to my inner Allen Ginsberg was intuitively perfect. I wanted to be free, less rule-bound, licentious. When I drove her home she kissed me passionately, and begged to be taken back to my flat, promising anything I liked by way of the unspeakable. I demurred: she was my student, she was married, she was that little bit unstable. I might have settled for any two out of three, but together they hardened my resolve. I've always regretted it. She was right.

I carried on, not with her, but with a book on Lawrence, which had been commissioned by Methuen two years before. I wasn't much good at that either. I had begun a chronological novel-by-

novel account, but there was something dead about the whole enterprise. I started again, informing Methuen that the book would
now be entirely about *Women in Love*. Curiously, they seemed
happy enough about this, probably because they had despaired of
ever seeing a final script from me.

A year later I wrote again to tell them that I was now writing a
novel about a university lecturer, unhappy in life and love, who is
writing a critical book about D.H. Lawrence. This novel would
correlate Lawrentian experiences and ideas with events in the
lecturer's life. After some time, this book was published, not once
but twice. The first version, by Bernard Malamud, was entitled
Dubin's Lives, which came out in 1979, when mine should have
been published, and wasn't. The second, in 1997, was Geoff Dyer's
Out of Sheer Rage: Wrestling with D.H. Lawrence, a great title, and
a good book. So mine was a viable idea after all, only I was the
wrong person to have it. I never wrote a single word.

Rereading *Women in Love* after some thirty years, it is hard to
escape the question: how is it that I was so taken in by all of this
overheated nonsense? How pleasurable it now is to quote Lawrence's
excesses, and to conclude: now I know better, how callow is youth,
how easily fooled. How agreeable it is to age, and to mature, and
to come finally to sound judgement.

This is fine, as far as it goes, but it leaves something out. There
is a memory trace running through *Women in Love* not of the
passages and sentences that I remember from last reading it thirty
years ago, but of me – could I call him a literary 'little Rick' –
who was struck by those passages so deeply as to remember them
almost verbatim on rereading: of the drowning of Diana Crich,
the smashing of the lapis lazuli paperweight on to Birkin's head,
the wrestling scene, those obscure moments of 'Excurse', multiple
individual lines and sentiments, all come back virtually intact.
And what returns, too, is a ghostly version of my former reading
self, captured by the lines, reading them attentively and with

respect, aware that, if the rhetoric is sometimes strained, the repetitions insistent, nevertheless there is a powerful presence in the words, a project worth taking seriously, and personally. Rereading Lawrence I re-encounter my previous self, and recover for a moment something fresh and young, eager to believe, open-minded and open-hearted in ways that I had almost forgotten were possible.

Is 'Sailing to Byzantium' wrong? This *is* a country for old men, worth revisiting and remembering, imprinted with a fading intensity which is recoverable, but can't be re-experienced: like visiting a house one has lived in as a child, filled with wisps of partial memories which emerge not as feeling, but as something like feeling, which recalls feeling – of truncated narrative, partial glimpses half-perceived, visual traces of persons like ghosts, wispy and insubstantial, echoing with half-remembered conversations and lullabies.

Listening intently to this distant music, after rereading *Women in Love*, brings me back to John Bayley and the memory of that tutorial. Let me return to the passage with which the novel ends, in a conversation between Birkin and Ursula, after Gerald's death in the Alps. Birkin, happy now in his love of her, yet laments his lack of a similar intimacy with a man.

'I don't believe it,' she said. 'It's an obstinacy, a theory, a perversity.'
'Well –' he said.
'You can't have two kinds of love. Why should you!'
'It seems as if I can't,' he said. 'Yet I wanted it.'
'You can't have it, because it's false, impossible,' she said.
'I don't believe that,' he answered.

After thirty-five years of reflection I still don't get it, not entirely. Highly orchestrated? The ending, which reaches delicately outside the confines of the novel into some future in which the striving goes on, is highly *considered*. There is nothing gratuitous about it, the mastery is complete. But highly orchestrated? Perhaps Bayley was thinking of chamber music, and I (misunderstanding him) of Wagner?

For many years this example of sensibility – like those of John Newton at Warwick, or of Dr Leavis – haunted me, and made me acutely aware of my own shortcomings. Earnest, intelligent in some prosaic, linear fashion, lacking fineness of discrimination, *tactless*. So when I encounter this recurring English strain of high sensibility, I often feel patronized, as if the message were *I am more delicately aware than you, I'll bet you couldn't have put this quite so acutely*. Though this is not, I suppose, the intent, it is certainly the result.

Surely it is possible to read English literature without aping this peculiar, parochial form of sensitivity? Wallace Stevens observes that 'Americans are not British in sensibility', and it is a danger of expatriation that the voices, procedures and tonalities that are sanctioned by English culture are, for an American visitor, tempting roads to self-betrayal. During my previous year at Oxford, my tutor Steven Wall had criticized one of my essays for 'lacking its own voice'. (Auden, more interestingly, accused Americans of all having the same *face*.) What Wall meant, almost sneeringly, was that I had not the advantage of Englishness, and lacked sensibility.

But I had a voice, and it was American, and I lost confidence in it. Ceased to be, even, Richard A. Gekoski, and became R.A. Gekoski. I began to acquire something of an Oxford persona, and to mime its tones and inflections. Yet what I had really needed to learn, however admiringly, from John Bayley was how *not* to be. He was, as he would happily admit, a terrible model. For many years I lost track of myself, and foundered in a miasma of mock-Englishness, of writer's block and incomprehension. The book on Lawrence, unsurprisingly, was never finished: the only time I have failed to meet a deadline, and one of the best things that has ever happened to me.

12

ALL YOU NEED IS LOVE?

> All prize-giving and marks and exams sidetrack proper
> personality development. Only pedants claim learning
> from books is education. It robs youth of its right to
> play and play and play; it puts old heads on young shoul-
> ders.
>
> A.S. Neill, *Summerhill*

After voting for my girlfriend to be the Prom Queen in high
school, I never again voted in an election. My reasons for this
shocking abnegation of responsibility may be characterized as
psychological and aesthetic. The mere fact that a person puts himself
forward for high office is frequently a sign of a personality defect
so profound that it ought to disqualify him. And having been raised
in America, I am disgusted by the sheer ugliness of political life:
the dispiriting level of most of the candidates, the fortunes wasted
on the interminable campaigning, the balloons, the pompoms, the
polyester, the flag-waving, the sabre-rattling, the yawning abyss
between what is promised and what delivered. *God Bless America!*
I loathe all of that phoniness, the false smiles and strained body
language. Are these real people, or androids? How could any right-
thinking person tolerate such company? Matthew Arnold makes
the point neatly:

Now for my part I do not wish to see men of culture asking to be entrusted with power; and, indeed, I have freely said, that in my opinion the speech most proper, at present, for a man of culture to make to a body of his fellow-countrymen who get him into a committee-room, is Socrates's: Know thyself! and this is not a speech to be made by men wanting to be entrusted with power.

And so when faced with a choice, even between the bumbling but mildly estimable John Kerry and the loathsome George W. Bush, I could not force myself to push the button, or whatever it is you do. Not voting is a kind of vote: an abstention. If more of us did it – and almost half already do – maybe we could be offered something more serious and palatable. More real.

But there is something disingenuous about this. I am interested in politics and follow elections attentively. I have favourites amongst politicians, and amongst policies. I espouse a murky but not entirely inarticulate liberalism, and believe in letting the other man live in his own way, as long as he will agree to leave me to do the same. I like differences, and I cannot abide being bossed about. I detest Ken Livingstone, the former Mayor of London, for getting rid of the Routemaster bus, the iconic walk-on walk-off double decker that has characterized London since the 1950s. And I will never forgive Tony Blair (the buck stops there) for one single act of crass stupidity. For it was under the Blair government in 1999, that the Department of Education tried to close A.S. Neill's Summerhill School.

Founded in Germany in 1921, and soon relocated to Leiston in Suffolk, Summerhill is a tiny, progressive boarding school for students aged between five and sixteen. Its aim is to raise children *in freedom*, and to generate what an admiring school inspector once called 'the atmosphere of a permanent holiday camp'. The founding premises, based largely on Freud and Homer Lane's Little Commonwealth, were radical but simple.

Self-government for the pupils and staff, freedom to go to lessons or stay away, freedom to play for days or weeks or years if necessary, freedom from any indoctrination whether religious or moral or political, freedom from character moulding.

Underlying this, of course, is the necessary belief in the innate 'goodness of human nature'. How children develop is the direct result of how they are raised. It is the task of parent and teacher alike not to get in the way: to facilitate rather than to impose, to trust that the unimpeded growth of a loved child must result in the creation of a loving adult. A child doesn't want to learn to read, can't be bothered to dress properly, prefers playing guitar to going to class? *Leave him alone.* He'll read when he finds that it is necessary and useful. No one ever left Summerhill illiterate. Personal happiness is the criterion and the goal, which sounds cloistered and selfish, and is in Neill's view just the opposite. Only happy people can make a happy world, as Neill concludes in the final sentences of his preface to his book, *Summerhill*:

If Summerhill has any message at all it is: Thou shalt not opt out. Fight world sickness, not with drugs like moral teachings and punishments but with natural means – approval, tenderness, tolerance . . . I hesitate to use the word love, for it has almost become a dirty word like so many honest and clean Anglo-Saxon four letter words.

Yet soon enough, like Rupert Birkin, he has need of the forbidden word. The closing lines of the chapter 'The Future of Summerhill' are unequivocal:

the future of Summerhill is of the greatest importance to humanity. New generations must be given the chance to grow in freedom. The bestowal of freedom is the bestowal of love. And only love can save the world.

Neill's words were sufficiently radical in their educational context, but reading them in 1971 it was hard not to feel that they encapsulated the spirit of the time. It had taken fifty years, but the world had finally caught up with A.S. Neill. 'All you need is love.' How could I sit in Oxford pursuing my dusty doctoral ends? I'd never wanted to be a university teacher, not really. Until my final year as an undergraduate, I still wanted to be a lawyer, and had been offered a place at Harvard Law. Granted a brief moment of lucidity that loosened my unconscious emulation of my father, I decided instead to do graduate work in English (which, anyway, was what he'd really wanted). But working towards my DPhil I would study and write sporadically, teeth gritted, without belief or pleasure, and in between I would read what really interested me, particularly the works of A.S. Neill. I was most intrigued by his four early autobiographical books, in which he traced his development as a schoolmaster, a dominee. How did a relatively ordinary Scottish boy, born in the late nineteenth century, with his fair leavening of Calvinism, become the century's most famous progressive educationist? For if he could transform himself in such a thoroughgoing manner, surely even I could, just a little?

Freedom was in the air: progressive education, or de-schooling, was hip. In that time at Oxford I read George Dennison, John Holt, Ivan Illich, and remembered fondly my time at Burgundy Farm Country Day School. Barbara, herself a victim of dreadful schooling, concurred with the new lines of thought, and suggested that we needed to pay a visit to Summerhill, to see what Neill's ideas looked like in action.

It was, thank goodness, much as we had expected. Many of the kids looked as if they'd been shipped in from a California commune, brightly and eccentrically dressed, long-haired, cheerfully androgynous.

The main house looked equally shabby, if less colourful, surrounded by a series of randomly located outbuildings, the children sloping about with varying degrees of purpose, 'Sergeant Pepper' playing from the dormitory. Visitors were greeted by the school secretary, and herded into the main hall, where Neill gave a ten-minute talk. He was eighty-seven, the very incarnation of Jung's wise old man, erect of carriage and bright of eye, smoking his pipe, shambling, radiant and benign. He gave a brief summary of what his visitors (there were about twenty of us) already knew about the school, and then left us to our own devices. I wanted to talk to him, perhaps introduce myself and ask about a job, but he didn't encourage contact. It was clearly drudgery for him to go on welcoming strangers every week, but it was also an opportunity to find the occasional parents who might send their children to the school. Always financially uncertain, Summerhill could not afford to neglect such public relations.

The main treat was the kids. They didn't look like school children at all, rather like a flock of talking free range chickens, pecking about here and there. A few, not many, were playing with a football, two boys were weeding the garden in a desultory manner, in a studio pots and paintings were being made, groups lounged about chatting and laughing. *Doing their own thing.* Summerhill, all of a sudden, wasn't alternative, peculiar, isolated: Summerhill was cool. We didn't encounter any of the aggressive tribalism that I associate with children in school playgrounds, nor witness any of the teasing, bullying and bitchiness, the cruel exclusions that children inflict on each other with such frequency that one would swear it was part of their nature.

The Summerhill children were exactly as Neill had characterized them: fresh-faced, friendly and open, relaxed in body and mind. Several came over to us to say hello, ask who we were and if they could show us around. They were all the advertisement the school needed. What was remarkable was that many of these children were there because they had failed to settle elsewhere, and come to Neill with that mournful disaffection so characteristic of unhappy children. If they got there young enough ('before the age of twelve') Neill could help. He gave 'PLs' – short therapy sessions, or 'private lessons' – to the most disaffected, which seemed to help some of the children, but no more, Neill acknowledged, than got better simply by being at the school. Being in a free community was all the therapy they needed.

We returned to Oxford confirmed in our beliefs, and I composed a letter applying for a job. I outlined my qualifications gingerly, and added a gushy good deal about my love of children, playing and telling stories. I got a letter by return informing me that there were no vacancies, which though I expected it, was nevertheless disappointing. I kept it for some time, treasuring Neill's signature, if only on a letter of rejection.

When I later arrived at Warwick to take up my lectureship, still full of Summerhillian yearning, I astonished our founding professor, a Scot but no A.S. Neill, by asking earnestly if I was required to examine our students, because I didn't believe in examinations. Professor Hunter looked at me intently, as if trying to figure out how I got there, and why he had colluded in the process. He firmly believed that 'when you teach literature, you also teach your own way of life', but he would have had no doubt that his was preferable to mine.

'Read your contract,' he said tartly. 'That is what we do.'

'I'm sorry to hear it,' I said. 'I think the more you are examined the less you are likely to learn.'

'Education,' he said, 'is about achievement. Examinations are how we determine the level of achievement that has been attained.'

'Do you still believe that? We must talk at length about this one day.'

He didn't respond, and neither of us broached the subject again. I was glad, really, for my position on the matter wouldn't have stood up to interrogation. I was there because I was good at examinations, and proud of it. If you had taken away my academic qualifications I would have felt naked and bereft. I knew this, yet still felt that my progressive attitudes were tenable.

Unfortunately, my experience at Oxford had been good for my self-esteem. I am told that one should feel proud of oneself and one's achievements, but I frequently value the wrong things for the wrong reasons. Pride resulting from, say, academic achievement, is a kind of false pride based on false goals. Does high academic achievement make one happy, or good? Does it fill you with laughter and goodwill towards man? Look round the universities, and despair. No, I rather prefer moderate, vigilant self-esteem, scepticism directed inwards, self-doubt: those qualities of mind that lead to humility, and to that irony which wryly registers the differences between the apparent and the real. And, ironically enough, I still feel proud of my academic achievements, when I'm not mildly ashamed of them.

I may have been a success by academic standards, but that was a sign of some inner weakness in me, a capitulation, a failure of ego strength. If I'd had the guts I would have abandoned my studies, and sought a way to have fun, to play a lot and to be happy. In 1967 I was offered a summer job as assistant professional at a tennis club in Mykonos. I should have taken it, and stayed, given lessons and played in local tournaments, learned Greek, eaten in the taverna, drunk the local wines (except Retsina) and entertained the local women. I could have rented a little villa overlooking the sea, got brown as a berry, kept my own hours, read whatever took my fancy, tried to write a novel. I might have become like that Lawrence Durrell. He seemed to be having a lot of fun.

But being 'in school', as Americans continue to call it even while one is at university, was all I had ever done, and it rather frightened me to think of leaving it. I had no experience, indeed no memories of *not* being in school. And the only genuinely happy ones were from my time at Burgundy Farm. It was the only school where I ever felt comfortable.

But schoolteaching wouldn't have suited me. I haven't the patience, the sheer grind would have worn me down. What I needed Neill for, I recognized, was not as a guide to good teaching, but to good parenting. In 1973, reunited after a second separation, Barbara and I decided that, to make things work, we ought to have a child. My father, told the news, was rightly sceptical. 'But I feel biologically ready to be a father,' I said, pulling myself up to the full height of my twenty-six years. I could virtually hear him not saying, in the ensuing silence of that long-distance phone call, that it was *psychologically* ready that he was worried about.

Nothing prepares you for the birth of your first child, but I had been heartened by Neill's description of the childhood of his daughter Zoe, raised with the freedom and generosity that her father demonstrated and recommended. According to her proud father 'scores of outsiders from all over the world' had said of her: 'Here is something quite new, a child of grace and balance and happiness, at peace with her surroundings, not at war.' Do we get a glimpse of the magi hovering round the Christ child here? I don't mind the proud hyperbole, it is wonderful for a parent to feel like that. I hoped I would too, and with equally good reason.

Anna entered the world as if reluctantly, struggling towards the light from a posterior position, almost as exhausted as her mother was. I'd done my bit at the top end with Barbara, joined her in breathing exercises, massaged and encouraged, but when the going got rough, and the forceps came out, I was banished to the waiting room, and was chagrined at how relieved I felt. She had a hard time, a stressed and unsympathetic doctor forcing the pace, and by the time I returned, baby Anna had been mysteriously removed, and Barbara was beyond consolation. Twenty minutes later I was presented with a tiny red-faced bundle, and clutched her to me almost dangerously.

She had matted black strands of fine hair, a grumpy, rubbery little face, forehead skewed from the trauma of birth, and, magically, when she caught my eye she looked at me steadily for a long time, as if to inquire what had just happened, what might have been done to avoid it, and who the hell I was. They say babies can't focus, but it's new born fathers who can't. I wept, squeezed her involuntarily, then gave her back to the hovering nurse, who was anxiously diagnosing a possible case of squashed baby syndrome, kissed Barbara good-bye, and went out to buy an Indesit washing machine. We'd prepared a pink nursery with an adorable crib and lots of girly bits for Anna to come home to, which took a good few days while both she and her mother recovered. I wandered the house, restlessly, reading Dr Spock, and thinking about A.S. Neill.

We'd agreed on the ground rules: baby Anna would eat when she wished, sleep as nature guided her. If she cried it would be for a reason, and we would comfort her, whenever. We had terry towelling nappies, not having discovered disposable ones, and vowed that she could use them for as long as she wished: no toilet training for her. She could grow up in her own way and in her own time. I bought a blue corduroy sling and pouch, imported from California, that fitted round my back, so that she could rest comfortably on the porch of my stomach. I walked the house with her in the early hours, as Barbara tried to sleep and Anna wept with colic, and later the pains of teething. When she wished, whatever the hour, I would take her for a ride in the car, which was often the only thing that would soothe her. I pretended I was a taxi driver preparing for the knowledge, and learned many of the obscure byways of Leamington Spa and Warwick.

It was wonderful and awful. It wasn't long before I was claiming, ruefully, that until having a baby I hadn't believed in original sin. I hadn't expected the confrontations, the tears, the relentless neediness, the constant desire for attention, the unrelenting egotism. Not *her*, she was a baby, they're like that. I mean *me*. I'd never been asked so much, had to give up so much. My life was dominated by fatherhood, and I wasn't (as my father had feared) entirely ready for it. Too much for them, not enough for me. I was so overwhelmed that this palpable selfishness hardly even embarrassed me. I was too tired to be embarrassed. What happened to my sex life? What was it like to sleep for a full night? To see my friends? Play snooker or tennis? Go out to dinner? Travel somewhere, anywhere?

None of the above. Just the daily grind of unbearable love. We had given Anna her head, in the best Neillian manner: she lived at her own self-regulated pace, and we accommodated ours to hers. Barbara was better at it than I was. But within a year we agreed that maybe good old A.S. Neill had overstated his case (or maybe he was just better than us), and we decided occasionally to let Anna cry herself to sleep, and began gently to insist that she ate what, and when, we wished her to. It was a bit of a compromise, and it made life easier. After all, Neill insists that the innate selfishness of children lasts well into the teenage years, and it was exhausting merely to contemplate the carnage. Surely we could be a little selfish too?

But Neill is an absolutist here: freedom is not to be compromised, standards and regulations not to be imposed. It wasn't enough that little Anna, by the age of three, was utterly gorgeous, talkative, charming, pretty much self-regulating, and swore like a trooper. I wouldn't call her an entirely happy child, that would have been difficult in the context of her parents' marriage, but she was a considerable live wire, and a source of joy for us both. There are, Neill insists, no problem children, only problem parents, and we could see Anna paying some of the price in sleeplessness and anxiety. Was Neill wrong, or were we? I don't know, and there is no way to find out. The world in which Barbara and I found ourselves hardly allowed the rearing of free children, and to raise a Neillian little person in a relentlessly directive, frequently ugly, social environment is nigh impossible, as Neill acknowledges. We certainly would not have allowed her to go to Summerhill, however much we believed in it. Even if the home environment and schooling were worse for her, we wanted her with us, and she would have hated leaving home. She went to the free-est schools Leamington could provide, and years later Bertie spent a few years at King Alfred's School in London, where Neill had once taught. He loved it, and the kids were as free as birds, and almost as flighty as Mayzie.

In that very period, though, Summerhill was under attack, in a way that seemed to me shocking and inexplicable. Neill had been dead for many years, but much honoured in his time with honorary degrees and citations, and his works were required reading in education courses. Summerhill was a world famous school, and England should have been proud of it.

As early as 1949 the (rather enlightened) school inspectors who reported on the school praised Neill as a man of unusual integrity, described the children as 'natural, open-faced, and unselfconscious' to a remarkable degree, and gave their blessing to the school's ethos and continued existence. But it was a constant source of anxiety, at Summerhill, that one day the wrong inspectors might just turn up. Fifty years later, they did. A teacher at the time described their visit: 'I think the first image I have of it was when they came down the drive and there were eight of them marching with clipboards and suits. They were in twos.'

This ominous, robotic precision suggests a military attack – eight was an unusually large contingent – by bureaucrats who had clearly made up their minds before they arrived. The eight of them snooped about, quizzed teachers and children in a hostile manner, sniffed, looked down their educational noses, harrumphed in disapproval. The children didn't even have to attend classes! Lazy little buggers! They could play all the time if they wanted! How were they ever going to pass exams?

This was hardly news. It had been like that since 1921, but the disapproving inspectors were determined that, after seventy-eight years, something was going to be done about it. They recommended the closure of Summerhill unless it modified its practices. Estelle Morris, then Secretary of State for Education, gave a typically Blairite account of the matter: *of course* Summerhill was entitled to its own philosophy, how marvellous, they just shouldn't practise it. Surely the children could at the very least be encouraged to attend lessons? Otherwise, they might (in the inspectors' words) 'confuse the pursuit of idleness for the exercise of personal liberty'.

Summerhill was hardly likely to capitulate to such an attack, and the inspectors soon ruled that it be shut down. The school appealed, citing the report as manifestly biased and incompetent in a remarkable number of ways. The details of the ensuing battle are disturbing, and comical, but the essential case was simply and eloquently put by Geoffrey Robertson QC: 'It is freedom or nothing, because if it is less than freedom it is not Summerhill.'

The loss of such a school, such a national asset, should not be contemplated. Summerhill fought and fought, and won. Distinguished educationists and former students spoke up on its behalf. Statistics were produced that showed that Summerhillians, in fact, did rather better than the national average at examinations. The ensuing case cost the school £130,000, and contributions flowed in from round the world. An attack on Summerhill was an attack on one of the foremost incarnations of the very idea of freedom. Freedom to be and to grow as one wants, freedom not to be directed, freedom to have one's own voice. Freedom from *schooling*, as it is usually understood. 'We are faced,' said Bertrand Russell (who founded a progressive school with his wife Dora in 1927), 'with the paradoxical fact that education has become one of the chief obstacles to intelligence and freedom of thought.'

Called 'the oldest children's democracy in the world', the school has always been run on a one-person one-vote basis, and at school meetings the five-year-olds had as much right to speak, deliberate and vote as Neill did. (They fired him once, and he pottered about contentedly in his workshop until he was rehired a couple of weeks later.) The system works wonderfully well, and has been a model for those mitigated examples of student representation in the student councils that are now commonplace in most schools.

But that's just a sop, and everyone knows it. Administrators and teachers actually run schools, and though they claim to be keen to hear student opinion, it is their own that counts. All animals are equal, Orwell's *Animal Farm* reminds us, only some are more equal than others. Except at Summerhill. I wish I'd got that job. I would have loved it, all of it, even – particularly – the voting. But I'd bet that Summerhill graduates are even less likely than I to vote for politicians. How could you participate in such a farce when you have direct experience of what a real democracy feels like?

The answer to this sceptical dismissiveness may be found in a single word: Obama. I had managed, in my fastidious withdrawal from political engagement, to resist the political attractiveness of Bobby Kennedy (spoiled rich kid), George McGovern (boring), even of Bill Clinton (rather fun, but smarmy). But Obama? I began my engagement with him in ignorant scepticism, and was gradually won over, and finally converted. He was both one of us and different. He carried himself with perfect ease, was not disfigured by either ideology or a need to be liked. If anyone could make one less embarrassed by America and Americanness, it was this remarkable hybrid. Though obviously highly ambitious, he struck one not as a politician, neither on the make nor (like Tony Blair) in love with the mere taking of power, but as a complex and highly admirable person, offering himself wholly and humbly. How could one not vote for him?

I did.

13

MATILDA, ALICE
AND LITTLE RICK

Matilda longed for her parents to be good and loving
and understanding and honourable and intelligent. The
fact that they were none of these things was something
she had to put up with. It was not easy to do so.

Roald Dahl, *Matilda*

The winner of the Booker Prize in 1988 was Peter Carey's *Oscar
and Lucinda*. A great romp of a story about an unlikely couple of
émigrés from Victorian England to Australia, the novel has epic
proportions, is crazily engaging, perfectly wrought, felt, and visu-
alized. But *Oscar and Lucinda*, much as I love it, was not the best
novel published in 1988. That honour should have gone to Roald
Dahl's *Matilda*, which is more likely to be read in a hundred years'
time, even, than Peter Carey's great novel. *Matilda* is Roald Dahl's
masterpiece, and loved by everyone who reads it: by children, by
parents who read it to their children, and by adults themselves, all
on their own.

That is how I first read it, anyway, when I bought a copy in
December of 1988. It was intended as a Christmas present for Anna
and Bertie (then fourteen and eight), and I duly inscribed it, wrapped
it up clumsily, and added it proudly to the vast mound of other presents Barbara was stashing away under our Christmas tree – a ghostly

glittering object teetering uneasily in a bucket of dirt in the kitchen, having been thoroughly 'vulgarized' by Bertie, who thought it essential that no bit of green emerge from the decorated object. The finished tree was submerged in tinsel, chocolates covered in gold and red foil were attached to every branch, baubles and hanging glass balls, both clear and coloured, balanced precariously and, at the top, a painted angel panned its unconvincing eyes spookily over the proceedings.

On Christmas morning the kids tore through the wrapping paper with scant regard for the enclosed contents, so anxious were they to get on to the next present. 'A football? Oh, thanks.' Tear, tear. 'Nice blouse, mum, thanks.' What else, what more? 'Oh, is this the new Roald Dahl? Cool!' The book, with the winsome Matilda staring out from the dust wrapper, was cast aside like an abandoned child.

As the gluttonous procedure went on, I was hardly able to suppress my usual spasm of distaste. I didn't grow up celebrating Christmas, and the sheer excess of it has always disturbed me. I was in constant conflict with Barbara about this, me trying to rein her in, she trying to get me to unbend a little and curb my rampant scepticism about the holiday. She was, after all, right. Christmas is what one does, everyone does it: it's not for enjoying, it's for getting on with. I consoled myself, on this particular Christmas morning, by picking up *Matilda*, and coiled in a chair next to the fire, still half-asleep, looking up occasionally in what I hoped was a benign manner, sipping coffee and reading. The book was wonderful, utterly engrossing from the first page.

The presents were soon opened. We stuffed the fire with the wrapping paper – *hours* of wrapping paper – and started making pancakes for Christmas breakfast.

'Will you play Cluedo with me, dad?' asked Bertie, tearing the cellophane off his new game.

'Sure,' I said, with a lack of enthusiasm that Barbara and Anna both noted, but which Bertie was too young to register.

'Great!' he said. 'Teach me how to play.'

'You want to play too, Anna?' I asked.

'No thanks,' she said. 'I'll help mum with the dinner after I get dressed.'

Lunch was served at two. The Cluedo game was put away, the presents stashed in a sad and still unregarded pile in the corner, Grandpa Freddie and Grandma Catherine tucked in to the mounds of food, Barbara hunched wearily but benignly in her chair, the kids and I wolfed our portions and came back for more. Glasses were refilled, the wine flowed more freely than the conversation. Afterwards they would eat their sweets – I *hate* mince pies and Christmas pudding, if I had my way they would be banned, or executed – and then waddle across the room to watch the Queen's Speech on the telly.

'Excuse me for a second,' I said, drawing my chair from the table. I went over to the pile of presents, picked up *Matilda*, and headed upstairs to the loo.

I knew I'd have twenty minutes before the alarm bells started even to tinkle. By that time I was already on page 45, and had not the slightest desire to go back to the festivities.

Ten minutes later – page 63 – there was a knock at the door.

'Dad,' came Bertie's voice. 'I need the loo.'

There was little urgency in his tone. I suspected somebody had sent him.

'Use the downstairs one,' I said grumpily. 'I may be some time.'

'Grandma's using it,' he said.

'Piss in the garden then,' I said stiffly, turning to page 64, 'because I'm not coming out, not soon. Then go and watch telly.'

'I'm bored,' he said grumpily.

'Well, I'm not.' I said. 'I'm having a great time.'

'You're not pooing, you're reading!' he said.

'They go together. Now go away.'

He went downstairs to report this to the waiting crowd.

A few minutes later – page 87 – there was a further knock on the door.

'Dad,' said Anna in her strictest voice, 'I know what you are doing! You've got *Matilda* in there! I looked on the presents pile and it's gone! And it's mine and Bert's and I want to read it right now.'

'*I* am reading it right now,' I said. 'Possession is nine-tenths of the law. You get it next. Bad luck. You'll just have to wait.'

And she did, on the carpet right outside the loo. After a few minutes – page ninety-nine – she was joined by her brother.

'Dad!' they'd expostulate together, knocking ferociously on the door. 'Mum says you're to come out right now!'

'Bugger off!'

'It's our book!' they'd shout, knocking recurrently.

And it was, and they got it, but not until I had skimmed my way to the end some half an hour later, deposited it in their greedy little hands, and made my way to the kitchen. The old folks were asleep in front of the TV, and Barbara was furious.

'I hope you're thoroughly satisfied,' she said icily.

And I was. It was a wonderful book. 'Certainly,' I said. 'Anna and Bertie must read it as soon as possible.'

A 'tiny girl, with dark hair and a round serious face', loveable, independent and preternaturally precocious – illustrated with heart-rending sympathy by Quentin Blake – Matilda has been cata-strophically born into the wrong family. Her father is a flagrantly dishonest second-hand car dealer, her mother a bingo addict, her brother a cowed daddy's boy. Thoroughly ignored when she isn't being derided, Matilda quietly teaches herself to read, and before she is five has read virtually the entire stock of the local library. Books have 'transported' her into new worlds; if only, she wished, her parents would read rather than watch the telly, for literature could give 'a view of life that they had never seen'. She reads most of the classics of adult fiction, though, she admits, she doesn't entirely understand Hemingway's stuff about men and women. (Neither do I.)

Books are soon banned from the house, and Matilda's cleverness – she can also do huge mathematical calculations in her head – is mocked, when it is noticed at all. Her response to this abuse, fortunately, is not withdrawal, but anger. She counter-attacks: puts superglue on her father's porkpie hat, stuffs a parrot up the chimney so that it seems there is a ghost in the sitting room, pours peroxide in her father's hair tonic: 'her safety valve, the thing that prevented her from going round the bend, was the fun of devising and dishing out these splendid punishments.' The phrase 'going round the bend', while lightly stated is nevertheless fully considered. It is only Matilda's remarkable capacity to marshal anger that can save her, as she is to find when she begins a primary school experience that consists not of neglect and belittlement, but of outright sadistic abuse. The headmistress of Crunchem Hall primary school, Miss Agatha Trunchbull, loathes children, particularly the littlest ones. (She denies having been one herself.) An Amazonian ex-athlete, now much given to the throwing of children instead of hammers, she is universally feared and detested.

It is only the presence of the young teacher Miss Honey that makes Matilda's ordeal tolerable. Astonished by the child's brilliance and maturity, she takes the little girl to her heart, but (being herself under the control of the headmistress, who turns out to be her aunt) she cannot offer much protection. But a child of Matilda's resourcefulness, having found such a mentor, is more able to cope for herself. She has, she soon finds, remarkable telekinetic powers: she can make objects move just by concentrating hard on them. She topples a glass of water (with a newt in it) right on to Miss Trunchbull's lap.

The parallels with Harry Potter's uncongenial family situation and gradual discovery of his true nature have been remarked. Like the boy wizard, Matilda's magical powers are most useful when she is angry, as a means of self-protection. The results are astonishing and gratifying. When she performs the 'miracle' of the tipping of the glass, Matilda is freed from fear, and the experience is little short of transcendent: her 'whole face was transfigured . . . quite beautiful in a blaze of silence'. When she recovers, her face registers a 'seraphic' calm: 'I was flying,' she reports, 'past the stars on silver wings.' She has become an angel, but not a soppy one. She is an angel of vengeance.

Soon enough Miss Trunchbull is defeated and banished, and Matilda's parents embark for Australia in a *great* hurry, abandoning her to the loving care of Miss Honey, now reinstated in the family home that had been usurped by her wicked aunt. Matilda's magical powers, no longer necessary, have faded, though her emotional and intellectual ones are now free to flower. We end, as fairy tales should, with a happy child, loved and loving, free to be herself, as all children ought to be, and so often are not.

One can easily imagine a real life Matilda, lacking only the spunk, precocity and anger, who instead withdrew into herself, festered and shrank, ending up not in a Miss Honey's happy home, reclaimed by love, but on a therapist's couch. I love Roald Dahl's works about children because he is entirely on their side, remarkably able to understand their point of view. To do so, he once said, you need to get down on your hands and knees to observe the adults towering above, issuing demands. Thus we have his first description of the kindly Miss Honey, who 'possessed that rare gift . . . to understand totally the bewilderment and fear that so often overwhelm young children who for the first time in their lives are herded into a classroom and told to obey orders'.

The language reminds me of Alice Miller, the Swiss psychotherapist, known for her advocacy of what she called 'the inner child', who has written at length of the 'fear, despair, and utter loneliness' of her own early childhood and schooling. It was Miller's experience – a common one in her view – that the pressure of expectation imposed on her caused her to shut down emotionally and creatively, withdraw into herself, and develop a persona that suppressed all memory of the 'psychic terror' of childhood. And as an exemplar of that psychic terror there can be no bettering Agatha Trunchbull, the incarnation of everything uncontrollable, arbitrary and overpowering about adults, seen from a child's point of view.

If there appears something farfetched in this leap from Roald Dahl to Alice Miller, it seems natural enough to me, but then again I was (at the time I gave *Matilda* to Anna and Bertie) in therapy with a Hampstead therapist trained in the Alice Miller school. And, funnily enough, I never made any connection between my love of Matilda, and my admiration for Alice. Sometimes I can't see what is in front of my face, but in any case it has been a recurrent fact about my adult personality that I have continued to love children's books and films.

Not in some nostalgic way, as elderly men often go goocy when they read *Winnie the Pooh* to their grandchildren. No, I have read all of the classics of children's literature, but I keep up with a lot of the new things too: have queued at midnight with Anna to get each new Harry Potter, and finished all of them within a week; read all of Philip Pullman with surpassing admiration, including the insufficiently admired Sally Lockhart mysteries; loved *The Wind on Fire* trilogy of William Nicholson. And films like *The Jungle Book, Short Circuit, Back to the Future*, and especially *E.T.* are more likely to give me pleasure, on re-viewing, than are the films of Jean Renoir or Ingmar Bergman.

So going into therapy to get into closer connection with some inner and largely forgotten 'little Rick' should have been easier for me than many people. I am, in most respects, thoroughly childish (or, as I prefer, child-like). I'm fidgety, noisy and attention-seeking, love watching cartoons and reading comics, am greedy, over-anxious to please and easily hurt, competitive and self-referring, have a short attention span and hate doing chores, am likely to blurt out inappropriate things about myself or others, and am guided almost entirely by the pleasure principle. If I have problems with my inner child, it is in keeping him in, rather than letting him out. He doesn't need an advocate, he needs a keeper. What I need to discover is my inner *adult*. I said this repeatedly to my therapist, but he wasn't having any of it. Continuing to act out little Rick's anxieties, he observed, was hardly the same thing as going back, re-experiencing them, and allowing their resolution through new understanding and empathy.

It's generally a bad idea, when in therapy, to read the relevant texts. It is regarded as intellectualization, and hence some form of defence: one ought to concentrate on feeling, not on obtaining some mastery of the theory on which the analysis is based. But you can't pretend to be someone you're not, so I consulted the relevant Alice Miller books anyway, finding pretty quickly that I didn't actually need to *read* them. I flicked through *The Body Never Lies, For Your Own Good, Thou Shalt Not Be Aware, Banished Knowledge*, and *Breaking Down the Wall of Silence*. The titles are remarkably similar, in that they all point to the same phenomenon. As a theorist, Alice Miller is a one trick pony. But it's a good trick, and it takes some learning, which is presumably why she keeps repeating herself, like some evangelist intent on saving souls.

She is particularly good on the ways in which childhood unhappiness manifests itself in adult illness and somatic symptoms, some of them serious, many apparently trivial. You don't have to develop asthma or cancer to pay the price of an unhappy childhood: cigarette smoking, nail-biting, and obsessive dieting (to pick just those symptoms that fit me) are all apparently adult signals of childhood abuse: 'all these illnesses or addictions are screams of the body that want to be heard.' In an interview in 1987, Miller put her core insight perfectly:

We do not need books about psychology in order to learn to respect our children. What we need is a total revision of the methods of child rearing and our traditional view about it. The way we were treated as small children is the way we treat ourselves the rest of our lives: with cruelty or with tenderness and protection. We often impose our most agonizing suffering upon ourselves and, later, on our children.

Surely this is an insight worth repeating. But quite how it would help me with the problems that had driven me back into a therapist's arms was unclear. I was, still, in an unhappy and uncreative marriage. I could not, still, write with any freedom or pleasure. How could these blockages diminish by reference to some putative inner child?

Alice Miller seemed unable to offer anything more satisfying than an explanation, which isn't much use. But she was unexpectedly helpful with regard to the problem of writer's block. The least known of her books, probably, is *Pictures of a Childhood*, and gives an account of her life as a painter, together with colour plates of a number of her pictures. Small in scale, semi-abstract and highly coloured, like a mixture of Klee and Miro, they have a numinous quality, with tiny, haunting figures seeming to peer out of the grounds as if crying for attention.

The pictures depict something of the artist's unconscious, and give unmediated access to that unhappy, 'inner' little girl with whom Miller (despite two full analyses) had never quite been able to recall or to sympathize. She had painted as a child, and been 'encouraged' (by which she means bullied) by her mother into excelling at her work. The young Alice's response to this putative 'support' was to dry up entirely: '. . . it is clear to me in retrospect that my strong resistance to formal training, to thought and planning in the area of my painting, was highly significant, perhaps even saved my life.'

Only in adult life did she resume painting, and found that she could only paint if she did so 'spontaneously', for unless she did 'the child in me rebelled and immediately became defiant'. But if she simply played with the paint, and allowed whatever wanted to be expressed to come out in its own manner, then she took immense satisfaction in the process, and the pictures flowed, as if naturally. They gave her access, she found, to the child within, and gave that long suppressed little girl, at last, a language of her own.

Whether the pictures were any good (they are) was not the point. They were free, unmediated, and responded to no pressures except those from within, demanding release. The implication was clear to me. Though it is easier to see how the process would work with painting rather than writing, nevertheless there was something to be learned. Might it be possible for me to write like that? Spontaneously, without premeditation, playfully? 'First thought, best thought,' as Allen Ginsberg put it. It was an unlikely proposition: after all, my academic training had taught me exactly the opposite process. Writing is the highly meditated, careful and considered outcome of mature consideration. *Avoid error!* There is nothing playful or spontaneous about it, it's a thoroughly conscious, largely defensive process.

I thought about this for a time, talked about it with my therapist, wondered how to take the first step.

'Trust your unconscious,' he said. 'It'll tell you what to do if you don't fuss about it.'

I listened intently, but all I heard was a voice saying, 'Just do it for God's sake!' A week later I started a novel. It was finished in six weeks. It was harder *not* to write than to write. If I put it down for a moment my head teemed with thoughts, scenes, images and conversations, and I had to get back to the typewriter. I banged away at it, surprisingly happy.

Entitled *Bottom's Dream*, it was predictably enough about me (in the guise of a psychotherapist with doubts), unhappily married to a difficult painter, trying to find a comfortable way to live in the world, and failing. (The poor old protagonist commits suicide.) The novel was personally and sexually explicit to a ridiculous degree, but it was really only a symptom of my angry and demoralized psychological state, and I didn't show it to any publisher. My therapist thought it 'remarkable', but I'll bet he said that to all the girls. I got a more disinterested opinion from the novelist Peter Ackroyd. When I told him I was writing an autobiographical novel he wrinkled his nose: 'Darling,' he said, 'why don't you write about something *interesting*?' I haven't reread *Bottom's Dream* since, and would not wish to, though I am curiously resistant to throwing it away. If there is anything worth returning to, it is in the nature of the doubts about Freud and psychoanalysis that it adumbrates, about which more later.

What was thrilling was that the writing came as if naturally, and was a cause of pleasure. All you had to do was believe in yourself, let it go spontaneously, allow whatever is in you to find its own voice, and fill up the page. The author of the book was called 'Rick Gekoski'. He had never written anything before, 'R.A. Gekoski' having been responsible for my previous works. I liked this new fellow better; if he was sometimes desperate, at least he wrote in a voice that I recognized as my own. I had Alice Miller to thank for this. And it wasn't just my inner child who came to my aid, but my inner Matilda as well. All you need to do to banish your Miss Trunchbull, after all, is to concentrate entirely, direct your eyes, and let the energy flow, and you will end up, victorious, feeling like an angel. (Whether you write a good novel is quite another issue.)

The key to such triumphs lies, I think, in the kind of stories that you listen to, read, and make up for and about yourself. That's how Matilda, aged four, releases herself into an imaginative world, to deal with and to supplant the realities of an inadequate real one.

In effect, she makes herself through reading, and in so doing offers a model, and a hope. And yet – this is too easily missed – she is also a sad example of a child who has had to become, prematurely, an adult: Matilda forfeits her girlhood because of the abuse she has suffered. She has been 'robbed', as A.S. Neill put it, of 'her right to play'. I suspect that Roald Dahl would have regarded Crunchem School as a representative, if exaggerated, example of what happens to most children in their early education. It didn't happen at Summerhill.

Anna and Bertie adored *Matilda*, and he went on to read all of Roald Dahl's books with passionate delight. When he had finished the last one, he asked what other writers he'd like? I didn't know what to say – there aren't any, quite, in the same league – and he's been disappointed ever since. (Just like me as a child, wanting more writers like Dr Seuss.) Bertie thinks nobody is as good to read as Roald Dahl, and I rather agree. Perhaps he should have won the Nobel Prize?

14

AYER AND ANGELS

> We say that a sentence is factually significant to any given person if, and only if, he knows how to verify the proposition which it purports to express – that is, if he knows what observations would lead him, under certain conditions, to accept the proposition as being true, or reject it as being false.
>
> A.J. Ayer, *Language, Truth and Logic*

Sixty-eight per cent of all Americans, I am told, believe in the existence of angels. This fact is frequently cited – I have done so myself – as an instance of the gullible religiosity of the American people. I can be quite rude on the subject. I have recently, though, begun to wonder if it is fair of me, quite, to be so dismissive. My unease is not philosophical: I know that the concept 'angel' is unclear, and that it is equally uncertain what 'believing' in such an entity might entail. Nor is it because I don't believe in angels myself, under *any* construction of those terms, but because I wish I did.

Not in that self-serving way in which I want to believe in an afterlife, the thought of which would be consoling while alive and (I presume) agreeable when dead. There is nothing self-interested in my search for my lost angels. By which I don't mean those banal beings who loiter listlessly on clouds, playing harps, translucent and bored: that's what happens when you can't eat, smoke, play poker or kiss girls. No, God forgive me, I never want to be one of them; give me a short sharp shock of damnation any time, something bracing and sexy.

What I want to believe in is not the bloodless seraphim of popular Christian iconography, but the angels of the poets: in Donne's angel with 'wings of aire', Blake's perky friend the angel in *The Marriage of Heaven and Hell*, Byron's angels hoarse with singing out of tune, Yeats's 'great angels' who visit us in our hours of need, Eliot's 'dark angel'. One could go on and on, citing angels: dear Matilda, enraptured, like an angel, or Emily Dickinson's, with 'even feet – and uniforms of snow'. When we peruse the imaginative world of writers, it appears that without their angels they are as nothing. I wish that I could have some, even one, to rescue me from the mundane linearity of my mind, its relentless proseyness.

Not that we Jews get a lot of angels, they're largely the province of the Goyim. I went, reluctantly, to Temple until my Bar Mitzvah provided the desired presents and freed me from further theological obligation, and I cannot recall any talk of angels or devils, though the Old Testament is stuffed with them. But we didn't care. It is one of the many charms of my religion, weak though my practice of it may be, that it focuses so entirely on this life, and on the moral obligations attendant on being a person in a community. All of that Christian insistence on doing good in order to be rewarded – *why not?* asks Pascal, *what do you have to lose?* – strikes me as the very worst reason to live a moral life.

So when a Jew comes up with angels, they're likely to be peculiar ones, like Allen Ginsberg's panoply of angels, Mohammedan, Indian, blonde and naked, mad but sane – hardly angelic at all really, more like Allen in fact, who no doubt thought himself one of them. Such an angel is an emblem of translucent otherness, of the ideal towards which the imagination strives, yet which is only just imaginable. Ginsberg wants the company of angels, in order to escape from the confines of the mundanely rational.

Keats, after all, had exactly the same concern and he wasn't even Jewish. Consider the lines from *Lamia*:

Philosophy will clip an angel's wings,
Conquer all mysteries by rule and line,
Empty the haunted air, and gnomed mine,
Unweave a rainbow . . .

If I had to choose the one philosophical text that most clearly and powerfully exemplifies the hostility of philosophy to poetry, it might well be A.J. Ayer's *Language, Truth and Logic*. Though published in 1936, Ayer's text maintains the capacity to shock. I first read it at Penn, and admired its lucidity and bravado, regarding logical positivism (as it was called) as the *ne plus ultra* of Humean scepticism. Indeed, one of my reasons for wishing to go to Oxford was that I would have a chance to hear Ayer lecture, for he was one of the luminaries of an excellent school of philosophy. Freddy (as he was known, later Sir Freddy) and his foxy motorcyclist wife, the American journalist Dee Wells, were central figures in both the Oxford universe, and that of North London's intellectual classes. Ayer was media-hungry, anxious to make philosophy widely available. He appealed to the kind of people who read the broadsheets, and listened to the Third Programme, the BBC's highbrow radio broadcast that began in 1946, and which was sometimes derided as merely 'two dons talking' – one of whom was frequently Ayer. Because his philosophical position was radical, surprising, even shocking, to persons of all persuasions – virtually all you needed, to be offended by Ayer, was to *have* a persuasion – he was much in demand. He was a controversialist, loved to argue, and was a formidable opponent.

What he opposed were those metaphysical concepts and

statements that he labelled 'nonsense', and those further proposi-
tions – like those of ethics or aesthetics – which he regarded as
simply 'emotive', and consequently impossible to verify (in effect,
further forms of nonsense). The use of 'nonsense' as the category
into which the non-verifiable was tossed, willy-nilly, was inten-
tionally provocative. God is good? Turner is a wonderful painter?
It is better to do good than evil? Steak and kidney pie is delicious?
One finds contentment in nature? Any football team is to be
preferred to Manchester United? Shakespeare is the best writer?
These are not truths, all are nonsense of one sort or the other. It
made it impossible to be English without embarrassing oneself
philosophically.

Of course Ayer, a genial and literate man burdened with the
normal baggage of belief, who passionately supported both the
Labour Party and Tottenham Hotspur, was having some fun with
his key concept. He was, after all, in his early twenties when he
wrote *Language, Truth and Logic*, and anxious to make his name.
(Isaiah Berlin described him at the time as 'an irresistible missile'.)
He later renounced his major arguments, but it didn't matter: the
book has sold over a million copies, and never gone out of print.

I was persuaded by Ayer for a time, at much the same age at
which he had written and published his book. He seemed so daring,
so assured, and so difficult to follow, that he must have been right.
But rereading it after many years, the book feels facile and dated,
and it's easy to see how it engendered the parodies in both *Beyond
the Fringe* and *Monty Python*.

Even so, one has to find a way to reject one's inner Ayer without
throwing one's sceptical babies out with the positivist bathwater.
Scepticism is a defining quality of intelligence, its free working is
essential to democratic culture and education (as opposed to indoctrination) is impossible without it. But you don't need to label a
good deal of man's deepest and best beliefs 'nonsense' to prove
yourself a sceptic. You have to be sceptical about your scepticism.

After all, as Robert Frost observed, scepticism is merely that sort of inquisitiveness that takes nothing for granted: does it consist of anything more, he asks, than 'Well, what have we here?'

Like *Finnegans Wake*, which Joyce was writing at the same time, *Language, Truth and Logic* represents both the apotheosis and the *reductio ad absurdum* of a tradition. After Joyce's exhausting work, it is hard to imagine what further innovations a novelist might undertake: it is a book from which you can only go backwards. So, too, *Language, Truth and Logic* defined so clearly the outer limits of philosophical scepticism as to make one back away from it, aware that if such a frame of mind leads to such conclusions, there must be something wrong with the entire enterprise. Ultimately, Ayer is the Holden Caulfield of philosophy, childishly obsessed by phoniness. Indeed, if you throw out the term 'nonsense', and replace it with, say, 'difficult to verify using rigorous criteria', then the force of Ayer's argument is greatly diminished.

Great works of literature contain and convey truths, and if the processes needed to understand them are different from those of philosophy, they are truths nonetheless. Otherwise it would be impossible to learn from literature, which certainly contradicts one's constant sense of enlargement and enhancement in relishing the metaphysical poets, suffering through *Lear*, or smiling at the modulated ironies of Jane Austen. The 'truths' one is exposed to through such reading are not simple ones, and are often, sadly, transmitted by sloppy readers as truisms: gather ye rosebuds while ye may, be kind to your daughters even when they seem difficult, make a good and sensible marriage. Those are truths of a banal but universal sort, and we do not need our great writers to remind us of them, only to make them glow. As George Eliot observed, 'the angels come to visit us, and we only know them when they are gone.' It is the obligation of poet and novelist to invite them back. And you don't find any of them in *Language, Truth and Logic*.

Life was easier without Freddy Ayer, and I became, I think, a more agreeable and less contentious person released from his influence: less likely to reflexively seek counter-arguments, repel 'emotive' excess, demand verifiability. In any case, I had begun to believe that verification was an unsatisfactory principle, best replaced by Karl Popper's insistence that falsification is a more reliable procedure. If you sit, for the first time, under an apple tree and watch the apples falling, it may be some time before you regard it as inevitable that they will continue to do so, and longer still until you posit the law of gravity. But if just one apple goes up rather than down, you will know that there was no such necessity after all, and no such law.

So: goodbye Freddy? It didn't turn out that way, not quite. Being infected by radical scepticism is like contracting malaria: you may seem to get over it, but it recurs unexpectedly. It's in your system, ineradicable. I'd experienced a decade of partial remission when I had a renewed outbreak of the fever, and it wasn't difficult for me to locate the cause. It was called by various names, but if I say 'post-structuralism' you may recognize what I mean.

It is a difficult term to define: indeed, since none of the associated figures (who included Barthes, Foucault, Lacan and Derrida), all responding to and rejecting structuralism, would have described himself as a 'post-structuralist'. The term is a generic one, and there is no adequate single definition, save an ostensive one. You want to know what post-structuralism is? It's him, and her, and this, and that. And if these writers didn't themselves have imperialist ambitions, their followers certainly did. These crusaders invaded English departments round the world, uncombatably aggressive, grimacing weirdly, speaking in a hideous foreign tongue, anxious to conquer and to convert.

All of a sudden, instead of English we seemed to have French, not the mellifluous French of Mallarmé, but an ugly, polysyllabic, hybrid tongue only comprehensible to members of the tribe.

Literature was superseded by *écriture*; the common pursuit of true judgement replaced by a culture in which readers replaced authors, relativism (and an associated multi-culturalism) prevailed. A whole variety of 'readings' were suddenly creditable, and the text came to be regarded as a signifier for more important issues that lurked latently behind it. Texts were puzzles, signs and symptoms, cultural artefacts.

I am, as I have said, an unregenerate practical critic. I believe that the greatest and most rewarding of readerly activities involves painstaking attention to the words on the page. And so it was distinctly uncongenial to me to observe, over a period of years beginning in the late 1970s, that my best and brightest students were increasingly influenced by continental linguists, philosophers, and psychoanalysts whose approach to literature – if they distinguished the 'literary' from other forms of 'signification' – had nothing of the painstaking particularity that I associate with good reading.

English Studies has always suffered from a certain methodological softness, and these new writers seemed to offer something harder-edged and more intellectually challenging. There were difficult new concepts to be mastered, and newly problematic ones (like 'the author', 'the reader', and 'the text') to be jettisoned or radically refined. Soon nobody wanted to 'read' texts, they wanted to deconstruct them.

In spite of all post-structuralist argument to the contrary, the reader is not the maker of what he experiences. He is subjected to his author, imposed upon, invaded, possessed. He hears the voices, is totally exposed to the characters of a novel, and has no control over their presence or absence. You can't simply put a book down or away. Books are peculiarly adhesive. A throng of characters clamorously demand attention, voices rise and fall, fade in and out of our consciousness. We suspend the everyday, ignore the telephone and doorbell, eat with our eyes fixed to the page, overcome, ravaged by the demands of the text. It is no wonder that writers – who are the best readers – claim that books provide them with the best of friends. Dickens refers to 'the friendships we form with books', and Charles Lamb regarded books as 'the best company'. Would Jacques Derrida agree?

Derrida's *On Grammatology* (roughly: the science of writing) was a much-cited example of this radical new line of thought. Here is a representative paragraph, from Chapter 2:

Now from the moment that one considers the totality of determined signs, spoken, and *a fortiori* written, as unmotivated institutions, one must exclude any relationship of natural subordination, any natural hierarchy among signifiers or orders of signifiers. If 'writing' signifies inscription and especially the durable institution of a sign (and that is the only irreducible kernel of the concept of writing), writing in general covers the entire field of linguistic signs. In that field a certain sort of instituted signifiers may then appear, 'graphic' in the narrow and derivative sense of the word, ordered by a certain relationship with other instituted — hence 'written', even if they are 'phonic' — signifiers.

And, what is worse, imagine someone less intelligent than Derrida trying to think along similar lines, and then applying their conclusions to English literature. The results were harrowing. I remember sitting through lectures, seminars and presentations by over-excited practitioners of this new art, who were positively writhing with delight at their capacity to play with this new set of linguistic structures, analytic tools, and conceptual categories.

I tried, oh how I tried. I'd had problems with these aggravating continentals before: Like Freddy Ayer, I'd never got on with metaphysics. What the hell is 'time'? Or 'being'? Or, indeed, 'nothingness'? And who cares? I read the major texts painstakingly, then read them again because I forgot everything almost as soon as I had read it. Even the second readings didn't stick. (Try reading that Derrida quotation twice, and then make a précis of it.) It wasn't that I wasn't interested. I was. How can a teacher not be interested in material that excites his best students? No, the problem was that I hated it. Hated as in loathed and detested.

Hated as in A.J. Ayer: dismissively, contemptuously. 'Nonsense!' What a useful concept to revert to, what a terrific rejoinder. I slipped seamlessly into default mode, back to the ludicrously self-assured, judgemental self of my high school years. I had the perfectly annoying habit, at seventeen, of lifting my index finger into the air and announcing – while in discussion or argument – either *False!* (left finger) or *True!* (right finger). I thought of the fingers as Holden (left) and Allen (right) and believed that they provided sufficient guidance to make my way through my emotional and intellectual life.

I thought of these inward voices and their finger-manifestations as opposites. I had need of both: of the capacity to distinguish the phoney from the true, to be both sceptical and enthusiastic. It did not occur to me – curiously, stupidly – that my Holden and my Allen were manifestations of the same impulse. Both were outsiders, keen to subvert established values, unable to enter into a community of like-minded fellowship. It was on the basis of such inward counsel – am I tempted to say, alas? – that I came to live in a foreign culture, to marry a women maximally different from me, to choose a profession in which I was uncomfortable. To make of myself even more of an outsider, and to derive what comfort and amusement I could by observing the distance between my inner world and my surroundings. Though I am now a dual citizen, both American and English, I am also neither, and now feel equally uncomfortable in both cultures, except on those days when I don't. When I finally came to locate a voice in which I was comfortable writing, I found that whatever my apparent subject, my real subject was me, observing myself, indulging the discomforting ironies of a displaced person.

Nothing made me feel more alienated, more out of place, than this post-structuralist stuff. It was an example of an utterly un-verifiable rhetoric, like a private language, which a clan of initiates speak amongst themselves, like Yeats's silly theosophists and Rosicrucians. Gibberish, as Evelyn Waugh would have pronounced it, with a hard 'g'. My students (and their teachers who were given over to this new material) had begun to behave like members of a secret society. They not only talked a different language, their faces registered varieties of self-satisfaction and scorn usually reserved for scientologists. The jargon was appalling, and has been described by V.S. Naipaul as 'a way for one clown to tell the other that he is in the club'. I began to dislike them – my own students! – and was appalled by my reaction. If I couldn't overcome it, surely, it was time to go: to become the old that is swept out by the new. I was only in my middle thirties, and it was humiliating to be prematurely tone-deaf, prickly and antagonistic.

This defensiveness was personal, almost neurotic. I felt *offended* by post-structuralism, and (as any psychotherapist would tell you) there is something in need of analysis in such heated resistance and denial. Derrida makes the point himself, with uncharacteristic concision and elegance: 'Certain readers resented me when they could no longer recognize their territory, their institution.' That would be me.

And yet, to be fair, there was plenty to admire in this new discourse, if one were allowed to pick and choose. From Lacan, for instance, there was the arresting concept of *absence*, a way of attending carefully to what isn't there, and is thus present in its very absence. Trivially, like Sartre's Monsieur Simonnot in *Les Mots*, whose non-attendance at a party seemed so much more powerful than anyone else's presence; more provocatively, in Freud's account of women, where lack of a penis becomes a defining quality. The further implications of the notion of absence, as applied to Freud, were to become a major topic for me in the coming years.

From Derrida my major borrowing was the idea of using concepts 'under erasure', which is a clumsy phrase that I try never to *say*, but which has proven conceptually useful. The idea, first mooted by Heidegger, is that there is a set of concepts which one needs, but which are nonetheless inadequate. We have already noticed the process in Philip Roth's need to use the term 'self', while at the same time denying its existence. Derrida's method is straightforward, if curious: first you write the word which is causing you difficulty, then cross it out, and then you print both the word and the deletion. Because the word is conceptually compromised, you have to cross it out; since it is necessary, it has to be employed.

Think, for instance, of *Women in Love*, in which Rupert Birkin professes himself disgusted by the very concept 'love', all that merging and mingling, the two-as-one loss of identity and separateness. But, asks his wife Ursula plaintively, 'don't you love me?' And he does. Being 'imprisoned within a limited, false set of concepts', he has to use what the language allows him. The received word is worn out, inadequate. If he has to use it at all, he wishes at the same time to disavow it. Love? Yuck. Cross it out. Do you love me? Sure. This rings true: we've all experienced something similar, though it makes it tricky writing a love letter.

But the fact that one can root about in the post-structuralist miasma and find some things worth taking home does not endear one to the whole project. If you want really to understand your post-structuralism, you have to correlate the new form of language to its essential form of life. Get yourself a table and some companions at Deux Magots, drink a lot of espresso, smoke Gitanes, talk all night, shrug and wave your hands about, purge all specificity and observation from your vocabulary and replace it with abstraction. Close your eyes, philosophize, and it will all make sense in a way quite inconceivable in a senior common room at an English university.

I had become, by these new standards, increasingly fusty – even I could see that – and if my chosen domain was indeed an English university, it had been taken over by these Gallified intruders. I couldn't even have a coffee (instant) and a cigarette (Benson and Hedges) in the common room without overhearing conversations which I could hardly understand, and which made me recoil with dislike. It wasn't very long before I regarded the entire project of 'reading' English 'literature' as itself under erasure, and before long the major *absence* was me.

I resigned from the Department of English in 1984. It would be inaccurate to claim that I had been pushed aside by the alien hordes; in fact, I'd wanted to leave almost from the very moment I got there. By the early eighties it had become clear to me, as I rose every morning, that it was becoming increasingly easy to distinguish work from pleasure. Though I still enjoyed a lot of what I was doing, my next attempt to escape had to be successful, or I would desiccate like a split coconut lying in the sun.

There was nothing there to compel me. Finish my book on Lawrence? It had gone dead some years before. Write another essay on the relations between Philosophy and Literature? I had nothing much further to say, and had ceased to care. I was only thirty-seven and I would say I'd burned out, if that didn't imply that there was once a flame. I never had that kind of passion, more a sort of fizz, and now I'd gone flat.

It was wrong for me. Becoming a university teacher was a bad choice based on insufficient self-knowledge. The life I was choosing wasn't zappy enough, nor was it ever likely to accommodate the rackety nervous energy that has always characterized me, nor the subversiveness, nor the need to play. I'd been seduced into going on with my studies by the mere fact that I was good at them. It is characteristic of the prevailing narcissism of academic life that teachers encourage their brightest students to emulate them, and the students are flattered and wish to follow. Perhaps this is true in most fields. Don't patients in therapy want to become analysts?

But the proof of the academic pudding is in the writing. I generally liked teaching, of that certain sort that kept its critical eye strictly on the text. But you can't go on doing that forever. The activity that defines the true academic – and that included only a small percentage of my colleagues – is the ongoing passion to do literary research, to write that new account of Dryden, or to investigate the link between the English and French romantics. You have to do more than want to pursue such topics, you have to need to. And that never made sense to me. *Need* to write a book on D.H. Lawrence? No, I *had* to, because the institution required it.

William James observes that, for a serious thinker, there are two possible imperatives: *Seek Truth!* or *Avoid Error!* As a younger man I had been greatly influenced by truth seekers – by Blake, Whitman and Ginsburg, say – but I had insufficient self-confidence to write with such freedom. No angels. To be a truth-seeker, the imperative implicitly is *Be Like Nietzsche!* – in which case you have actually to *be* like him: to have something to say, something new, and urgent. I didn't, and I don't. That's a good lesson to learn young, it saves you looking a considerable fool.

Avoiding error was the safer trail for me. I remained a sceptic, though not a radical one. I wasn't a radical anything: you can shed your Ayer without finding your angels. So you play it safe. Most academics do that: the work they produce is generally worthy, well-researched, competently presented. It makes certain that you, the reader, are aware of the context in which the debate takes place, and what other people have said about the topic. If most such work is fundamentally uninteresting – even those of my colleagues in the same field as me didn't read my work, nor I theirs – it is, at least, not *wrong*.

I suppose there is something likeable and modest in this: '*not*

Prince Hamlet, nor was meant to be.' So we academic Prufrocks were growing old together, mildly disappointed, listening to the mermaids singing in the distance, observing and commentating from below, as a crustacean feeds on the droppings of the freer and larger forms of life swimming above, and the angels wheel in the heavens unobserved.

When I announced my early retirement, a kindly colleague slipped in to my office, closed the door carefully, and whispered, 'I just want to say I think it is very brave of you, what you are doing.'

I knew what he meant: I had two young children, and my income as a part-time book dealer was just over £5,000 a year, or roughly a third of my salary as a senior lecturer. I was giving up the security of a tenured position. It was a risk, leaving. So what? At least it would get me out of an environment in which I felt increasingly crimped, where I had never found my own voice, and had long ago ceased to be any fun.

'I must say,' I replied, 'that when I think of another thirty years in this department I think it is very brave of you to stay.'

15

THE ROYAL ROAD

Insight such as this falls to one's lot but once in a
lifetime.

Sigmund Freud, Preface to
The Interpretation of Dreams

On Wednesday nights the nuts came. After dinner, Ruthie and
I had to promise to keep out of the way and to lower our voices.
No clomping up and down the stairs – it was a noisy, open-plan
'split-level' house, ill-designed and badly built – and it was essential, mom said, that her clients felt comfortable coming to their
sessions. She had set up her therapy room (which Ruthie called
the Nutcracker Suite) on the ground floor, and left the garage
door open so that there was private, if insalubrious, access at
that level. We were fascinated, and would peer through a cunningly
constructed gap in the venetian blinds in the living room above,
to see which 'nut' was arriving. I'm sure they must have seen us,
but mom never knew. She would have regarded our behaviour as
an example of 'hostility', which was one of her favourite terms.
Apparently there was a lot of it about, like teenage drunkenness.

We didn't realize it, of course, but Ruthie and I grew up in a
Freudian household. We'd been bottle-fed and toilet-trained
according to the precepts of Dr Spock, began our education at a
progressive school, and constantly encountered in our daily lives

the vocabulary and conceptual apparatus of the committed Freudian. When we didn't want to do what we were told, Mom called it 'resistance', and if we argued that was called 'denial'. If you denied denial, now that was 'hostile', and required both an apology and an interpretation. But to get fully interpreted you had to be 'open', and we remained resolutely closed. That was 'infantile' of us, even if we were children.

We were frequently told what we *really* wanted and *really* meant. What we thought we felt was often interpreted as projection or displacement, and was either felt by, or towards, someone else. Our mistakes and forgetfulness were greeted with raised eyebrows, and our slips of the tongue revealed, apparently, repressed truths and wishes. When I was thirteen, my mother accompanied me on my yearly check-up at the optician. He explained the mechanics of my growing short-sightedness, which had led to the recent humiliation of having to wear glasses. I made up for my disability by demonstrating my knowledge of the physiology of the eye.

'Does this myopia indicate,' I asked, 'some malfunction of the rectum?'

There was a long pause.

'Do you mean the retina?' asked the bemused doctor.

My mother peered at me intently, and avoided the optician's glance. I was lucky she didn't make me an appointment with a therapist, or a proctologist. We hurried home in the car, silently, both of us embarrassed by whatever it was I had revealed about myself, after which she disappeared upstairs for a time, presumably to consult her psychoanalytic library. I'd skimmed through much of it myself, but Freud's books – of which there were many – were a relatively poor source of stimulating material. He was, obviously enough, obsessed by sex, but not in a way that generated a reciprocal excitement. I looked, particularly, at *The Interpretation of Dreams* – having had some pretty hot ones myself – but didn't learn a lot from it.

Though *The Interpretation of Dreams* was to become one of the defining books not merely of my own life, but of all of our lives, I am not sure I have ever read it, as in read it through from cover to cover. There is a lot in it that is pedestrian, repetitive and boring. I have consulted it, quoted it, referred to it, admired it. My experience is not, I suspect, uncommon. Kant and Hegel are misunderstood only after a proper reading of their works, whereas Freud has penetrated the common realm so comprehensively that it might be regarded as a sign of pedantry to have to read him. His terminology penetrates our common discourse, his central concepts – neurosis, the unconscious, id, ego and superego, the processes of repression, displacement and projection, the Oedipus complex, penis envy and castration anxiety – are confidently, if inaccurately, deployed by a public who can instantly interpret the 'Freudian' implications of anything from one banana to two peaches. And if it is now common to deplore the results of Freud's speculations – the narcissism, permissiveness and promiscuity that are alleged to be his legacy – it is impossible not to see the world through Freudian lenses: seamlessly relating childhood to adulthood, motivation to behaviour, the intended or manifest to the symbolic or latent.

Freud's work provides the model for introspection in the twentieth century, in which the implications of the child being father to the man have been the focus of the inward journey. Freud was a remarkable observer of infantile experience, and recaptures the child's experience of the world, from the first relations to the breast, through the growing awareness of selfhood and of the body, the struggle for bowel control and growing sensual awareness, to the rise of Oedipal feeling, and subsequent sexual awakening: the maelstrom of feeling that every child experiences, and which is our common heritage. *The Interpretation of Dreams* is the first stage of Freud's personal exploration of these themes, and of himself. The book is not, as claimed, a scientific treatise, nor is it a handbook to dream interpretation. It is Freud's autobiography, and it provides a template for one's own.

Self-analysis convinced Freud of the importance of dreams as the 'royal road' to the unconscious: it was through the interpretation of his own dreams that he recovered in himself that distressing matrix of hostility and desire towards his father and mother that was later to be termed the Oedipus complex. Audaciously, he decided that this apparently idiosyncratic disposition must represent a universal human tendency, that what he found in himself must be found in others: an intellectual procedure equally characteristic of brilliant people and of very stupid ones.

My formal immersion in Freud's work, while initiated at school by Miss Wyeth, accelerated, under the pressure of necessity, at Oxford. Barbara had nabbed Oxford's only Freudian therapist as her daily companion, confessor (he was, nicely, an ex-cleric) and consolation. It was relentless, this systematic and all-encompassing reflection, and it was no time before I wanted 'to get help' in my mom's phrase, of my own.

I think I was lucky in finding a Jungian, not because I was much interested in Jung, but because he was not a Freudian. Jung was obsessed by archetypes – the various manifestations of anima and animus, or the wise old man – in which I was uninterested, and none of which I managed to locate in myself. But I still preferred his view of the world, with its insistence on the *creative* powers of the unconscious, the use of active imagination, and the individuation process, to the grinding specificity and obsession with sex of the Freudian. Which is odd, given how obsessed I was by sex, and how fond I was of talking about it. But I would have found psychoanalysis too slow, too invasive, and thoroughly embarrassing.

The Freudian process goes like this: you lie down on a couch, while the therapist sits behind you and out of sight. He initiates a process designed to allow expression of repressed material. This is difficult, and the patient frequently feels blocked. The therapist subtly probes, encouraging the material to emerge. Freud likened the patient's resistance to this process to fears of an extraction at the dentist. So too a psychoanalytic patient may 'put up a struggle' against the invasive insistence of the analyst. But though the ongoing process is embarrassing and shaming, it is also accompanied by feelings of release, which led Freud's close associate Josef Breuer to call it the 'cathartic method'.

Barbara did this every day, while I went and individuated once a week. The rest of the time we read and talked, informing ourselves of the theory behind the practice. We shared the contents of our sessions, interpreted each other's dreams and fantasies – which therapists *really* don't encourage – and lived in an over-heated attempt at making the unconscious conscious that dwarfed our other activities entirely. We didn't see any of this, any more than the orchids see the hothouse in which they are growing. And there were benefits. We were not so much exploring as creating new worlds in ourselves and for each other, redescribing what we had been, what we were, and what we might hope to become. We'd tuck ourselves up on the sofa and the beige donkey-cord scoop chair that Freddie and Catherine had given us for our wedding, put on the Incredible String Band LP, drink copious quantities of Earl Grey tea or brew a Cona coffee, and read and talk far into the night, pausing only to dream and then to talk some more.

It would be quite wrong to describe the following decade as lost, but at the very least it was defined by the routines of teaching, parenting, negotiating the complexities of marriage, and trying to do the sort of academic research for which I had modest ability and less taste. But following my decision to take (very) early retire-ment, a number of wholly unexpected factors combined to re-ignite my interest in Freud. In the preceding few years my major commit-ment to his works was in trying to acquire them. In those pre-internet days, you actually had to go round the second-hand bookshops, asking, 'What Freud (or Jung) do you have in stock?' It was great fun, and I gradually acquired a full set of the Hogarth

Press *Collected Edition* of Freud, and most of the volumes of the Bollingen *Collected Works of C.G. Jung*.

In 1984 the AIDS virus was first diagnosed, and within two years even the Thatcher government was aware of the catastrophic potential of the new disease. Newspaper and television commercials reminded us all to practise safe sex, use condoms, and warned more or less obliquely of the particular dangers associated with anal intercourse, which was assumed to be an exclusively gay activity. An embarrassed heterosexual population turned its head discreetly aside, only to be forced back to full attention by an apparently correlative pandemic of child abuse.

The first cases – loads of them, an astonishing number – were 'diagnosed' in Middlesbrough, where two local GPs convinced the local hospital that they needed to be allowed to examine large numbers of children, even babies, for signs of sexual abuse. Their diagnostic procedure consisted of an 'anal dilation test', in which the poor, humiliated children had their buttocks spread by the doctor. If the anus remained open this was taken to be unimpeachable 'evidence' of sexual abuse. Hundreds of screaming children were taken away from their protesting, horrified, and helpless parents – eighteen over one weekend – and placed in care. Frequently their siblings were removed as well, 'for their own protection'. The media carried daily reports of cults of 'satanic abuse' of children who, when recovered from their devilish tormentors, frequently could not pass their dilation tests. England had, of a sudden, become a country of unrestrained paedophile buggers, whose apparently unchecked activities were threatening the health of the nation, and fascinating its public. I don't know if the Chinese have such a thing, but surely 1986 was the Year of the Anus.

It was wicked, stupid, unfounded and unfathomable, this medical and social hysteria, and there was scant empirical evidence for the test on which the doctors placed such confidence. It called to mind a similar decade of hysteria, in the 1890s, when Breuer and Freud reported widespread sexual abuse of children based on their 'seduction theory', which relied on the accounts many adults gave, while in therapy, of their sexual abuse at the hands of fathers, uncles, doctors, nursemaids. But Freud, when required to posit an unlikely number of incestuous attacks on children, was less gullible than the doctors some hundred years later. It simply couldn't be; what he was observing in his patients, he decided, was not the memory of an abuse, but a wish that such abuse might have taken place. It was, if anything, an even more shocking line of thought.

One thing leads to another, thoughts coalesce in unexpected ways, and these thoughts and images were percolating away in my unconscious. It became clear to me, of a sudden, that only writing a novel could calm me inwardly, purging my unhappiness on to the page. Purgation, catharsis. It's peculiar, isn't it, how the processes have their twin meanings? My dictionary allows the following for *catharsis*:

1. the relief of strong suppressed emotions, for example through drama or psychoanalysis.
2. evacuation of the bowels, esp. with the use of a laxative [Greek *kathairein* to purge, purify]

And suddenly – in that odd unconscious way in which Lawrence's characters realize things – I saw what it was that I had been sensing, and missing, in my long engagement with Freud, which seemed to clarify for me the deep unease that psychoanalysis had always awakened, to elucidate what was so creepy about that figure lurking behind you as you lay vulnerable on the couch, invisible yet so powerful.

Remember what happens when you go into psychoanalysis: the lying down, the figure probing insistently behind you, the repressed material, the blockage and release, the feelings of shame. That's more or less it, isn't it? But it always had, for me, a shadow, or something shadowy, unsaid or unacknowledged, something *absent* in the Lacanian sense. This sense of the unconscious underpinning of our experience is, of course, the stuff of classical Freudianism: a child is being beaten, a primal scene enacted. Our adult lives are shadowed by the potency of unremembered childhood fantasy and desire. There is such a shadow here too, in the relationship between analyst and analysand: an underlying metaphor that Freud, curiously, never acknowledges. Because the operating analogy is not with the extraction of a tooth, but with the giving of an enema.

Feelings are repressed, and become impacted when they cannot be released. The process is like constipation (from which Freud suffered for his entire life). The internal material festers, becomes painful, and threatens the health of the entire organism. When this happened to Viennese children in the 1890s they were regularly given an enema to re-establish regularity. One can imagine the resistance with which it was received, the discomfort, the sense of violation which may have been accompanied (as Freud observed) by pleasure.

Germans sometimes use the term *Bescherung*, which means bestowal, to refer to a child's bowel movements. The gift is frequently understood to be a form of gold – my grandmother would look in my sister's diaper, grateful that her bowels had emptied, and murmur *gelt* – and the association is enshrined in German folktales in a character who actually shat gold coins. If toilet-training becomes prolonged the child may fixate at this stage, and we get the development of that obstinate, anally retentive type who withholds faeces, and in adult life finds it impossible to give emotionally, is both literally and metaphorically miserly: the association is explicitly made by Freud's early disciple, Sandor Ferenczi: 'Money is nothing other than odourless, dehydrated filth, that has been made to shine.'

Money is shit, shit is money? The identification of the two leads to curious conclusions, for if our excreta is actually a gift of gold, why should it be given away? Each time the child takes to the toilet he is a loser, under the coercion of toilet-training. The parent becomes a sort of lavatorial highwayman: *Sit down and deliver!* is the demand, and punishment is threatened for the insufficiently generous.

Freud acknowledged that analysis ends when the money runs out. So the demand of the analyst – keep producing! give! – recapitulates those ancient demands of the parents to the costive infant. The analyst demands: *Lie down and deliver!* This may sound perilous, but it is also central to psychoanalytic procedure. The analyst inherits the crucial roles in the patient's life, and is emotionally regarded as if he were a parent: resented and loved. The possible result of this transference of feeling is that unresolved infantile dramas may be re-enacted, and resolved, in the therapeutic setting. For Freud this applied, crucially, to re-enactments of the Oedipal drama, but little attention has been given to the ways in which psychoanalysis re-enacts the battle of the chamber pot.

I wrote my novel *Bottom's Dream* in an attempt to find some dramatic form for these new ideas, unlikely as this may sound. If the plot sounds unpromising, the result was even worse, and confirmed what I had always suspected, that I am no novelist, nor was meant to be. (I don't much mind: if something is worth doing, it is worth doing badly.) My characters lacked depth, and spoke in the same voice, the descriptions of faces, rooms, food, trees, skies, lacked texture, detail, colour, particularity. There were too many overheated conversations, everything was pitched at the same intensity, climax followed climax, as in a pornographic novel. Nothing came alive, nothing was adequately envisioned, nothing except the ideas.

My novel was intended, I proclaimed proudly, to do for the anus what *Moby Dick* had done for the whale. I offered to send the draft to various literary friends: to Graham Greene, William Golding, Faber director Charles Monteith, Salman Rushdie. Funnily enough, they didn't seem very interested, though D.M. Thomas (perhaps predictably) liked it, and was encouraging. But when I sent the text to a Professor of Freudian Studies at the Institute for Advanced Studies at Princeton, I was gratified to hear that he regarded my line of thought as both true and original, if a little peculiar, and he urged me to publish it in some form or other.

Instead, I took the manuscript and put it in a drawer, and haven't looked at it since. What would be the point? It had served its purpose, allowed the release of some feeling: it was cathartic, and now it's embarrassing. Anyway, it seemed to me unlikely even then, and inconceivable now, that someone hasn't made the same points, more carefully and thoroughly than I had, or wished to.

No, what *Bottom's Dream* did for me was to signal the end, not of my belief in psychoanalytic concepts and apparatus, but of my reflexive turning to therapy when in personal trouble. The problem is that therapy privileges feeling without testing it. Feelings are treacherous things, and we are as likely to be misguided by what we feel as creatively informed by it. Nor does therapy sufficiently assess or value how we behave, partly, of course, because your average analysand is likely to offer a deeply sympathetic account of their own behaviour, and to suppress critical reactions to it.

But we are frequently the worst judges of how we act, what we feel, and how we need to change. If you want to learn about such things – about what you are *really* like – you will do better by consulting your spouse, children, colleagues and friends, in a spirit of curiosity and humility. Psychotherapy, like mumps, is something you should have when young, get over, and remain immune to for the rest of your life. A lifetime addiction to it – like some compulsive fixation on internal cleansing – is obsessional, narcissistic and counterproductive. Otherwise, psychoanalysis may become the illness from which you need to be cured.

Ruthie and I certainly wanted to rid our lives of therapy, sitting quietly upstairs as one nut followed another for their sessions with mom. It wasn't fair: the TV was in the downstairs den, next to the Nutcracker Suite. What were we supposed to do for three hours, homework? It was time, we agreed, to make a point. Resistance, that was what she called it, didn't she? Now we *were* the Resistance. There was no sense denying our hostility. We hated being stifled like this, keeping our feelings in. It's not healthy, it's infantile. Better to do some acting out.

When the last nut left, at ten o'clock, we watched the lights disappear as he drove away, and listened for mom coming out of the Suite. We turned out all the lights in the upper part of the house, which meant that she would have to come upstairs in the dark before she could locate a light switch. A door closed, she walked over to the stairs, and stopped.

'Ricky? Ruthie?'

We didn't say anything. Ruthie hid behind the sofa, and I secreted myself behind a kitchen door – the two avenues towards the light switch.

'Ricky! Ruthie! You'd better not!'

This was how our game began, and she loved to play, especially when she wasn't the victim. Lights out, victim terrified, hidden person jumps out and yells: 'BOO!' Now we had her where we wanted her, helpless, tip-toeing up the stairs in the hope that we might have gone to bed.

Timing is everything in the BOO game. If you get it wrong your victim is not unlikely to fall back down the stairs and die, and that would be hostile even for us. You have to wait until you hear at least three steps from the top of the stairs, and then strike.

One-two-three.

'Ricky? Ruthie? I'm scared!' But she was already starting to giggle, because BOO! – which she had, after all, invented – released something childlike and zany in her that all of us cherished. She started turning round in circles, trying to see by the pale light that came from the lamp posts through the living room window.

'No, no, no, don't! I'm scared!' Her laughter became a shriek, as Ruthie screamed the first BOO!

'NO! NO!'

BOOS are best delivered in pairs, and I got mine in with impeccable timing. Mom rushed past the light switch and out through the kitchen door, hysterical, on to the front lawn.

It was dark there too. We stalked her from opposite ends of the garden, stealthily, giggling just enough to add to her terror. Lights came on in the neighbour's kitchen, which overlooked our garden, but we were too entranced with our hunting ritual to care if we were observed. Mom was laughing helplessly now, turning round and round in circles on her tiptoes, clenching her thighs together.

'I'm wetting!' she cried, 'I'm wetting!'

Perfect. That meant we'd won, and we relented gracefully, ushered her back to the house, and made hot chocolate while she went upstairs to shower and change. She came back down a few minutes later, in a terry towelling robe, her hair wet, glowing.

'You really got me!' she said.

16

BETTER THAN LITERATURE!

> The thing I have to do, it's so important . . . If you
> knew it all you'd see the point.
>> Carl Hiaasen, *Double Whammy*

I issued my first catalogue as a rare book dealer in the autumn of
1982, while still teaching at Warwick. In those days individual
catalogues had names, to serve as shorthand for telegraphic orders.
My first was called *Barbara*. I got a telegram after I sent it out,
from a delighted potential customer (who didn't buy anything)
proclaiming 'Barbara is Beautiful!' a response grudgingly shared
in the rare book trade. (Along with: 'who the Hell does this guy
think he is?') The catalogue was printed on glossy paper, with illustrations, which was uncommon at the time. I thought it rather
grand. But by the time it was issued, though, I'd learned that *Barbara*
was actually a bit of a tart. When my printer handed over the first
copy, he looked at it fondly if not admiringly. 'Not bad,' he said,
'cheap and cheerful.'

I wished my father, who had died two years earlier, had been
there to see it. He would have been so proud. On my visits home
over the last few years of his life, he'd become fascinated by my
new vocation as a book scout, and would sit in his Eames chair,
put his record of *The Magic Flute* on his new Danish teak modern
hi-fi, and quiz me on points, issues and values of first editions. He

was uncommonly engaged with this my incarnation, possibly because it was the first time I had deviated from the directions he'd laid down. No one in the family had ever been good at business, and my combination of literary and financial acumen fascinated him. I would come home from New York after a day scouting for rare books, with a few hundred dollars profit in my pocket, and we would both be lost in admiration. We contemplated setting up a business together: Son and Gekoski, Rare Books.

I wished this name might have been on my new catalogue, but I liked it anyway, whatever it was. I loved it. I took that first copy home, made myself a cup of coffee, and sat at the pine table in the kitchen leafing through it happily. I was shortly joined by our neighbour, the rather strict academic wife of one of my colleagues. I should have known better, but I was so chuffed with my little green catalogue that I handed it over excitedly, saying, 'Look: My first catalogue!' She flipped through it in a desultory way, taking in the occasional details, mostly, as far as I could see, of the prices. She paused for a moment, and looked me squarely in the eye, as anyone fearlessly committed to the telling of truths should do.

'How disgusting!' she said. I don't recall how I responded; I'm not sure I said anything at all. I was aware, of course, that academics are hostile to 'trade', as well as ignorant about it. And though happy to deploy this prejudice, she would also have known that much of the material she'd worked on as a graduate student – rare texts, letters and manuscripts – would have found its way into special collections departments of libraries through the rare book trade.

It may be that rare book dealers, like rubbish men, are necessary, but that doesn't make them smell good. The problem was compounded by the fact that I had gone into business in rare *books*. Books, to my colleagues – indeed, books to most sane people – are objects of utility, designed to convey information and give pleasure, and esteemed accordingly. To value a book not for what is in it, but (as it were) in itself suggests a fetishization of the object that many people in the academic and literary worlds find offensive. Why should a first edition of some novel be worth more than its reprints? Why does the presence of its dust wrapper – for God's sake! – render it much more valuable? Why should the mere fact that an author has signed a book make it more desirable? Surely fetishizing the object simultaneously demeans its contents?

From that time, colleagues would occasionally inquire, sniffily, 'And how is *business*?' My regular response to this – 'Terrific! And how are you finding *academic life*?' – generally signalled an end to the conversation, a confirmation of the distance that now separated us.

When I gave up teaching, in 1984, I found – I don't know why I should have found this so surprising – that the major emotion that accompanied my retreat from university life was anger. I kept banging on about my feelings obsessively, like someone with post-traumatic stress syndrome. I could recognize the symptoms, but I couldn't stop. I bored myself, I bored everybody. I was scathing about the form of life that I had just left, sulphurous about many of my ex-colleagues, and particularly furious with myself for following such an uncongenial path. Though I was ostensibly having a terrific time in my new career as a rare book dealer, I could neither purge the regret I felt at having wasted my time and energy, nor give up the social cachet of being a university teacher. As I still taught part-time (for three years) as part of my redundancy package, I now described myself as a 'university teacher and rare book dealer', unwilling to give up the prestige of my old position at the same time that I professed to detest almost everything that it represented.

In order to purge this anger, and to eradicate the hold that university teaching still had on me, I conceived a cunning plan which I hoped would rid me of the toxicity of my academic persona: the fearfulness, the hyper-scepticism, the pomposity, the anxiety not to be found out for the drudge I was. I called this new project 'becoming less intelligent'.

It was fun. I hardly needed to cultivate my philistinism, which was pretty much full grown already. I've always preferred sport to high art, and have a positive dislike for people who regard themselves as 'cultured'. Next time you go to the opera look at the body language of most of the patrons: the stiffness of demeanour, the noses held that extra ten degrees skywards, the strangulated voices. There is little so repellent as the English in high culture mode. Nor did it take much for me to give up going to the theatre, which I have always disliked: all that spitting and declaiming, the audience's anxiety that something might go wrong, allied to the vague hope that it might. (Holden Caulfield hated actors, whom he regarded, though without having met any, as the very incarnation of the phoney.) I abjured philosophy – that was easy enough – but also swore off 'literature'. No more fancy reading, no more highbrow talking. Simplify, if not to refine then even to coarsen. Become less intelligent.

For years I confined my TV watching to sports and movies, and my reading to detective fiction. I opened a standing order for twenty thrillers a month with Otto Penzler of Manhattan's Mysterious Bookshop, to be chosen by his bright and knowledgeable staff. When the boxes arrived I would pile up my new treats, start at the top and work down, handing them over to Anna when I was finished. When asked what I had been reading – even what I was reading on the day – I could rarely remember either author or title (or, much of the time, the plot). I gorged myself, grew fat and indolent with reading. I read dozens of thriller writers, and hundreds of books. Like Kingsley Amis, who complained that he was quickly bored by a novel that did not begin with the words 'A shot rang out', I demanded nothing but finger-on-the-trigger entertainment.

I am pretty sure that none of Otto's shipments contained a novel by Carl Hiaasen. Even in my befuddled state, getting less intelli-

gent by the minute, I would have remembered that. So when in
the Hampstead branch of Waterstone's one day, I spotted a book
called *Double Whammy*, by an author unknown to me, I hardly
gave it a thought until I read the puff on the front cover: *'Better
than literature!'* P.J. O'Rourke. Perfect! Something other than literature was what I was looking for, something *better* than literature
was a bonus. Anything that P.J. O'Rourke is that keen on is OK
with me. He may be laughably right-wing, but he's funny and sharp
as a tack, and I reckoned that this Hiaasen person must be worth
a look.

He was. His novel was blackly comic, with a one-eyed protagonist called Clinton Tyree, a drop-out Governor of Florida who
becomes a hermit in the Everglades under the name of Skink,
living on road kill. There was a cast of characters ranging from the
wacky to the totally deranged. *Double Whammy* is in a tradition
of the grotesque Southern novel, but the enterprise was animated
and informed by Hiaasen's rage at the desecration of the landscape
of South Florida by planners, developers and associated con-men
intent on making a sleazy quick buck. The writing was wonderful,
totally surprising in tone and content, and made me cringe, howl
with laughter, and contract in righteous indignation. The novel
culminated in a scene in which a psychopath who has been bitten
on the arm by a rabid dog, and is unable to prise its jaws open
even when it is dead, simply cuts off the body, and goes about his
business with the dead dog's head attached to his arm. (Hiaasen's
villains often end up with something peculiar attached to their
arms. When asked why this was, he admitted that he'd never noticed
it.)

But there is something more than sheer mayhem going on.
Skink is a great comic creation, but his story is a black parable of
the Fall. He enters politics, naively, in order to do good, and is
brought down by the massed forces of greed and corruption that
are endemic to South Florida. Entrusted with an Edenic garden –

a 'virgin' territory – he presides over its destruction. His with-drawal into the swamps is an act of penance:

> 'Want to know who I am? I'm the guy who had a chance to save this place, only I blew it.'
> 'Save what?'
> ' . . . Everything. Everything that counts for anything.'

An investigative journalist by training, Hiaasen has worked since 1985 for *The Miami Herald*, and writes a regular column which, he acknowledges jauntily, 'at one time or another has pissed off just about everybody in South Florida', including his own bosses. His indignation at the institutionalized desecration of the prelapsarian South Florida landscape is the animating impulse of both his columns and the string of delicious novels that began, in 1986, with *Tourist Season*. His only regret, he says, is that the books haven't put tourists off visiting his homeland. He hates tourists as much as he loves South Florida.

The *Irish Times* review of *Double Whammy* called it 'seriously funny', which ought to have meant both serious *and* funny – an admirable goal – though it probably didn't. I enjoyed it so much that I did something I've never done before, or since. I went to the excellent Primrose Hill Bookshop and ordered ten copies to give away. My kids each got one, the guys in my office, various friends. I gave Salman Rushdie one, and in exchange for the tip he insisted I read Stephen King.

Stephen King! What an odd notion.

'He's terrific!' Salman said.

The publisher Tom Rosenthal turned down my offer of a copy.

'Of course I've read him,' he said, 'he's a genius. I tried to sign him for Deutsch but my co-publishers let me down, and we lost the deal.'

Hiaasen was clearly serious, but he wasn't high serious. He was low serious. I preferred that, and it set a sort of example. He seemed to be having fun writing, and all of a sudden I was having fun reading. It had all the freshness of a new experience. Was there something frivolous about the way he wrote, and the way I read him? Absolutely, though by no means entirely. That's what I yearned for, and what I had been missing, in making reading into my profession. And, yes, I am aware that people don't have fun in their professions. Do accountants adore all that yummy adding up? Do lawyers love all that obsessive prevaricating? No, most of the ones I know come to dislike it, as I came to dislike the profession of letters. Literature, as taught at universities, has become an institution: syllabus-bound, examination-driven. You get marks for how well you understand Dickens. I gave them. I'd become institutionalized too.

How did all of this happen? I don't mean: to me. I mean: to us. How did the reading of imaginative literature get hijacked by the pedants? English Literature as a secondary and tertiary subject is now so popular, and seems so natural to us, that we seldom pause to inquire where it came from, and why. We make the assumption that it is as obvious a university subject as history, or classics, much less law, medicine, or engineering. In fact, though, 'English' is pretty much a Johnny-come-lately of academic subjects. Curiously little has been written about this, most of it in obscure academic journals that are hard to find, and embarrassing to be seen reading.

The story, once you begin to piece it together, is surprising and revealing. In eighteenth-century England a gentleman studied the classics of Greek and Roman literature, in the original languages. The classics didn't confer gentility, they confirmed it. If he went to university at all, it was most frequently to become a cleric. It was only in the 1820s that the first university courses in English appeared, at the newly founded University College and King's College in London. These institutions differed substantially, the former being egalitarian and utilitarian, while King's was informed by a romantic, neo-Platonic aesthetic, in which the study of English encouraged its students to rise 'above what is apparent and transitory to what is real and permanent'.

These new educational courses and practices – both utilitarian and transcendental – were soon appropriated by government, and sent to the colonies. If English literature was good for us, surely it would be even better for our overseas subjects, for whom some such civilizing influence was so palpably necessary. Talking to the House of Commons in 1833, Thomas Babington Macaulay recommended the conscious propagation and study of 'that literature before the light of which impious and cruel superstitions are fast taking flight on the banks of the Ganges . . . And wherever British literature spreads may it be attended by British virtue and British freedom!' The study of literature, nauseatingly, was both useful and good. It was, of course, particularly good for those who needed to be improved, whether they be on the banks of the Ganges or amongst England's emerging mercantile classes.

One can feel this spirit pervading the introduction to Vicesimus Knox's *Elegant Extracts*, published at the same time as the London colleges were being founded, and one of the first anthologies of literature for use at schools. The emerging middle classes, Knox maintained, should use their leisure to peruse 'polite literature': 'Nothing perhaps contributes more to liberalize their minds, and prevent that narrowness which is too often the consequence of a life attached, from the earliest age, to the pursuits of lucre.' The mere study of 'English' thus confirmed its students, either indigenous or foreign, as inferior educational citizens. But it still might confer, if not the class of the classics, at least the saving grace of the vernacular.

English universities were based to a large extent on Germanic models. Disciplines were strictly divided from each other, methods of examination and conferment of degrees were controlled centrally, teachers achieved ranks culminating in professorships, students divided into undergraduate and postgraduate. But if the study of English was the coming thing, there was no clear agreement on how it was to be taught within the structures available. The transition from the reading of books as a polite drawing room activity suitable for young ladies, to an examinable discipline of higher education was a complex and hotly disputed subject during the nineteenth century.

Oxford and Cambridge, typically, had been slow to react to these changes, and only entered the arena once English had established itself, but had yet to find an agreed academic form. Oxbridge didn't lead the way in this process, but entered at the point at which guidance was sorely needed. The first Oxford Chair of English Literature was established in 1904, though the original Oxford syllabus in English was severely philological and historicist. At Cambridge, though it had been possible to read English as part of the Tripos since 1891, it was impossible to do a single Honours degree in English until 1926, exactly a hundred years after the formation of UCL. The Cambridge degree included an element of practical criticism as well as a paper on 'Life, Literature and Thought', and provides the basis of English Studies in the Anglophone world.

This new degree had an evangelical flavour: it aimed to train 'sensibility', to promote moral awareness, and to produce a cultural elite of readers who were highly sensitive to the demands not merely of literature, but of the life from which it was drawn and with which it was engaged. The message was explicit: reading literature is good for you, and good for us all. It may not confer gentility, but (as Matthew Arnold observed) it gives a leavening of culture. The great literary models provide instruction and guidance, and may supply that bedrock of value that religion once offered. If Arnold was the priest of this revaluation of the importance of letters, F.R. Leavis was his curate. It is impossible to miss in Leavis's tone and demeanour the grimly entrenched, almost medical, belief that literature is good for you if you take it in the prescribed texts, forms and doses. Literary criticism, after all, has some of its root structure in Biblical exegesis.

We remember Arnold's definition of God: 'There rules an enduring Power, not ourselves, which makes for righteousness' and his conclusion: '*therefore* study your Bible and learn to obey this.' This isn't much of a formulation (you may as well define soap as the power, not ourselves, that makes for cleanliness) but it points the way: if no longer to the Bible, then at least to Wordsworth, Austen, George Eliot and Lawrence. Study the right texts in the right way and you will become wise. Read English!

This is an attractive position, and you can see why it became necessary, if the study of English was to shed its historicist and philological biases. But it is also an empirical claim, with a clear implication. If the study of literature conveys wisdom – much less righteousness – then it should follow that proper students of literature are the wisest and best of persons. Yet I have scanned myself in vain for traces of wisdom and exceptional goodness, and wondered whether my former colleagues exhibited these qualities. Certainly the splenetic Leavis was hardly a proper role model for the young and impressionable. (The opposite assertion, that a lifetime study of English makes you *worse*, seems to me more feasible.)

So by the end of the first hundred years of the teaching of English at universities there was no common understanding of what a course should consist of, no shared methodology, no common teleology. English sat uneasily in that Teutonic structure in which the study of a discipline demanded rigour, accountability, methodological clarity, clear aims and values. By these criteria it was not clear that English was a discipline at all, and it is to this day regarded as a soft option by, say, scientists or mathematicians.

On these grounds, V.S. Naipaul has recently suggested that English should no longer be offered as a university subject, and all English Departments disbanded: 'I think it would be a great fillip, a great boost to the intellectual life of the country. It would immediately have a great impact. It would release a lot of manpower. They could go and work on the buses and things like that.' I sometimes argued similarly to my colleagues (who wouldn't have made good bus conductors) that the 'common pursuit of true judgement' of literature, if it is to be enjoyable as well as serious, would better take place in forums like reading groups or adult education courses.

No one listened to me, but when a Nobel Laureate talks like this one assumes that people may pay attention, even when he is notoriously iconoclastic and grumpy, and the potential academic audience famed for not listening. But no debate ensued, and Naipaul's provocative remarks have by now been pretty much forgotten, if not forgiven.

Had Sir Vidia gone on to say that teaching in an English Department is bad for you, I would have agreed with him. It had stiffened my emotional and intellectual sinews, drained my reservoirs of delight, made me (more) pompous and domineering. 'Becoming less intelligent' was an attempt at reforming myself, and I suppose it had to begin with deforming what had preceded: detoxifying, I called it. There was nothing pretty about the process.

One afternoon, playing golf with my friend Simon Grogan, I was having a particularly bad round. On the elevated ninth tee I hit my drive into the lake, teed up another ball, hit that into the lake, teed up another and scuffed it along the ground. It rolled down the gentle slope of the hill and came to rest in a bush about forty feet away.

'Fuck!' I screamed. 'Fucking fuck!' I took my driver and flung it down the hill. It turned in an ungainly parabola and landed next to the bush where the ball lay.

Simon looked at me disapprovingly. He had no objection to the bad language – which he was rather partial to himself – but throwing clubs was definitely rotten behaviour.

'You know this project of yours – becoming less intelligent?' he said, tartly.

'What? What!' I started walking down the hill. You don't talk to a man who is lying five in a bush. It is neither polite nor safe.

'You could be taking it too far,' he said, walking quickly ahead to avoid having anything else to do with me.

He was right. You can't deny who you are, or abandon what you have read and cared about. What I had read defined me, informed my judgements, influenced every moment of who I was and what I did. It is all very well: become less pompous, be less intelligent. But you can't live by Carl Hiaasen alone. If he is funnier, more enjoyable to read, and more passionately committed than many of our syllabus's canonic authors, he isn't as good a writer. That still matters. There is something to be said, after all, for literature.

When I was teaching at Warwick, we used to interview all prospective students. (I gather they no longer have the time or energy to do so.) In answer to my question: 'Why do you want to read English?' I would often get some variety of the answer: because I am interested in people, and in how they work. Why, in that case, I would ask, don't you read psychology? Or history or philosophy or sociology? Surely that is where you learn about people and how they relate to each other? Reading English is for people who care about literature. Not about the truths that literature may reveal (the paraphrases and 'meanings') but the literature itself.

I still feel this passionately. We have to preserve some area in which literary language and form and tonality are foregrounded: to preserve the practices and virtues of close reading; to stake out this territory, to define it, and to defend it. To keep our eyes and fingers on the page, warmly. What you then do with these skills, once acquired, is up to you: do 'readings' of literary works if and only if you know how to read: do post-structuralist ones, even. I don't care. It took me a while to reach this position, and when I did I was no longer angry, nor so dismissive of my former incarnation as a university teacher. I believed I had transcended 'literature', with the help of Carl Hiaasen, but – what a lovely irony! – it seems that I was wrong, or at least that my concept of 'literature' needed refining, not my concept of intelligence. In 1999, the redoubtable literary partnership of Colm Tóibin and Carmen Callil published *The Modern Library: The 200 Best Novels in English Since 1950*. They included *Double Whammy*.

17

SPYCATCHER AND THE LOST ARCHIVE OF KIM PHILBY

If I hadn't been a novelist I would have been a rare book
dealer – it's like a constant treasure hunt.

Graham Greene

I have never read Peter Wright's *Spycatcher*, by all accounts a pedestrian
tale of life in the security services that gained its fifteen minutes of fame
when Mrs Thatcher was foolish enough to ban its importation, upon
its overseas publication in 1987, for contravening the Official Secrets
Act. The resultant publicity catapulted the book into prominence, and
copies were smuggled to the UK from Australia and America in their
thousands. Within a year the ban was overturned by the Law Lords,
and the book could be assessed for what it really was: a dull and ill-
written, self-serving account of a former minor spy.

I have no interest in the world of espionage, all that pretending
and betraying, skulking about in trench coats and hats, save for an
admiration for the works of John le Carré and Graham Greene,
both of whom served in the English secret services. Greene, who
maintained a taste for a well-cut trench coat, tended to write his
espionage books as a form of relaxation from the more taxing and
morally heated novels that explored crises of faith engendered by
human frailty.

In the late 1980s I was a regular visitor to Antibes to see Greene (from whom I was buying a number of manuscripts, letters and books), making my living as a full-time rare book dealer. I was happier than I had been for years, my decision to leave Warwick fully vindicated by my new form of life. It hadn't been a hard decision to leave, it just took a while, and then one day I'd woken up and said to Barbara, 'I'm going to quit.'

'I've known that for ages,' she said, 'it always takes you a long time to recognize what you've already decided.'

She was the key, and it wouldn't have happened without her support. The children were fourteen and eight, and abandoning a safe £15,000 a year for an uncertain future might have looked irresponsible from her point of view.

'It's fine,' she'd reassured me, 'if we need more money we can always sell the house.'

There was no need. The first year after leaving I made £30,000, and I never made as little as that again. But the business I was doing with Greene was headier than any I'd yet encountered. In his modest flat at La Residence des Fleurs, in Antibes, he pulled manuscript after manuscript off his shelves and out of his bureau: two volumes of travel diaries, five books filled with daily accounts of his dreams over twenty years, his letters to his mistress, Yvonne Cloetta, and, finally (I had to pick these up in Paris), all of his copies of his own books. I wrote cheque after cheque, to his puzzlement and delight.

'Surely this is too much! Are you a gambler?' he asked, after pocketing a cheque for £35,000.

'Not at all,' I said. He seemed disappointed. 'What I am is a poker player.'

He looked puzzled.

'It's a matter of skill and reading the odds and the situation,' I said. 'I have great customers for this sort of material. I'll make a very good profit.'

The next time I showed up in Antibes it was in a new white

Saab convertible. I filled it up with bibliographic goodies, bid Graham and Yvonne a very fond farewell, set the cruise control on 170 kph, and headed north. After six hours (equals 600 miles) I stopped in Joigny at La Côte Saint-Jacques, a small luxury hotel with a three-star Michelin restaurant, and gave the doorman £20 to carry all of my new books and manuscripts – some ten boxes full – into my suite. I ate and drank exceedingly well – there was a young waitress whose only job was to dispense a variety of chocolate truffles – and then went and wallowed like a pig in books on the floor of my room.

Two months later, the treasures dispersed and the large profit banked, I took the family on a holiday to Block Island, between Long Island and Connecticut, renting a Victorian house so grand that we kept finding tourists walking round it, guide books in hand, under the impression that it was open to the public. I hardly noticed them. I was upstairs, moping about. 'It will never be that good again,' I moaned, like a teenager granted five minutes of bliss with Marilyn Monroe.

But it soon was. Some time before he died, in 1991, Graham (a lifetime friend of Kim Philby's) suggested that it might be enjoyable and profitable for me to go to Moscow to meet Philby's widow, Ruffina. According to Greene, Mrs Philby might be willing to sell some of Philby's books, and all of the papers that he had accumulated during his Moscow years. The archive was of considerable historical importance, and provided the clearest indication possible of what Philby was up to between 1963, when he defected, and his death in 1988.

Kim Philby was the cleverest, most important and elusive of that set of spies – Guy Burgess, Donald Maclean and Anthony Blunt were the others – who had been Cambridge undergraduates in the 1930s and subsequently worked for the Soviets. Though Philby had been rumbled and largely discredited by a series of inquiries into his behaviour, he'd never been arrested, and was working as a journalist in Beirut when a defector from the Soviets informed MI6 – what they had suspected for some time – that Philby was indeed a Soviet agent.

What happened next could only have come straight from a *Carry on Spying* film. An agent was dispatched to Beirut to confront Philby and to bring him back to London. The ensuing conversation, apparently, went more or less like this:

'We have you banged to rights!' said the agent. 'You come back to London, you bad spy!'

'Shan't!' said Philby.

'Would you come if I said please?' said the agent.

'Certainly not!' said Philby firmly, and commenced packing his bags.

Disconsolate at this rejection, the MI6 man returned to London. By the time he arrived, Philby was on a boat to Moscow, where he was soon to be reunited with Burgess and Maclean.

But if MI6 didn't quite know how to handle Philby, neither did the KGB. He had been the source of some useful information, no doubt about that. But there was something, even to the Soviets, a little . . . shall we say, untrustworthy about the urbane and unflappable Englishman. Could he be some sort of triple agent after all? Philby protested his innocence – or do I mean his guilt? – but the KGB were unmoved. They set him up nicely, with a good two-bedroom flat and a toothsome red-haired interpreter called Ruffina, who later became his fourth wife, for Philby changed his sexual allegiances even more frequently than his national ones.

Ten years passed, slowly: a time that he spent reading and writing letters home, wandering round Red Square trying to find the latest cricket scores from English tourists, and occasionally in bed with Maclean's wife Melinda. But, at last, the barriers came down, and Philby began to present his 'English seminars' at the KGB. Their purpose was to train Soviet agents how to pass when they were working in England, which involved a lot of astonishing nonsense about MCC ties and the laws of cricket, which accents to acquire and clubs to join, and the arcana associated with a public school and Oxbridge education.

I met one of these 'students' – let's call him Michael B– on my trip to Moscow in 1993 to examine Philby's library and papers. He was, he told me, acting as Mrs Philby's 'agent' in our negotiations.

'How delightful to meet you,' he said, shaking my hand. 'I do so miss London. I had the most marvellous time there. Such a delightful city!'

'You worked in London?'

'Yes,' he said suavely, 'I was a Tass correspondent for seven years.'

'Hold on a minute,' I said. 'I'm new to this. You were a student of Kim's? And then you went to London?'

He nodded.

'So you were a KGB spy?'

'Of course,' he chortled. 'Now . . . entrepreneur!'

In Michael's charming but vigilant company Mrs Philby and I began to go through Kim's library. He had thousands of volumes – he'd had plenty of time to read, and various friends (like Greene) had been generous in sending him reading material. As I browsed, a few of the books virtually demanded a return to England. There was Kim's heavily annotated *A Handbook of Marxism*, from the 1930s, which was wonderful. A couple of books from Guy Burgess's library were rather fun.

But best of all was a copy of *Spycatcher*, inscribed to the Philbys by Graham Greene: 'For Kim and Ruffina from Graham and Yvonne.' That sounds homey enough, as if the book were a Christmas gift of some innocuous volume. Perhaps that is how Graham thought of it. But seen from the outside, and after a few years, it was a remarkable find: a celebrated book about spying, presented by the finest writer about espionage to the third man himself.

I had to have it! Mrs Philby had a distinct interest in money, and was constantly anxious about inflation in post-Communist Moscow. The fare on the palatial underground system had recently doubled to the equivalent of 1p a trip, and Ruffina was in a stew about it.

'But Ruffina,' I said, 'you just sold one of Kim's unpublished essays to an English newspaper for £600 . . .'

'You don't understand Russians,' she said wearily, and fairly. 'It is always a struggle here.'

'Perhaps you'd sell me a couple of books then?' I asked.

She would. During the afternoon, with both of us feeling a little carefree due to Michael's uncharacteristic absence, she and I did a deal, and I gave her £1,500 pounds in cash for four books, of which £1,000 was for the *Spycatcher*. Her eyes glowed. I considered making an offer on the one further book I craved – I forget the title, it wasn't anything particular – but it bore a warm inscription to Maclean's wife: 'For Melinda – an orgasm a day keeps the doctor away. With love from Kim.' It is possible to press your luck too far, and I regretfully put the book back on the shelf.

Mrs Philby was a tireless host, and during my four days in Moscow she showed me around the local parks, churches and places of interest. On several of these perambulations it was impossible not to notice that we were being followed by a sauntering, portly, slightly florid gentleman, dressed in a cravat, spats, a bright waistcoat, and a hound's tooth tweed jacket. He didn't look local. He made no attempt to conceal himself – how could he? – rather the reverse: he wanted me to know that he was there.

It was the man from Sotheby's.

It's no wonder he was on the chase: the Philby papers were wonderful. There were all of the notebooks containing his English Seminar material, an unfinished draft of an autobiography, documentation concerning his status at the KGB, letters from various important Russian and English figures, diaries, unpublished articles. There were also a number of kitsch plastic trophies – of the sort Bertie got in his under-twelve's football league – awarded to Comrade Philby by the KGB. (He must have scored a lot of goals.) Considered together the material provided a wonderfully clear, and hitherto unknown, picture of Philby's Moscow years.

Ruffina, Michael and I agreed that I could offer it to the British Library at a price of £60,000. Ruffina's eyes were wet with anticipation, Michael looked distinctly pleased. We shook hands happily, and went out to eat at one of Moscow's crassly ostentatious new hotels, stocked with ex-KGB men (now entre-preneurs), higher echelon government officials, international businessmen, Russian Mafiosi, and the occasional (anxious-looking) tourist.

An enormous bowl of Beluga caviar, suspended over a bowl of ice, was placed on the table before us. Ruffina took out her hand-kerchief, filled it with half the contents of the bowl, folded the corners over neatly, and replaced it gently in her bag.

'Momma loves caviar!' she explained cheerfully.

How adorable! In the midst of this post-Soviet mayhem, here is the fourth Mrs Philby calling herself Momma, like a parody of an old Negro plantation slave, and gobbling caviar as if it were shortnin' bread. I wondered if Momma's l'il babies loved it as well?

I smiled over the table to Michael, in wry approbation.

'Her mother is rather elderly, and lives with Ruffina,' he explained stiffly.

Another bottle of champagne arrived, what was left of the caviar was finished and replaced. We talked cheerfully, ate, drank some vodka. I paid.

Things progressed slowly after my return. The British Library were keen, but needed governmental approval before they could proceed with such a potentially controversial acquisition. Shortly after the proposal was sent to the Foreign Office, I received a phone call from Moscow. It was Michael.

'Rick?' he said in a tone lacking his customary charm. 'We are not happy.'

'What's the matter?'

'Those books you have purchased from Ruffina? I do not like the price you have put on them.'

This was genuinely astonishing. I had put the books on a shelf behind my desk, having jotted a provisional price in each (I wasn't yet ready to part with them). They added up to £5,000, with the *Spycatcher* the most expensive of the lot. No one other than myself and my working colleagues had seen them. At night we close the shop, and a very good burglar alarm is set.

'Those are not prices, they are insurance valuations,' I said. 'Anyway, how do you know?'

'Never mind,' he said. 'I have lost confidence in you.'

'Listen, Michael,' I said, unsure where this was going, 'I flew to Moscow, I spent four nights in a hotel, I gave Ruffina a free, detailed appraisal of the papers and the books in the library, I spent hundreds of pounds entertaining you both. And I need to make some profit. That is called capitalism, and it is how my wife and children come to eat.'

'We do not understand this, we are just simple Russians.'

'Simple Russians! Simple Russians? You got to be kidding! You were some sort of big shot in the KGB, and I am just a simple bookseller!'

'The deal is off,' he said, and put the phone down.

At the British Library Department of Manuscripts, the unfailingly genial archivist who had painstakingly negotiated the purchase of the papers, was distinctly unhappy.

'It's obvious, you stupid boy!' he said testily. 'Did you offer him a bribe?'

It was by now abundantly clear that I was out of my depth, as if I had wandered into the script of a Graham Greene story without being taught my lines. My instructions were to bribe an ex-KGB agent on behalf of the British Library, so that the Foreign Office-sanctioned purchase of a traitor's papers could be concluded.

I rang Michael back in Moscow. He didn't sound pleased to hear from me.

'Michael,' I said, in a tone both casual and insinuating. 'I am calling to apologize. I have been so tied up with the purchase and details of the archive that I neglected to mention your introductory commission.'

Silence.

'In such cases, it is customary in my trade to pay the seller's agent a fee of 10 per cent of the price . . . That would come to £6,000 for you. You can have it in cash if you want!'

'Are you trying to bribe me?' he asked, sounding genuinely shocked.

'Yes!' I said. 'Is it working?'

He put the phone down.

Maybe the man from Sotheby's paid him more? Who knows? Perhaps Michael simply did it for love of his old mentor, or of his younger wife.

When the Philby material came up at Sotheby's London, in August of 1994, Ruffina had taken the decision to split up the archive into its constituent parts, presumably to increase the take, though the final sales figure achieved was more or less what the British Library would have paid. But the individual items were purchased by a wide variety of buyers, most of them unidentified, and Kim Philby's papers were distributed, in bits, round the world. None of the material was lost, but the archive was broken. Anyone wishing to do research on Philby's Moscow years would now have to search desperately, and sometimes fruitlessly, to reassemble his papers.

There must have been something I could have done. Maybe I shouldn't have bought the four books that caused the problem? If I hadn't the deal might have gone through. But, after all, I am a book dealer, and Mrs Philby was happy to take the cash. Maybe I shouldn't have put the valuations in them? But why not? They represented a fair profit after expenses, and I don't think I can be faulted for failure to anticipate an infiltration of KGB agents with x-ray eyes.

Perhaps, after my phone call from Michael, I should have caught the night flight to Moscow, my pockets stuffed with cash? At least, in person, I could have put the case: not for my sake, or theirs, but for the integrity of the archive. After all, it is through such combinations of pieces of paper that a society defines and records itself. And it is in our libraries that such paper is best protected, made available and studied.

By the time the Philby archive was dispersed, it wasn't only Michael who had lost confidence in me. But at least I still had my *Spycatcher*, and a chance to recoup some of my expenses. Yet it proved curiously less attractive to my customers than it was to me. For months I had it on my shelves, where it was more admired than purchased.

'If they don't buy it when they're still smiling, they won't buy it at all,' said my colleague Peter Grogan helpfully.

I'm a sucker for books with great stories behind them. It's a rarefied sort of taste, but you have to believe that your sensibility isn't so arcane that no one else will share it. Whether they also have the money to buy is a separate question. My late literary agent and friend Giles Gordon had both. Every so often, after one of his famously indulgent lunches at the Garrick, he would roll merrily into my office, in search of some gossip and a book or two for his collection, his primary-coloured Paul Smith tie signalling his arrival from across the courtyard. Normally genial, with a few drinks in him he became manically sociable, burbling and giggling, breaking off into accents and impersonations (he gave good Tom Maschler, Anthony Cheetham, Tom Rosenthal), his voice dropping into an exaggerated – rather loud – whisper when he had a particularly juicy bit of gossip to relate.

He was, of course, not merely the source but the subject of good stories. With an eye for a pretty girl, he was often to be found at literary parties chatting up some attractive young copy editor or personal assistant. At such a party some years ago, when he was between marriages, Giles was interrupted in a promising tête-à-tête by the boisterous figures of Bernice Rubens and Beryl Bainbridge, the Abbott and Costello of the literary world.

'Giles, dear,' said Bernice, pushing her way past the promising young thing at his side, 'Beryl and I are having an argument, and we want you to settle it.'

'One's memory,' said Beryl in her best fey manner. 'It plays such tricks when you get to our age' – she put her arm round Giles to include him in this superannuated category – 'doesn't it, darling?'

'Happy to be of service,' said Giles. 'What is the problem?'

'Can you remind us,' said Beryl earnestly, 'which of us it was you had the affair with?'

Giles loved tricky moments.

'Both of you, darlings, both of you,' he chortled. 'And if you don't remember it, I *certainly* do!'

Beryl and Bernice toddled off, obscurely satisfied, and Giles returned his attentions to the new object of desire, his attractiveness undoubtedly enhanced by this example of both urbanity and sexual desirability.

The fun thing about Giles as a book collector was that although he had his tastes – David Jones, illustrated books, Wilde and Beardsley – he would buy anything that seemed interesting. He once purchased one of Ted Hughes' cancelled passports, and another time a book by D.H. Lawrence (whom he didn't admire) inscribed to E.M. Forster (whom he did).

So, his resistances already lowered, and certain, at least, that I had something to amuse him, I put the *Spycatcher* on the table.

'Have a look at this,' I said.

He did, and his eyebrows lifted a good inch.

'Well, you know I *have* to have this!' he said.

'For the Greene connection or the Philby?'

'Neither really, though it is marvellous. I agented this book, you know.'

I didn't. Giles put the book into his briefcase, wrote me a cheque for £4,000, and went home distinctly happy.

Happier than me. *Spycatch*er joined the relatively short list of books that I have regretted selling – not, like the inscribed first editions of *Ulysses* and *The Waste Land*, because it had overweening literary importance (certainly not!) – but because of what it reminded me of. Of Graham Greene, Ruffina Philby and Michael B., my trip to Moscow, Sotheby's, the British Library, and the loss of the Philby archive.

It would be wrong to say that the book haunted me after Giles bought it, but it nagged and niggled. I tried to buy it back from Giles, at a good profit to him, but he loved it, and had just as intimate a connection with it as I did. After his sad and unexpected death a few years later, I approached his wife to ask if I might borrow it, to use to illustrate a talk I was giving at the *London Review of Books* bookshop?

Reunited with the book, I found reason after reason to delay returning it. Some months later, offering to give it back at last, I suggested as an alternative that she might sell it to me instead.

'I don't want to sell anything of Giles's', she said. 'I want to keep it all with me.'

I wanted to keep it with me too, but quite understood, and demurred with something approaching good grace. But I still miss my *Spycatcher*. I would like to have it with me, indeed have it mounted on a plinth on my desk, as John Donne had his human skull, a bibliographic memento mori. I like the thought that it would puzzle others to see such an indifferent book so curiously elevated, but I would know what it signified. You don't have to read a book to be changed by it.

18

BIRDS OF A FEATHER

I'm as good as anybody you've got at the cop stuff, better at some things. The victims are all women and there aren't any women working this. I can walk in a woman's house and know three times as much about her as a man would know, and *you* know that's a fact. Send me.

Thomas Harris, *The Silence of the Lambs*

. . . fascination with murder is dangerous. It invites a kind of paralysis of the mental and moral faculties, a blind state of wonderment, featureless and useless. It merely soaks up images and sensations which lodge in the mind and threaten to fester.

Brian Masters, quoted by Anna Gekoski, *Murder By Numbers: British Serial Sex Killers Since 1950*

I don't know what it is teenagers do in their bedrooms that requires they be in there so frequently, and I'm not sure I want to know. Especially these days, when a typical teenage bedroom is like an electronic warehouse, with computers with wi-fi and broadband, the latest mobile phones, television, camcorders, whizzo speakers and all sorts of gadgets I can't understand. Becoming instantly intimate with strangers in chat rooms, transmitting images of themselves over MySpace and YouTube – *Broadcast Yourself!* Be a Celebrity! – why do they feel so comfortable, so secure, in this electronic environment? Why can't they just go upstairs and spritz over their books like we did?

It was bad enough twenty years ago, when Anna had access to none of the above, yet was still largely absent from ongoing family life, doing something or other in her bedroom. Talking on the phone incessantly, trying on skirts to see which was shortest, and blouses to confirm which could be seen through most comprehensively. But Barbara and I knew what she was mostly doing up there, and that was reading. We'd find her propped up in bed at any time of day or night, a paperback in her hands. We felt relieved, and proud of her: she read voraciously, at almost a book a day pace, so there was no need to worry about her time being used unproductively. This was reprehensibly naive of us, and dated from that period in which I felt that reading was, in some simple way, good for you.

Within a couple of years, I began my becoming less intelligent period, reading a thriller a day, and immediately passing them on to Anna. It was immense fun reading together, and discussing our favourites – Carl Hiaasen, Michael Connelly, James Lee Burke, Harlan Coben, Lawrence Block, James Harvey – at least when we could remember them. We ingested books together like sharing meals, and remembered as little about most of them as of last Thursday's breakfast. Cereal? Bacon and eggs? What does it matter?

I had purchased a flat in Primrose Hill in 1986, and opened it as an office for my new rare books business. I'd spend three nights a week there, and return home for long weekends, which was both a sensible business plan and a necessary marital one, because it was yet another period in which Barbara and I found each other's constant presence abrading. I purchased the flat entirely on my own, using money from my father's legacy – she never even came down to look at it – as a bolt hole into which I could escape for half the week. It initiated a period of great happiness and excitement for me, in my London incarnation, with the tricky marital negotiations of the weekends small price to pay, amply compensated by the chance to see the children. Bertie, then aged seven, didn't like the look or smell of it.

'Are you and mum separated?' he asked me, when it became clear that I was going to be away half the time.

'I wouldn't say that,' I prevaricated. 'Separations are for people who only have one house. We have two, and we use them both. And I need to be in London for my business, don't I?'

He was smart enough to see through this, and continued to seek reassurance.

'Look, dad,' he said, 'I'm a simple boy and I like a simple answer. Are you separated or not?'

'Not.'

He looked relieved, though not entirely satisfied. The 'simple boy' persona was, already, one of his life strategies. Of natively cheerful disposition, his way of dealing with discord was largely to deny it, which worked pretty well for him most of the time. Relentlessly positive in his selection of memories – an admirable quality – his account of his childhood has managed to blank out many of the problems of his parents' marriage. If he was later to pay some price for this psychic vigilance, in occasional sleeplessness and need to recheck that the doors are locked, it seemed, on the whole, rather a good deal.

Anna took the opposite position. When I got home from London on Thursday evenings she wouldn't talk to me, stayed in her room reading a book, her head turned away when I went upstairs to say hello. Reading was what she did when she was particularly angry; it is no wonder that she soon became addicted to thrillers and tales of serial killing.

She was often, sadly, a better reader of the state of our marriage, of how dangerously the tensions had risen, how fragile the emotional situation was, than Barbara and I were, and she had assumed from an early age the anxious role of watchdog and peace-maker. She knew what my regular absences meant: that Barbara and I were estranged, and that I had abandoned *her*. She glowered with that ingrowing rage that children who are powerless to halt the inevitable frequently feel, as their lives slowly morph into undesirable new forms.

On a Friday morning she still hadn't entirely forgiven me, but she was genuinely glad that I was home, and we would meet over the neutral ground of the kitchen table before she went to school. I'd give her a huge hug, and she would respond tentatively at first, firming up the pressure as the seconds went by. It was an immense relief to me each time, and heartbreaking.

'I'm glad to be home, chicken,' I'd say. She loved being called 'chicken', a nickname that dated back to her infancy, when I made up stories of a family of chicken-midgets who lived in my beard. She was one of them, and was happy psychically to remain so in some small part of herself. It was a process fraught with regressive possibility, which made it necessary that she develop at some point a strong alter ego to counterbalance this ongoing childhood persona.

I don't think it was on my recommendation that Anna first read Thomas Harris's *The Silence of the Lambs*, which was published in 1989. It wasn't the sort of thriller I much like. I think I read it at her suggestion, rather than she on mine. I hope this is right, because I would feel guilty having introduced her to such contagious material. There was my little chicken, filling her head with horrible images. Not like those from normal thrillers, which are usually sanitized by genre, for *The Silence of the Lambs* insistently reinforces and recommends its grisly core images of cannibalism, kidnapping and murder, gloats over them. Assuming one is susceptible, how is one to get that out of one's head?

The novel is based on an absurd premise, which sadly never quite becomes laughable – a serial killer is kidnapping fat girls to harvest them for their hides, which he wears as special party outfits – and features the chillingly memorable Hannibal Lecter, incarcerated for multiple murders and acts of cannibalism, restrained in his cell, masked, and kept at more than arm's length by his warders, who fear for their lives if he gets his teeth on them. Dr Lecter, ironically and alas, is psychiatry's most brilliant interpreter of the fantasies and procedures of serial killers of the most pathological sort. So it is to him that the FBI turns when they are stumped by the murders of one 'Buffalo Bill', as the newspapers have christened him, whose victims have begun to show up as eviscerated corpses in a series of watery sites. Surely, reasons Jack Crawford, Section Chief of the FBI's Behavioural Science unit (that deals with serial killers), Dr Lecter might have some insight into the crimes which the Bureau's vaunted VICAP profiling system is not helping to explain? But it's a remote possibility – even if he does know something, Lecter is unlikely to do more than play with his interrogators – and Crawford, whose adored wife Bella is dying of cancer, has neither the time nor the energy to pursue the lead. He sends Clarice Starling instead.

It is a sign of how little hope he has invested in the line of thought. Though she (like Anna) has degrees in criminology and psychology, as well as having worked in a mental health centre, Starling is only a first-year Quantico trainee, and palpably no match for Lecter. Nobody is. Crawford sends her anyway, prompted by an unspoken desire to test her and to further her career, and on a hunch that Lecter might speak to an attractive (and naive) young woman more openly than he would to a more seasoned operative. Anyway, there's nothing to be lost, and Starling is keen.

The book then plays itself out predictably. Starling and Lecter form an odd mutual attachment, more murders take place, Lecter offers some ambiguous clues, and then escapes from gaol, Starling ends up in deathly battle with the killer, almost loses her life, but emerges, heroic and triumphant, having rescued the most recent hostage on the very morning on which she was to be flayed. Recovering from her ordeal, she receives a letter from Dr Lecter, predicting that this will be the first of many such experiences for her: 'Because it's the plight that drives you, seeing the plight, and the plight will not end, ever.'

Identification with the victim is the key: the heroine is saving herself, and will need continually to do so. You can see how a girl might be moved by such an image. Anna was not then, never has been, an extroverted person. She has a bruised tender heart, conducts her meditations inwardly, comes slowly and undemonstratively to her conclusions. So it was quite impossible to assess or to measure the effect that the figure of Clarice Starling was having on her inner world. (A starling was a curiously appropriate bird, having Anna's own dark plumage and relative shortness of stature.) She contracted Clarice Starling much more violently than I had, at the same age, caught Holden Caulfield. But in Anna's case, aside from acknowledging that she thought both the book and film of *The Silence of the Lambs* 'pretty good', one had no idea what subtle transformation she was undergoing inwardly.

She didn't either. Just as a tourist returning from an obscure land may contract a disease but not have the first outbreak for a number of years, so too Anna was unaware of harbouring a dangerous virus, caught like some sort of avian flu. There were occasional clues, but too easily misinterpreted. A few years after first reading *The Silence of the Lambs*, when she had started at York University, she went to Paris with her boyfriend (later her estimable and loving husband) Steve Broome, and he bought her a baseball cap as a souvenir. It wasn't very Gallic. It was a simple French blue, to be sure, but it bore the white letters FBI on the front. She wore it like a uniform, proudly and incessantly. We all thought it was cute, this pretty, slight-figured girl in her FBI hat. We didn't know she was serious.

Like me, and pretty much like my father, she'd gone to read English and philosophy at university, though she individuated herself a little, in family terms, by dropping the English within a few weeks.

'I don't understand the questions they keep asking,' she said of her professors, 'much less what would count as an answer to them.' She felt happier with the hard edges of philosophy, which was less vague, less personal, based on argument rather than opinion. In those days Arts professors announced that their subjects should be pursued for 'their own sakes', though what English or philosophy were, such that they had a sake, was never divulged. Anna certainly didn't want to teach – she was too diffident even to lead a seminar when requested to by her teachers – so I assumed she was simply educating herself, developing the tenor of her rather sharp analytical mind, and that vocational yearnings were not part of her short-term thinking.

It came as some surprise, then, towards the end of her final year, when she announced she was applying to do post-graduate work at Cambridge in criminology.

'Why would you want to do that?' I asked incredulously, unaware of her identification with Agent Starling.

'So that I can apply to Quantico, and train as a profiler.'

'To the FBI? Like your hat?'

'That's where they do it.'

'You're kidding, right?'

'I could qualify. I'm an American citizen.'

I paused, to give this my full attention, and to take it seriously. We were about to define a turning point in her life. I thought for a while. She waited patiently.

'What're you, crazy?'

The next thing I knew, of course, was that I was helping her to fill out the application. We read the course description with care, and I was relieved to learn that what most criminologists did was to study the effects of street lighting on urban crime, to tabulate *this*, and provide a statistical model for *that*. Anna sneered. A criminologist studies crime, right? And the biggest and worst crime is murder, and the king of murderers is the serial killer, right? With this regal if peculiar line of thought, she began composing an essay describing her macabre interests, to accompany her application. Great! Given that ninety-five per cent of candidates for the course were rejected, Anna was positioning herself nicely for a quick dismissal, after which she could pick from some sensible options, like buying shoes for Harvey Nichols (she's addicted to shoes) or becoming an editor at a nice publishing house that does thrillers.

But she got in. She did well. She wrote her thesis on British serial sex killers. She revelled in Cambridge life, studied hard, drank and partied a lot, had fun. The year seemed over in a flash, and to have delayed the inevitable. No, she was not going to become a profiler – the very thought of the training as an FBI agent was a sufficient deterrent – and the question *what to do next?* arose once again. A PhD based on more of the same? No, I was unprepared to fund it. Doctorates are for people who want – or at least are willing – to teach.

Giles Gordon, who adored Anna, came up with the answer. Why not extend her MPhil thesis into a book? It was a sexy topic, and she was a sexy girl, and the combination of the two, he recognized, would be distinctly saleable.

'I can't write a book!' said Anna. 'I'm not that good a writer, and I don't have enough confidence.'

Giles smiled reassuringly.

'It's a terrific idea,' he said, 'starting with the childhood of a serial killer and seeing how and why they develop. Just do them, one at a time, like a series of essays. Don't think: book. You'll be fine.'

Over the next twelve months she read, did research, wrote letters to incarcerated serial killers, even consulted Hirschfeld's *Sexual Anomalies and Perversions* to read the chapter on Sexual Murder.

(I'd skipped that one.) In a further year she had finished a long book entitled *Murder By Numbers*, a study of British serial sex killers since 1950, which was published by André Deutsch, who had outbid Macmillan and Hodder for the rights. At exactly the same time I was selling – also through Giles – my book about Premiership football, *Staying Up*, and when Anna and I met, instead of swapping thrillers we would exchange chapters, and make encouraging comments.

But the enterprises were not comparable. I was hanging out with footballers Gordon Strachan, Gary MacAllister and Dion Dublin, and going to matches at Highbury and Anfield, while she was in the constant company, figuratively but harrowingly, of the Yorkshire Ripper, the Moors murderers, of Fred and Rose West, Dennis Nilsen and other predators and maniacs. It was radioactive material, contagiously unstable and explosive, and (like Homer Simpson) she was ill-equipped to handle it safely. Every day, at her desk or away from it, with frightening assiduousness, Anna was thinking and dreaming about sadists who raped and slaughtered vulnerable young women: of people who wanted to murder *her*, she fitted the demographic perfectly. (Interestingly, the major readership of true crime books is women in their twenties and thirties.)

Barbara and I worried for her, fussed over her, offered cups of tea, homeopathic remedies, and counsel, but were reassured by her stoic engagement with her task. She was fascinated by the material, and if she identified with the victims it was partly in order to give them a voice, and hence a symbolic reprieve. She was the agent who could go into the darkness and emerge, if not with a rescued girl, at least with a story, a point of view, and a cause. As a writer she also rescued the part of herself that had always felt raw, exposed, and vulnerable: she became the Clarice Starling both of, and to, her own darkest imaginings.

She wrote with frightening intensity, propelled by a series of forces of which fear was probably the greatest. *Writer's* fear: of not being good enough, of getting it wrong, writing badly, thinking slackly, opening herself to criticism. She was, after all, only twenty-two. Anxious on her behalf – my anxiety for her was psychological rather than intellectual – I attached myself to the emerging manuscript as if my presence could help to ward off the insidious forces with which she was grappling. She was writing every day about the murders of young women just like herself. How could she avoid being dragged into an abyss of identification with her victims, however much she was employing her inner Clarice Starling on their (and her own) behalf? She was aware of the dangers, she maintained, but in control of them. What she wanted was help of an editorial not a psychological kind. Was her Introduction good enough? Did the prose flow? Was the chapter on the Wests reading all right? How could she frame a Conclusion?

I edited that manuscript, blue pencil in hand like a sabre, as if I could defend Anna from the demons that it both described and threatened to unleash. They attacked me, certainly enough, and unless I was ceaselessly vigilant my head would fill with terrible images. Surely hers would as well? I have always been anxious for her. From the moments I first held her after her birth, she has seemed to me so delicate a gift that she would always need constant, unobtrusive and benign watching over. She developed into a remarkably loving and fiercely loyal little girl, whose attachments to both people and objects were almost comical in their intensity. When she was four, she howled when our old sofa was sold, and attached herself to its legs so the removal men couldn't take it from the house. In supermarkets she would insist that we buy the dented tins, so that they wouldn't be left alone, sad and unwanted on the shelf.

When she was little I would take her to our Victoria Park playground, and she would insist on climbing the steps of the large slide, all seventeen of them, to a height of some twenty feet. As she reached the top, and her hands let go of the rail, she would teeter slightly, right herself, and prepare to sit down. Below her, on the paved tarmac, I would shuffle from left to right as she swayed, arms held out, hoping to catch her, in her fuzzy brown jacket, as she lost her balance and plummeted down, to smash herself against the ground. I could envisage her little body, twisted and broken as she landed, just on the wrong side of the slide, as I dived and failed to save her.

I'd sit in the evenings with her manuscript and her blessing, correcting, editing, redrafting, inserting phrases and questions, crossing things out, connecting one bit to another, and I'd think, 'She's on the fucking slide again, and this is me diving and trying to catch her when she is in danger. It's all I can do for her now: I can edit.'

When Lucy's dismembered body was found, in 1994, there was cord and tape wound around her head, and many bones were absent. Horrifyingly, it seems that she may have been kept alive in the cellar for up to a week.

No, I thought, as I made my notes: '*Show, don't tell. Be specific: how and why "wound around her head"? Which bones were absent? Is there any need for "Horrifyingly"? Let the facts speak for themselves!*' I eventually crossed the comments out, and left the passage as it stands. Who wants or needs such details? Tell, don't show!

Lucy Partington, a twenty-one-year-old student at Exeter University, niece of Kingsley and cousin of Martin Amis, in the wrong place at the wrong time. An Anna Gekoski, making a bad decision, accepting a lift from strangers on a rainy Gloucester night. As soon as I began to think about it, about what happened to poor Lucy Partington, my mind capsized with images, and began to founder. Why should I have to think such thoughts: about her, or about her double, my daughter? *Why did Anna wish to?*

It was a mystery, curiously analogous to the mystery with which her book ended: why is it that a very few children grow up to be serial killers, and the rest don't? Anna is circumspect in her answer to this question, citing Wittgenstein's arguments against essence, denying some 'factor X' of the sort posited by Colin Wilson, instead sensibly laying down conditions, neither necessary nor sufficient, which may turn a child into a murderer. But there was a clear pattern: serial killers had abusive fathers and over-protective mothers, were introverted and often bullied at school, they withdrew into a toxic inner state as their rage transformed into sadistic fantasy.

As for why *she* should have developed such grisly interests, when most children don't, she was similarly careful, and tentative. In an article that she published in *Vogue* after *Murder By Numbers* came out, all she would offer by way of explanation was that she had been 'entranced' by *The Silence of The Lambs*:

The combination of intellect, sex-appeal, and violence was irresistible . . . I was, in 1990, a shy and tentative 16-year-old, still unformed and somewhat alarmed at the intensity of my interest in the book. Clarice Starling became my heroine and alter-ego. I wanted to be her because she was so unlike me. She was a powerful, fearless, gun-carrying hunter of the 'monsters' that preyed on the innocent. It was pure fantasy of course, and one which I shared with many other young women who read the book. But for most of these women the fantasy was transitory. Mine was not.

How did this happen? Most readers got over *The Silence of the Lambs*, but Anna was captivated and transformed by it. Some unexpected inner seed germinated, and there seemed little she, or her parents, could do to control the process. If it hadn't been Clarice Starling it would have been someone else. Or, and this was a radical and disarming thought, could it be that the furious little girl that

she had been, feeling abandoned, abused and enraged, had identified neither with the FBI heroine nor with the victims, but with
the murderer himself? Could it have been that the unconscious
role model was not Clarice Starling but Hannibal Lecter?

When she'd finished writing she took to her bed for two months,
utterly depleted. And when she rallied – denying all the time that
she was suffering the psychic effects of her long journey into the
underworld – she shook herself off, and got back to work: began
a career as a *News of the World* reporter specializing in crime ('It's
the job my alter ego has always wanted.'), and ghosted a book for
Sara Payne, the mother of the eight-year-old girl murdered by a
paedophile.

But she was restless and unfulfilled, and the incessant ugliness
of the *News of the World* drained her. For a time the demands of
the job had strengthened her sinews, made her more confident,
but it couldn't last. Soon she didn't want just to write about crim-
inals, but to study them eyeball to eyeball. She enrolled for an MSc
in forensic psychology with a view to working as a psychologist in
a prison or secure hospital. She wanted to hear the confessions of
the Yorkshire Ripper, to analyse the motivations of Ian Brady, to
recommend a course of action for treating Rose West.

Thank God it didn't work out, as following the fantasy began
to lead closer and closer to the reality. She soon decided that she
no longer wanted to work with rapists and killers, to spend days
confronting people who had done terrible things to others, and
who probably wanted to do them to her. So instead of applying
for jobs as a trainee forensic psychologist, she chose a related but
altogether gentler course of action, doing doctoral research into
how victims of crime may be re-victimized by their experiences
with criminal justice agencies such as the police and courts.

It's good work, and I suppose somebody has to do it, and teach
it, which she seems to enjoy more than I – or she – would have
guessed. But she confesses that she dreams of doing something or

other with shoes: 'fabulous, high-heeled, brightly coloured, happy-making shoes'.

Shoes? Why not? 'Sherlock Holmes became a bee-keeper didn't he? And that detective in *The Moonstone*, Sergeant Cuff, is addicted to rose-growing. So perhaps my shoe fantasies aren't so odd: roses, bees, shoes – they're all a way of seeing the nicer, brighter side of life.'

You don't have to be Alice Miller to understand the symbolism.

19

STAYING UP WITH BERTIE

'I am trained, as an academic, in habits of analysis, in trying to figure out how things work – whether those things are novels, or even football clubs. And I'm a supporter of the club, so I don't think there is anything to fear.' I was starting to babble . . .

Rick Gekoski, *Staying Up*

Gerald Crich's mother, in Lawrence's *Women in Love*, is an odd old bird, fierce and dissatisfied as a hawk sulking in a cage, given to embarrassing behaviour, and gnomic utterance. In an early chapter of the novel she is talking to Rupert Birkin, during a family party, surrounded by people she doesn't recognize:

'I don't know people whom I find in the house. The children introduce them to me – "Mother, this is Mr So-and-so." I am no further. What has Mr So-and-so to do with his own name?'

That is terribly funny and provocative: 'What does Mr So-and-so have to do with his own name?' Not because he is called 'So-and-so'. The newcomer is called Señor Fitzpoodle, or the Duke of Earl, or Dr R.A. Gekoski. Obviously something can be learned from such nomenclature, but nothing – to Mrs Crich – that is at all essential. Why have a name, in that case? Whatever can be learned from it?

The answer, Mrs Crich, is: a lot, if you are sufficiently interested. (She isn't.) I've had several in my time, and when I segue from one to the other it indicates that some major changes have occurred in my life. Since childhood, except for a short and unremembered period in which I was apparently called Richie, I became Ricky, and within the family have stayed that way since. In ordinary life I have always been Rick, a name that strikes me as lacking gravitas compared to Richard, which is my given name. But I have never felt like a Richard, always a Rick. Rick Gekoski, then. (I don't much like Gekoski either.)

But once I went to college, all of a sudden I had two names: one personal, and one academic, as if one were bifurcated by the very process of higher education. At Penn, we used the American format: formal first name, initial, second name: my essays were all written by Richard A. Gekoski, and I rather liked the dignity that seemed to confer upon them. They were marked by Professors William H. Marshall and Peter B. Murray. At Oxford I immediately changed my studying name to R.A. Gekoski, in deference to local usage, not having learned, yet, that when you change your language – especially when you change your name – you change your life. A few years later this person morphed into Dr R.A. Gekoski, a name I still use when making airline reservations.

The life changes that accompanied these alterations of name were imperceptible, to me at least. But what happened over the next years was that my voice changed. I do not mean that I acquired my characteristic mid-Atlantic accent, which often happens to Americans who emigrate to England. In fact, most of my English friends claim that I still sound American after forty years in the UK, though I am frequently mistaken for English when I visit America.

'Ah, you'se over from da old country?' said New York's Carnegie Delicatessen waitress when I ordered my pastrami sandwich.

'Excuse me?' Presumably I must have sounded Polish to her ears?

'Jolly old England,' she said, affecting an English accent which made her sound like Joyce Grenfell drowning in the bath.

'That's right,' I said. 'Can I have extra pickles? English people like pickles.'

'You have a good day,' she said.

Not *that* voice. The critical change was not in how I sounded, but in what I said, and how I said it. There was nothing conscious about this process, and it was understandable enough. When we go somewhere new we pick up not merely accents, but different ways of seeing and expressing ourselves. Over the next decade I found myself attempting to express myself more complexly, delicately, and ironically: to think and talk, that is, as if I were English. Or, more accurately, to take my relatively ill-informed notion of Englishness, and apply it to my own voice. The best way to illustrate this is to quote to you part of the second paragraph of a book by one R.A. Gekoski, entitled *Joseph Conrad: The Moral World of the Novelist*, which was published in 1978, and based on my DPhil thesis. He is talking about Conrad's portrayal of women:

His women attain to particularity only in the absence of those fulfilments that sentiment would ascribe to them. Like so many of Conrad's male heroes, they are all defined and particularised with reference to the test which they undergo, rather than by a challenge that they generate themselves . . . Conrad's heroes seem not to have depths discretely their own; their inner lives consist, in the most dramatic form, of a reflection or enactment of the universe in which they live.

My sister Ruthie, having read this far – we're still on page 1 – abandoned the book. It was, she said, 'too intelligent' for her. But it was, in fact, quite the reverse, her judgement a symptom of her loveably unflagging belief in my intellectual superiority, and lack of confidence in her own considerable critical abilities.

What the hell does 'attain to particularity' mean? It must be important because the term 'particular' is used again, almost immediately. (I suspect simple sloppiness here.) What is the 'most dramatic form' that 'an inner life' can have? How does that inner life 'enact' the universe? I could go on. The prose is immature and crunchingly academic, and its badness is multi-determined. If language could elicit psychotherapy this might be a good candidate. The obvious problem is the strain: nothing flows, there is no sense, none whatsoever, of a speaking voice. Its author is trying to appear more intelligent than he is, anxiously injecting a needlessly complex vocabulary to make relatively simple points. Desperate to impress, himself most of all.

Oh well, perhaps many brightish aspiring academics are like that, writing dissertations, and worrying. The strained tone, though, is characteristic of academics generally, and you can hear it in more mature (and better) writers than my immature self. It is the tone of people constantly anxious that their colleagues may be smarter than they are.

The second problem with my little paragraph is that it is an ill-conceived, thoroughly inadequate piece of ventriloquism. Ever hear an American – even a good actor – trying to do an English accent? Embarrassing. That is what is happening in my sentences, and I'm not even a good actor. This is a poor miming of English sensibility, and it rings false.

I am sorry to be so hard on my former self, it feels unpleasant of me: I wouldn't judge someone else who wrote like that quite so harshly. But it saddens me, and makes me cross, to have wasted so much energy on so little output. I didn't write another book for twenty years, because I couldn't. I started several, particularly the one on D.H. Lawrence that stuttered on for years. I tried desperately to make headway with it when on sabbatical in 1975 at Wesleyan University in Connecticut, soon after Anna's birth and my mother's death. Exhausted, thoroughly depleted, I went to the library every morning to write, leaving Barbara with a new baby and little in the way of infrastructure, friends or support. I came home every night guiltily pretending to have done an honest day's work.

I hardly wrote a single word, and it was unrelenting agony, trying, and failing, and trying again. Norman Mailer describes writer's block as 'simply a failure of ego', which is right in many ways that I couldn't recognize at the time. What caused this failure was unknown to me, and I attributed it to some internal force that didn't want me to succeed, *to make a name for myself*. The career of one R.A. Gekoski, DPhil and university lecturer, seemed to be going nowhere. I worried if I would ever get promoted, though I did, in 1981, when I became a senior lecturer. Then I worried that the promotion had been premature and unwarranted. I was certain I would never become a professor. Not that I liked professors very much, most of them were even more pompous and defensive – and competitive – than I was. Presumably you grow into the job.

It took me another ten years to realize – I am a slow developer – that my academic inability to write, this 'writer's block' as I described it, was in fact a creative method in which my unconscious was desperately trying to tell me something. The message was simple: *I do not like or recognize this 'R.A. Gekoski': he is not pursuing ends that are good for him, he is inauthentic and his efforts are those of an unhappy person manifesting his unhappiness. His tones are strangulated, pompous and unreal, a pretend voice and not a real one. I won't let him write like this, not without a fight. Every word he tries to write I will resist every letter of the way*. And that is how it felt. I didn't have writer's block, I had identity block.

Now read this, published twenty years later, by one Rick Gekoski in a book titled *Staying Up: A Fan Behind the Scenes in the Premiership*.

I had decided to go wherever I wanted until someone told me not to, a policy that proved remarkably successful as I accompanied the team onto the pitch for the pre-match warm-up. Airily announcing to two amiable Torquay stewards, 'I'm with the Coventry lads,' I ambled through the barrier and onto the pitch with Dion Dublin, only to hear one of the stewards say 'Who's he, the chairman?' The other considered: 'Nah, probably the owner.' I was exultant. Life was different on the other side of the barrier.'

The difference between this and my Conrad paragraph is not attributable to the fact that the first is academic, and the second popular: this is not an example of a high-minded person slumming it 'on the other side of the barrier'. The new prose is, if you will, the result of my former projects of writing more freely, and becoming less intelligent. Its author is clearly having fun, expressing himself simply, and if showing off, he is not doing so by trying to be cleverer than he is, just more important. It sounds, I have been told, as if I were simply talking, and the reader listening. That was the idea anyway.

I had talked the chairman of my beloved Coventry City Football Club, Bryan Richardson, into letting me write a behind-the-scenes book about the 1997–8 Premier League football season. I had no idea what to expect, but the idea of hanging out with manager Gordon Strachan and his team was thrillingly beguiling. I was given open access to the chairman, the team's administrative officers, and all of those on the management and playing side. It was my brief to write an account of what a football season is *really* like, not to talk about myself. Most sports books are written as 'fly on the wall' accounts, and make little reference to the writer's own experience, much less to his feelings. What readers are interested in, after all, is what the chairman does and Gordon Strachan has to say, what centre forward Dion Dublin is like once you get to know him.

This assumes a modest narrative presence: the fly must be invisible on the wall, which is appropriate, because that is how sports people treat not merely journalists but almost everyone else as well. I found this more than a little disconcerting. Players turned their backs on me, Strachan 'forgot' appointments, I was kept waiting for hours in offices, dugouts, practice grounds and stadia. Nobody gave a damn if it bothered me. I not only had no rights, I had no self.

'That's how we treat newcomers,' centre back Gary Breen confided to me, 'even when a new player joins the team it takes us a long time to let him in. We go all shy, like a herd of animals.'

I was not used to this, as an experienced journalist would be, and found it impossible to put aside my feelings of hurt, thwarted friendliness and anger. Talking and being talked to is how I make my living, it's what I like and need, and all of a sudden my normal resources failed. My curiosity met with indifference, attempts to charm were shrugged or laughed off, the merest request for simple attention was ignored. It was no fun at all, and the only solace was that I could, at least, write about the process. *Staying Up* thus became a kind of travel book, about a visit to a remote foreign land. The traveller doesn't know the customs or the language, he looks different, and is regarded with suspicion. He learns to speak slowly and quietly, if at all, and to move about unobtrusively. The natives warily keep him at a distance, and only slowly accommodate themselves to his ways, as he to theirs. It's a difficult process, and takes patience. It reminded me of my first days at Oxford.

And so I became, if not the hero certainly the protagonist. When you write you are inevitably describing yourself as well as your object (even in academic writing, as my Conrad paragraph demonstrates). *Staying Up* had to be in my *personal* voice because it was about trying to find and to employ that voice in a familiar but suddenly alien setting: the voice that could be heard on the terraces, and in my conversations about football, not about literature.

Most of these talks were with Bertie, then aged seventeen, who was my fellow traveller during the season, and frequently my guide. He had developed from the self-proclaimed 'simple boy' of seven into a remarkably genial, intelligent and artistic, highly rational young man. The only member of our family who could keep his head in a crisis, he tried to avoid disputes, but once in them had a remarkable knack for finding a resolution. In the continuing discord that was frequently our family life, I often tried to react as I thought he might, and often failed.

He took the opposite course to his sister's: if she was fated to plumb the abysmal waters, he was determinedly staying up on the surface of things. His choice of career – he was to read advertising and marketing at university, and later founded his own modelling agency – was inevitable and appropriate for someone who wanted to fill his head with positive images. Anna, he felt, looked into things too deeply and suffered for it, though he rather envied her, while she admired his capacity to protect himself from the darkness. If her fantasy was to skim happily across the surface of things in her magical shoes, he admits to a desire to become an underwater videographer.

His level-headed amusement at my floundering about became one of the book's topics, and supplied a measured response to my own amalgam of frustration and over-excitement. He was allowed much of the freedom of access that was offered to me, but had it in better perspective. He quite enjoyed standing next to the pitch while the players warmed up before a game – I *loved* it – but quickly (and rightly) got bored.

'Why are we here, dad?' he asked. 'What good is it doing us?' I was shocked.

'Look around you!' I said. 'See all the people in the stands? Any of them down here? We're here because we're allowed to be here, and they're not.'

He shook his head in mock pity, and headed back to the stands to read his programme, disregarding my shout that he had no soul.

I had better conversations with other City fans, more envious than Bertie of my new status, and anxious to be told what was going on. If I'd cravenly lost my confidence in the presence of Strachan and the players, I found myself treating the other supporters as if I were one of the elect converting the heathens. The only consolation I could offer myself for this shameful bit of psychic inflation was that what had happened to me was both interesting and right. It would happen to any fan allowed so extensively behind the scenes. The best part is not being there, but talking about it to people who wish they were.

I thus became a representative figure, living out the universal fantasy of sports fans. My desire to know was theirs, my privileged access to the inside story an instance of what they all yearned for. On the train up to one of the games, a Coventry City supporter had enjoined me, earnestly: 'Be careful! You're living this experience for all of us, and you're writing for us all!' He was identifying himself, then, as the ideal reader that every writer has in mind, however subliminally, as he writes. To whom is the story directed? Whose praise would mean the most?

After *Staying Up* was published, two responses stood out, and gave me the most satisfaction. The first was from the redoubtable poet and critic Ian Hamilton (himself the author of *Gazza Agonistes*, and a Spurs supporter) reviewing the book in the *Sunday Telegraph*. *Staying Up*, he wrote, actually told us things about football we hadn't known, 'was richly comic', and 'the year's best soccer book by far'.

I could hardly have imagined a more satisfactory response, but I got one, and it came, modestly enough, in a reader's report on amazon.com. The writer didn't give his name (he called himself 'A Customer') and was clearly at the other end of the literary spectrum from Ian Hamilton. He was obviously a passionate City supporter, though. He was one of us:

> Fantastic reading best book I have read. I bought this book the very first day it came out on sale and it took me 3 days to read. I thought the way the book was written and no holds barred with some of the stories which mentioning no names got offended by if it was about me I would have been honoured.

I had simultaneously satisfied, then, the old R.A. readership, and the new Rick one.

Benjamin Disraeli, asked if he had read *Daniel Deronda*, remarked, 'If I want to read a novel, I write one.' This is wry, and has some nice hidden truths, but I'll bet he *had* read *Daniel Deronda*. I like the notion that authors don't merely write their own books, they read them too – and that the processes are separable. As I sat and read the final draft of *Staying Up*, I recognized it was one of the most important reading experiences of my lifetime. The writing struck me, at last, as having the relaxed ease, and good humoured intelligence, that I had never found as a writer. My ideal reader, finally, was me.

The final chapters of *Staying Up* reflected just this process: during the early stages of my travels in football-land I had tried to adapt to customs that were alien to me, and lost confidence in my own voice, just as I had in academic life and in assimilating to Englishness. At the end of the experience there was an odd mixture of triumph and despair. Travelling to the final match of the season, I experienced a shy sense of loss and anticlimax, and again it was Bertie who helped supply perspective.

'I've seen you talking with the fans, and with our friends all year. I've heard every one of your opinions a hundred times. It's been "As Gordon was saying the other day", and "actually Bryan doesn't think that, the true story is . . ."'

'OK,' I said, recognizing the ring of truth when I heard it. 'You're right. So why do I feel so low?'

'Because you wanted it to be easy, and fun, and some of it was hard work. And because you're sad that it's over.'

He smiled, as much to himself as to me, adding: 'But I know you, and you've loved it.'

I had, and I was grateful to him once again.

A friend, reading *Staying Up*, remarked that although she had no interest in football, the book was really about how much I love Bertie. Going to the football games, like the golf that we played every week, was part of a normal process of bonding between father and son, but I have always had an additional tie to him, because he both recalls and replaces my father. Not merely in his sweet reasonableness, but because his birth was followed so quickly by my father's death – as Anna's had been by my mother's. Genetic replacement is ruthless in our family, and Bertie's charmed babyhood was linked to my father's last days.

Dad died of pancreatic cancer in 1981, at the age of sixty-eight. As he lay peacefully awaiting the end – he was as inspiring an example of how to die as my mother was a sad one – he confided, 'I never had much energy,' as if that explained it. Though he outlived my mother by eleven years, and she had bags of energy, most of it misdirected, my father wasn't built to last, and seemed not to regret it. I did, terribly. His virtues were Chaucerian: largeness of vision, freedom from cant, shrewdness, benignity. He treated everyone he met with the same quiet respect, lived an exemplary inner life, and would have died reconciled to his God if he'd had one. His example and legacy became part of my psychological and moral cellular structure and his death, like his life, formed and enabled me, and through me, Bertie, the star of *Staying Up*, who enjoyed the finished book but not as much, I think, as he had liked *Matilda*, which showed good judgement.

My diminished spirits on finishing the football season were further restored when Bertie and I were invited to dinner with the Coventry City directors, before the final game at Everton. Suddenly I found myself, surprisingly, at ease: 'The tone was familiar and cordial, and as I sat laughing, telling them all about the progress of the book, and the difficulties of the early months, I had the sudden, sharp realisation that I was speaking in my own voice.'

It had been a great lesson, and a coming into consciousness. Writing as Rick banished R.A. – I won't write under that name again – and reinstated myself to myself. Yet this Rick Gekoski, as author, incorporated what I had been, rather than simply obliterating it. The campaign to become less intelligent had served its purpose, and been misconceived. The better idea was to become differently intelligent. And so Rick Gekoski doesn't overwrite R.A., he ingests him and transforms his voice. One person, one voice.

I had managed to make reading and writing into work, and now they weren't. I began to rescue those worthy tomes – that 'literature' – that had made me feel alternately frightened and bored, and to take real pleasure in them once again: to reread Henry James, to ask myself how much of *The Waste Land* I could still recite, to cut down on my allowance of thrillers (except Carl Hiaasen) and replace it with more demanding fiction. Surely there was some significant gain in this reclamation of things past? I'd never had all that much learning anyway, which made it easier to wear it lightly.

It was a year in which a number of burdens eased. Though Barbara had been generous while I was writing *Staying Up*, allowing me to spend two nights a week at the house while I hung out with the City players, it had been some time since we had lived together. This new estrangement felt different from the old ones, had less fire and more resignation in it. We were simply worn out with each other, the children had left home, there was nothing substantial holding us together except the emotional scenarios that we seemed doomed to repeat without resolution, like players trapped in a script.

My understanding of my marriage is limited and incomplete, and my attempts to generalize about it leave me feeling foolish, unperceptive and vaguely fraudulent. Things happened, one after another, patterns seemed to suggest themselves and then recede, needs and feelings emerged imperiously and waned unexpectedly, the sheer immediacy of the moments overwhelmed either the desire or the capacity to link one inextricably to the next. So when I asked after thirty years of marriage and an impending divorce – *what went wrong?* – the answer was not, quite, that I didn't know, but that I could hardly imagine what would count as a satisfactory answer. Any that I might have given would have felt facile and incomplete. We'd met while on the rebound? We came from such different backgrounds that a computer would have spat us out as a bad match?

But lots of couples are animated by their differences, and many meet while on the bounce. These may have been factors, but they're not explanations. I can't do better than this: something didn't happen, that appears to happen in better and more durable marriages than ours. I hardly knew what it was, having little experience of it. My parents didn't discover it, nor did Barbara's. But dear Ruthie and Roy, in spite of the maelstrom of his ill health, were never engulfed, never ceased to love one another. I observed this with envious incomprehension.

It has something to do with trust, doesn't it? A reflexive cleaving together when the impulse is to fly apart, some reliable emotional disinterestedness. I hope this doesn't aspire to a definition. There isn't one, surely? It would be dreadful if there were.

Love resists its name, but it was simple, after all. I needed to feel loved, and I didn't, and hadn't. I suppose Barbara felt the same. We had settled for that for much too long, tried being together, and apart, and mixtures of the two. This protracted ambivalence was foolish and damaging, but it also produced a reservoir of cherished moments, images and memories. I don't regret any of it. It was what I chose.

The best, and least expected, result of the publication of *Staying Up* was that it introduced me to Belinda Kitchin, whom I was to marry in 2004. I'd gone to an opening at the Grosvenor Gallery – reluctantly, and only on the promise of an Italian meal with white truffles afterwards from my friend Michael Estorick – to view the work of some Irish artist or other. The pictures weren't very arresting, I didn't know anyone, and was thoroughly bored when, of a sudden, someone trod on my foot. An extremely attractive, immediately amused and friendly woman turned round, and without much embarrassment said, 'Sorry!'

'It's nothing,' I said, 'you must do it again.'

'I was just going outside for a cigarette,' she said.

'I think I'll join you,' I said, and we introduced ourselves.

We were standing outside companionably, puffing away, animatedly asking and answering the usual questions, when Michael came out and glared at me.

'I thought you'd stopped smoking!'

'I have,' I said, 'but you know how meeting a good-looking woman makes me anxious.'

She didn't though. She was instantly approachable, bright, curious, laughed with the easy openness of antipodeans (she is a New Zealander, though raised largely in Malawi), and made me feel that I just had to get to know her. I liked her immediately, more than liked her, *recognized* something in her.

Michael invited her to join us for dinner, and was soon apologizing for not having read *Staying Up*, which had just been published.

'What's that?' asked Belinda.

I explained that it was a book about football. She made a face. Like many of her generation of New Zealand women she has a disdain for big-time sport, is untouched, and a little bemused, by the adulation of the All Blacks, and had participated in the protests against the South African Springboks tour to New Zealand in 1981. Not an ideal reader for a book about my compulsive interest in Coventry City.

I could virtually see her estimation of me collapsing. 'It's not so bad, really,' I hastened to say, not exactly apologizing for the book, but attempting to interest her just a little. 'It's really a sort of travel book, with balls.'

She raised her eyelids.

'You know, stranger goes to a strange land, the natives and he don't understand each other, various funny things happen . . .'

'Maybe I should read it,' she said. I would have had a bet that she'd never read a book about sport before.

'I hope you'll like it, I'll send you a copy. What's your address?'

'I am,' she said firmly, 'perfectly capable of purchasing a book by myself.'

'I don't doubt that,' I said, immediately clear that she was perfectly capable of doing and saying anything she wanted. 'But I would be so delighted if you'd accept one as a present.'

She wouldn't. A week later we rang each other at exactly the same moment to make a date. I invited her to the opening of an exhibition at the British Library. Fancy party, wine and canapés, pretty impressive venue for a first date.

When we got there the building was dark, the gates locked. I wandered about shouting for somebody to let us in.

'Are you sure this is the right night?' Belinda asked, peering into the gloom.

'Of course it's the right bloody night!'

It wasn't. I'd arrived a week early. Chastened by this sad example of bibliophilic premature ejaculation, I took her for champagne and oysters at Odette's Restaurant in Primrose Hill, round the corner from my flat in Chalcot Square.

She was remarkably forgiving, and we talked and talked, and slurped and drank. When we got to the flat I opened a half-bottle of 1983 Chateau Climens, a wonderful Barsac, and a token of my increasing esteem. She took one taste and seemed, of a sudden, to regard me with further interest and respect.

She'd liked *Staying Up*, and she came to love Rick Gekoski: author, voice, person. As I came to love her. She is a totally supportive but not unchallenging companion, with a remarkable emotional accuracy and integrity. I trust her entirely.

Good thing I didn't give Belinda my Conrad book, that would have been the last I'd have seen of her. She later tried to read it, but gave it up after a few pages, with a baffled look.

'How could you have written this sort of stuff?' she asked.

'It's a long story,' I said.

EPILOGUE

April is the cruellest month, breeding
Lilacs out of the dead land, mixing
Memory with desire . . .
>   T.S. Eliot, *The Waste Land*

I

From a man without a philosophy no one can expect philosophical completeness; clearness is the one merit which a plain, unsys-
tematic writer, without a philosophy, can hope to have. The words
are in fact Matthew Arnold's, but they are so apposite that I want
to make them my own. I wish that this investigation of myself
and of my reading amounted to something, something more than
it has: wish I had a theory, a wider perspective, something general
with which to conclude, and from which someone could learn
something. Something big, something Hortonish. But I have no
theory of selfhood, nor of reading, nor of psychological development, or more properly I have them in bits, which added together
come to nothing more than an unreliable set of dispositions, opinions and prejudices. I am sceptical about theory, do not believe
in essence, adore particularity, like to keep my eyes on the text

not the idea. This has its benefits, though my incapacity to generalize rather saddens me, and makes me feel as if I had started a job and had neither the wit, the energy, nor the penetration to finish it.

II

I do know some things. My books have made me, and through them I know myself, and through myself I know them. And nobody can take them away.

III

I still wish I believed in angels. De Quincey says that 'in an angelic understanding, all things would appear to be related to all'. What, then, would be the opposite of an angel: a practical critic? Who sees one thing at a time, observes his world closely but never whole, looks down because he is frightened to look up? As I once looked at the stars from the roof of the bungalow, was overwhelmed, and took up a book instead.

IV

I no longer know what I have read and what I haven't. Have I read *Tristram Shandy*? I know about it, I can talk about it. I think I haven't read it, though I am more familiar with it than, say, those thousands of thrillers I have read and forgotten. *Tristram Shandy*, oddly, is part of my reading.

V

Memory is reconstructive, and the assumption or hope that one can photographically recapitulate and reanimate the past is wrong. Even photographs don't do that. The past is what we make in the present, as the present is made by the past. We take the strands and feelings of our past lives as we experience them now, not then, and make them into narratives, themes, incidents. Such constructions are more or less reliable depending not on how strictly accurate they are to the past, but how authentic they feel, how fairly they make the case, how interesting they become. When Clive James calls his memoirs 'unreliable' he means that you might well produce contemporary witnesses to say that 'no, it didn't happen quite like that, it happened like this' and that, within a range of accountability, it doesn't matter. You are allowed to sex them up, not as an act of falsification, but because that is how memory works. There is nothing wrong with this sort of forgetting, forgetting is part of who we are and of how we describe ourselves. Forgetting enables us to make better stories.

VI

Is there something arbitrary about my choice of books? They were culled from a much longer list of possibilities, but my final list, once I had settled upon it, had an aura of inevitability that was both satisfying and puzzling. These were the right books. Freud tells us that things happen for a reason, there must be a reason. The answer only became clear to me after I had finished writing. What did these apparently disparate books have in common? They have formed the basis of some sort of intellectual and personal memoir. But the recurring motif, it surprised me to see, has been the search for an understanding of the nature of love.

No, that's not it, quite. That sounds intellectual and second-hand, in the wrong voice. It seems, baldly, that love is what I am interested in. I don't quite know what to make of this, it feels slightly embarrassing. It's surprising, reading yourself.

VII

I have re-read all of the books about which I have written here, though you don't have to reread a book in order to revisit it. I can remember the text of *Women in Love*, reread it, remember reading it at various times in my life, remember what I made of it at those times, take an attitude to those reading experiences, take an attitude to having taken that attitude . . . And so it goes on. Rereading we encounter the familiar strangers of our past selves, reading. It is a surprisingly complex process, and in tracing the lineaments of our reading experience we are most assuredly reading and rereading ourselves. It is too much for me, trying abstractly to unravel these processes, and I am certainly not going to make the attempt. Has anyone written about this? Perhaps on the phenomenology of reading? Or a book modelled on R.D. Laing's *Knots*? If so, I don't want to know about it.

VIII

We read together in anxious, attentive satisfaction, our fingers moving slowly, word by word across the lines. We have started with the opening of *The Waste Land*. It is the late afternoon, my favourite time to teach, and in my memory there is a wintery penumbral light as the sun sets, and a wood fire is burning in the fireplace. Often my students come by our house, which I greatly prefer as a teaching space: warmer, more personal, comfier. I have served coffee or tea at the start of the seminar, as I always do, accompanied by biscuits. We drink from our cups, nibble and consult, read with an increasing excitement and sense of incipient understanding, putting the images together, getting some sense of an emerging pattern. I love this activity, the slow, creative excitement of reading word-by-word, sharing the experience, understanding how the words relate, one to the other.

It is an advantage of having the seminar late in the day that we can exceed the stipulated time if we are still excited by the reading, go on until we are ready to stop, tired. And then I put on the LP of Eliot himself reading the poem, and we listen quietly, drifting in and out of the poem sleepily, as his cracked, rasping voice makes its way through the poem with a wry desperation. It is impossible not to close one's eyes, listening.

I didn't recognize it then – the process was entirely unconscious – but I see it now. I had done this before. It echoes that primal scene: the parent reading to the child, fingers on the page, the slow understanding, the delight. My class and I are learning to read, again, together. It is night-time, with an exciting, almost sensual drowsiness, cuddling up in soft chairs and sofas with our tea and cookies. Touching the text with fingers, being touched by it. In reading with this degree and kind of attentiveness, we reanimate the earliest memories, books and practices that have touched us. We are touched by how and who we read, and by what we read, and by those who transmit it to us, and to whom we transmit it. The excitement of reading widens and refines throughout our lives, but there is always the echo of the first times that we began to understand the power and mystery of words. 'In all things we learn only from those we love.' Reading is how we learn to attach ourselves to ourselves, and to others, and to the world: reading inhabits us with the tendrils of love. We are made and continually transformed by what, and how, we read: from Dr Seuss to T.S. Eliot, we are made by it.

IX

This process of self-making, of reading and re-reading both my books and my former selves is ongoing; why suppose that the formative ends at some moment, when we are made, perfected? It doesn't happen. Every reading experience vibrates subtly across the jelly of being, makes adjustments minute or transforming, recalls other reading and foreshadows reading still to come.

Now I'm sixty-four, I most look forward to that time when Anna and Bertie will have children of their own, and I can have a little Vera, Chuck or Dave on my knee, and introduce them to the admirable Horton and that little angel Matilda. And I shall recall little Rick snuggled up and listening raptly: connected once again to my parents, as through my children and my children's children the reading will go on.

And we will read until the light fails and the night draws in, and I can read no more.

REFERENCES

The author and publishers gratefully acknowledge permission to reprint the following extracts:

A.J. Ayer: an extract from *Language, Truth and Logic* (Pelican, 1971); Roald Dahl: an extract from *Matilda* (Jonathan Cape, 1988), reprinted by permission of David Higham Associates Ltd; T.S. Eliot: extracts from 'The Waste Land' from *Collected Poems 1909-1962* (Faber & Faber, 1974), reprinted by permission of the publisher; Sigmund Freud: an extract from *The Interpretation of Dreams*, edited by J. Crick (Oxford University Press, 2008), reprinted by permission of the publisher; Gerry Goffin and Carol King: song lyrics from 'Will You Still Love Me Tomorrow?' by The Shirelles from the album *Tonight's the Night* (Scepter label, 1960); Allen Ginsberg: extracts from 'Howl' from *Selected Poems 1947-1995* (Penguin Twentieth-Century Classics, 1997); Germaine Greer: extracts from *The Female Eunuch* (Paladin, 1976), reprinted by permission of HarperCollins Publishers Ltd; Thomas Harris: an extract from *The Silence of the Lambs* (William Heinemann, 1989), reprinted by permission of The Random House Group Ltd; Carl Hiaasen: an extract from *Double Whammy* (Pan Books, 1999); R.D. Laing: extracts from *The Divided Self* (Pelican, 1965); A.S. Neill: extracts from *Summerhill* (Pelican, 1970), reprinted by permission of the Estate of A.S. Neill; Dr Seuss: extracts from *Horton Hatches the Egg* (HarperCollins Children's Books, 2004); Ludwig Wittgenstein:

an extract from *Philosophical Investigations* (Blackwell, 1953); Tom Wolfe: extracts from *The Electrik Kool-Aid Acid Test* (Black Swan, 1989); W.B. Yeats: extracts from 'Among School Children', 'Brown Penny', 'The Song of Wandering Aengus' and 'Sailing to Byzantium' from *Collected Poems* (Picador, 1990), reprinted by permission of A.P. Watt Ltd on behalf of Gráinne Yeats.

Every effort has been made to trace or contact copyright holders prior to publication. If contacted, the publisher will be pleased to rectify any omissions or errors at the earliest opportunity.